The Harvard Architecture Review · Volume 9

RIZZOLI NEW YORK

The Harvard Architecture Review
Volume 9
1993
A Journal of Architectural Research

The Harvard Architecture Review is a publication of the students of the Graduate School of Design, Harvard University.
Published by Rizzoli International Publications, Inc.
300 Park Avenue South
New York, New York 10010

Please address all correspondence to:
Editors
The Harvard Architecture Review, Volume 9
George Gund Hall
48 Quincy Street
Cambridge, Massachusetts 02138

Front cover from The Valparaiso School, Fernando Pérez Oyarzún
Back cover from Osaka Folly, Christopher Macdonald and Peter Salter

THE HARVARD ARCHITECTURE REVIEW

VOLUME 9

1993

A JOURNAL OF ARCHITECTURAL RESEARCH

Contents

INTRODUCTION:

Toward a journal of architectural research

The Editors

Inquiry is a challenge, not a passive conformity; application is a means of growth, not of repression.

John Dewey, *Individualism Old and New*

This issue of *The Harvard Architecture Review* began with a desire to understand better the architect's ways of perceiving and acting upon the world. The discussions and articles included here make up a chronicle of our ongoing inquiry into the processes and possibilities of architecture's distinct form of knowledge. They also constitute a proposal for how this understanding of architecture might form the basis for a new type of journalistic practice.

To initiate a public dialogue about these concerns, the editors, working with Storefront for Art and Architecture, organized two symposia in late 1990. The presentations and discussions that emerged from these sessions outline some of the theoretical and institutional implications of understanding architecture as a form of knowledge. They also provide a critical framework for considering the projects presented here.

Our efforts were partly a reaction to developments in the architect's role in society, and to certain trends in architectural publishing. Despite the continuing flood of books and magazines on and about architecture, doubts linger about the ability of the press to provide architects with a forum for the exchange and discussion of ideas central to their discipline. Readers of professional and trade journals, for example, face a dizzying barrage of images and information, new technologies, and ever-shifting stylistic trends. Those who turn to academic journals for a more reflective forum encounter instead an increasingly arcane discourse, dominated by languages and methods born of other disciplines. Implicitly, both types of publication acquiesce in the institutionalized separation of the production of knowledge about architecture from the production of architecture itself. In this climate, the role of the practitioner seems trivial; the architect is reduced to the manipulation of information on the one hand, and to the illustration of theory on the other.

However, the practice of architecture is certainly more than just a matter of technique, or translation. On what basis, then, might we construct an alternative conception of architectural practice that recognizes the architect's intellectual prerogatives and capacity for meaningful creation? How might architectural journalism support and build upon this understanding? Our approach has been to focus on the processes of inquiry and experimentation that are intrinsic to architectural practice, and to recognize in these practices a form of research that can provide a basis for the exchange of architectural knowledge. In adopting this approach, our primary goal has been to provide architects with a more rigorous framework for evaluating and learning from their differing practices. Therefore we present projects within the context of the choices and intentions that define the architect's field of action. This is in contrast to the custom of presenting projects as a stable set of conclusions. Our emphasis has turned from the end product of practice to the means and methods of the practice itself.

By publishing under the rubric *architectural research*, we are also making a claim for the legitimacy of architecture as a rigorous and distinct form of knowledge. The term *research* has traditionally carried connotations of progress, and, as John Whiteman noted at our first symposium, the promise of "going from a state of ignorance to one of knowledge and ability." In architecture, research has been most commonly associated with disciplines that employ positivist modes of ordering the world, such as structural engineering and environmental psychology. Only rarely are architecture's more intangible aspects, or the activities that occur within the context of design or professional practice, given serious consideration or recognition by the academic establishment. If architecture is to be taken seriously as a form of knowledge that contributes to our understanding of the world, it is precisely these concerns and practices that we must address.

The projects collected in this volume take up this challenge by reexamining architecture. They explore the gaps and contradictions contained within the discipline and profession of architecture: the divisions that separate knowledge from action and research from practice. The first series of articles, by Hillier, Sarkis, Lerup, and Whiteman, which were presented at our first symposium, are motivated by theoretical concerns. They reveal some of the hidden assumptions that underlie the ways that we represent, produce, and experience architecture, and attempt a reconciliation between the conventions of architectural thinking and other modes of rational thought. A second group of articles, including Pérez-Oyarzún's discussion of the Chilean School of Valparaiso, Kennedy and Violich's Interim Bridges Project, and Woods's proposal for "drifting architectures," challenge cultural and political limits on the architect's place in society. The projects that follow, by Allen, Cohen, Macdonald and Salter, and Williams and Tsien, present a diverse group of ambitions and methodologies. They question our received understandings of architectural form and method, and approach architecture as a discipline to be continually reconceived. Together they suggest that architectural inquiry can address the phenomena of everyday life as well as advanced technology; it can incorporate the chance and uncertainty inherent in the processes of design and construction, as well as the logic of scientific method. What unites these architects is a common dedication to the pursuit of knowledge and the communication of new discoveries. The view of architectural knowledge that they depict is a composite one, a tableau made of multiple and sometimes mutually limiting points of view.

In presenting this range of strategies for architectural investigation, we are not preaching a new orthodoxy. Although our consideration of the political dimensions of these issues reinjects architecture into ongoing debates over the uses and control of knowledge and the role of the professional in society, we are not advocating a program for institutional reform. Our interest lies rather in encouraging a more rigorous and inclusive understanding of architectural inquiry and experimentation, and in establishing a more integral role for these activities in practice. In doing so, we hope to support a discourse in which the professional and academic communities may share, evaluate, and build upon one another's questions, methods of inquiry, and discoveries.

This project of making public the inner workings of architectural inquiry has been arduous but rewarding for our authors and the editors. It could not have been undertaken without the advice and assistance of many colleagues and friends, including: William Adams, Catherine Cassety, Pamela Davies, Susan Joseph, Kevin Kieran, John Poros, William Mitchell, Jorge Silvetti, John Whiteman, our coordinator at Rizzoli, Solveig Williams, and the Board of Directors of *The Harvard Architecture Review*: Michael Lauber, Margaret Minor, Linda Pollak, and Ben Tate. Dean Gerald McCue and the faculty, staff, and administration of the Harvard Graduate School of Design were always ready with encouragement and support. The editors are grateful to Barbara Grzeslo and Bob Stern of the 2^b Group, who have given this journal clarity and beauty, and to Charrette Corporation and Anderson Schwartz Associates who provided much-needed financial assistance. We extend our thanks as well to Kyong Park of Storefront for Art and Architecture, whose early enthusiasm and efforts in organizing our second joint symposium added immeasurably to the breadth of our investigation.

Finally, publication of this volume would not have been possible without generous grants from the Daewoo Foundation, and Seoul Architects and Consultants International Ltd., of Seoul, Korea, to whom we are deeply grateful.

SPECIFICALLY ARCHITECTURAL THEORY:

A Partial Account of the Ascent from Building as Cultural Transmission

to Architecture as Theoretical Concretion

Bill Hillier

INTRODUCTION: ARCHITECTURE AS THEORY

Theories are forms of knowing that summarize experience into abstract principles, and thus transform the meanings we assign to experience and the way we act on the world. Architects use theories in design, knowingly or unknowingly, not only because the creation of forms must reflect how the designer understands the world, but also because architecture, unlike everyday building, seeks as yet unknown forms, whose nature cannot, by definition, be predicted from experience.

But what are architectural theories like? Are they intellectual styles, like semiotics or deconstruction, brought into architecture from outside and interpreted within architecture? Or is there also some harder edged sense in which architectural theories are specific to architecture, aiming to explain architectural phenomena as well as to guide design? Are architectural theories, in short, theories *applied* to architecture or are there also theories *of* architecture?

In this article, I argue that theories of architecture exist, and that they are to be found not in the changing intellectual context of architecture as a bookish appendage to practice, but within the practice itself, guiding the answers to kinds of questions that arise at the point of design. Architecture, I will argue, is an intrinsically theoretical act. The key to architectural theory lies, I will suggest, not in the invocation of external abstractions, but in a proper understanding of the processes and products of architecture.

I will argue my case for specifically architectural theory using the problem of space as a specific instance. Architects and builders already use theory-like constructs in creating built space, and I will try to show that it is possible to develop a much fuller theory of space, one with some pretence to objectivity, capable of augmenting our intuitions in explaining and predicting forms, and also capable of refutation. I will argue that although such theories challenge architects with much more powerful and precise tools of analysis than they have had before, they lead not to constraint but to liberation.

Better theories of space mean more freedom for the designer because they bring the deep structures of architectural and urban space into the realm of rational debate and creative intuition.

In this article I will first try to distinguish architecture from building to show how theory is central to architectural practice. Then I will look at the issue of space, first as a philosophical problem, then as an aspect of buildings, and finally as an architectural phenomenon. I will then turn to the theory of space itself and suggest that space has its own internal laws, and that it is only when these are properly understood that space can be fully a part of architecture. Finally I will draw some inferences on how this view of theory affects our view of architecture as science and as art.

SYSTEMATIC INTENT OF THE ARCHITECTURAL KIND

First, how is architecture theoretical? Let us begin with some elementary semantics. If we try to unpack the ways we use the word *architecture*, it seems to refer both to an activity and a thing, that is, to the activity we call *design* and to buildings where we note evidence of this activity. Does this imply, as it seems to, that architecture is not really an objective property, but only a record of a certain kind of activity?

This is a difficult question, of a kind familiar to philosophers and aestheticians, who often ask whether words like *beautiful* refer to intrinsic properties of things, or are more akin to words such as *appropriate* which clearly do not refer to intrinsic properties of things, but to the judgments that we make by comparing things to other things.[1] Putting the question their way, we might ask whether architecture is actually a property of architectural objects, or a judgment that we make about objects, aware that they are the result of architectural activity.

Let us try to throw light on this by examining cases where deciding what is and is not architecture is particularly difficult, as when looking at the origins of architecture, or at where to draw the line between architecture and the vernacular. A colleague of mine, in reviewing the archaeological record for the origins of architecture, suggests that we see architecture in the evolution of buildings when we see evidence of "systematic intent."[2] By this she means deliberate abstract thought applied to construction, to space arrangement, or to visual organization, either at the level of the building or the settlement.

This is an interesting and persuasive definition. But if we try to generalize it we encounter problems. Suppose, for example, that we try to use it to distinguish architecture from the vernacular. It doesn't work, because clearly the vernacular is full of systematic intent. To make the matter even more difficult, the demarcation between architecture and the vernacular shifts with time, in that aspects of the architecture of one generation may reappear as the vernacular of another, and vice versa. These difficulties really do begin to make it look as though architecture is not at all an intrinsic property of things but a judgment that we make about things in the light of other knowledge.

However, if we look a little more closely at the vernacular we find new possibilities. The outstanding work of Henry Glassie on vernacular housing adapts from Noam Chomsky a concept he calls "architectural competence," which, he argues, underlies the architectural consistencies and variations by which we recognize a vernacular tradition. For Glassie, "architectural competence" is a set of technological, geometrical, and manipulative skills relating form to use, which constitute "an account not of how a house is made, but of how a house is thought . . . set out like a program . . . a scheme analogous to a grammar, that will consist of an outline of rule sets interrupted by prosy exegesis."[3] Glassie's analogy with language is apposite. It suggests that the rule sets the vernacular designer uses are often tacit, taken for granted in the same way as the rule sets that govern the use of language. They are ideas we think *with*, rather than ideas we think *of*. The proposal that the evidence of systematic intent that we note in the vernacular might have its origins in some such rule sets seems a compelling one.

The implication of Glassie's idea is that "architectural competence" provides a set of normative rules about how building should be done, so that a vernacular building reproduces a known and socially accepted pattern. The house built by a builder sharing the culture of a community comes out right because it draws on the normative rules that define the architectural competence of the community. Buildings become part of what Margaret Mead calls "the transmission of culture by artefacts."[4] Through distinctive ways of building, aspects of the social knowledge of a community are reproduced.

Now whatever architecture is, it is clearly not just the transmission and reproduction of social knowledge through building, though it may include that. But this does suggest where the difference between architecture and building might lie. What we mean by architecture surely is not building by reference to *culturally bound competences*. What we mean, rather, is building by reference to a would-be *universalistic competence* based on general comparative knowledge of architectural forms and functions, and aimed (through understanding of principle derived from comparative knowledge) at innovation rather than cultural reduplication. The judgment we make that a building is architecture arises when the evidence of systematic intent is evidence of intellectual choice and decision making exercised in a field of possibility that goes beyond cultural idiosyncrasy and into the realm of principled understanding. It is when we see in buildings evidence of this concern for the abstract comparability of forms that building is transcended and architecture is named.

We may then generalize and say that building is transcended and architecture is named where we note as a property of buildings some evidence not only of systematic intent, but of theoretical intent, at least in embryonic form. In this sense architecture transcends building in the same sense that science transcends the practical arts of making and doing. Architecture introduces into the making of buildings a more abstract concern for the realm of possibility created through theoretical concern. In this sense, architecture is theory applied to building.

The demarcation between the vernacular and architecture is then no longer problematic. The reproduction of existing forms, vernacular or otherwise, is not architecture, because it requires no exercise of abstract comparative thought. But by the same criterion, the exploitation of vernacular forms in the creation of new forms can be architecture, because it does involve such thought. Architecture is thus both a thing and a judgment. In the form of the thing we detect evidence of systematic intent of the architectural kind. From the built evidence we can judge both that a building is intended to be architecture and, if we are so inclined, that it is architecture.

SPACE AS A PHILOSOPHICAL PROBLEM

Now space, I will argue, is one of the primary means by which the ascent from building as cultural transmission to architecture as theoretical intent is made, and is therefore one of the prime targets for architectural theory. This is to say that one aspect of the abstract comparability of forms in architecture centers on spatial form, which implies that space is, in some important sense, an objective property of buildings.

This is not obvious. Most of our common notions of space do not deal with space as an objective entity in itself but tie it in some way to human agency. For example, laymen tend to transcribe space as the use of space, or the perception of space, or concepts of space. Space as a thing in itself is harder to communicate. Common spatial concepts in architectural discourse are also similarly tied: personal space, human territoriality, spatial scale, and so on.

Even in architectural concepts of space where space is unlinked from direct human agency, we still find that space is not independently described. The concept of spatial enclosure, for example, describes space by reference to the physical forms that define it. Without them, the space vanishes. This tendency finds its extreme expression in writers such as Roger Scruton who think that the concept of space is a rather silly mistake made by rather pretentious architects, who have failed to understand that space in not an entity at all, but merely the obverse side of the physical object, the vacancy left by the physical building. For Scruton, it is self-evident that space in a field and in a cathedral are the same thing except insofar as the interior built surfaces of the cathedral create the impression that the interior space has distinctive properties.[5] All talk about space is in error, because it can be reduced to talk about physical objects.

In fact, this is a quite bizarre view, since at a practical level, space is manifestly the saleable commodity in buildings. We build walls, but we sell and rent space. Are developers who advertise space at so much per square foot making a category mistake? Should they be offering to rent walls and roofs? Why then is Scruton embarrassed by the concept of space? Let me suggest that Scruton is making an educated error, one that he would not make if he had not been so deeply imbued with the Western philosophical tradition.[6]

The dominant view of space in Western culture has been one we might loosely call Galilean-Cartesian. By this I mean that the primary properties of objects are seen as their extension—length, breadth, width, and so on—which are also their measurable properties. Extensions are the indubitably objective properties of things, independent of observers, unlike secondary properties such as "green" or "nice," which seem to depend in some way on interaction with observers. If extension is the primary property of objects, then it is natural to infer that it is also the primary property of the space within which objects sit. We can see this by the fact that when we take the object away from its space its extension is still present as an attribute of space. Space is therefore generalized extension, and as such the framework within which the primary properties of objects are defined.[7]

But once we see space as a general abstract framework or background of extension, then we are doomed not to understand how it plays a role in human affairs, including architecture. Space is never simply the inert background of our material existence. It is a key aspect of how our social and cultural worlds are constituted in the physical world, and structured for us as objective realities. Space is not the neutral framework for social and cultural forms. It is built into those very forms.[8] It is because this is so that buildings can carry within their spatial forms the kinds of social knowing that Glassie notes.

SPACE AS A PATTERN PROBLEM

But because space is built so pervasively into social and cultural life, we tend to take it for granted, to the point that its forms become invisible to us, and so much so that we have no rational language for the discussion of these forms. The only language is that of the forms themselves. If we wish to build a theory of space, then, we must first learn this language—although in a sense we know it already—and learn to talk about space in a way that allows its form to become clear.

Let us begin by defining the problem clearly: as a *pattern* problem. Consider the two notional courtyard buildings of figures 1a and 1b, showing in black the pattern of physical elements. Figures 2a and 2b show in black the corresponding pattern of spatial elements. The basic physical structures and cell divisions of the two building are the same, and each has the same pattern of adjacencies between cells and the same number of internal and external openings. But the locations of cell entrances means that the spatial patterns are about as different as they could be from the point of view of the permeability of the layout. One is a near-perfect single sequence, with a minimal branch at the end. The other is branched everywhere about the strong central spaces.

figures 1a and 1b
Arrangements of physical elements into structures

figures 2a and 2b
Arrangements of spatial elements into structures

figures 3a and 3b
Justified graphs of permeability relations in figures 1a and 1b

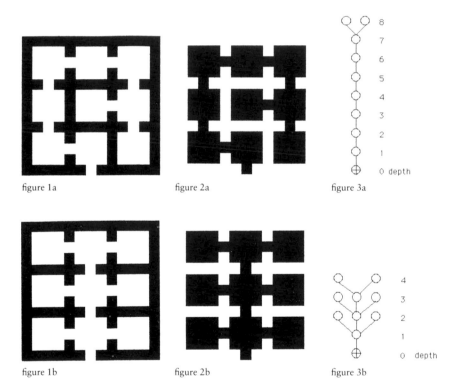

figure 1a   figure 2a   figure 3a

figure 1b   figure 2b   figure 3b

The pattern of entrances would make relatively little difference to the building structurally or climatically, especially if we assumed a similar pattern of external fenestration, and inserted windows wherever the other had entrances onto the courtyard. But it would make a dramatic difference to how the layout would work as, say, a domestic interior. For example, it is very difficult for more than one person to use a single sequence of spaces. It offers little in the way of community or privacy, but much in the way of potential intrusion. The branched pattern, on the other hand, offers a more flexible set of potential relations between community and privacy, and many more resources against intrusion. These differences are inherent in the space patterns themselves in terms of the range of limitations and potentialities offered. They suggest the possibility that architectural space might be subject to limiting laws, not of a deterministic kind, but ones that set morphological bounds within which the relations between form and function in buildings are worked out.

We can capture the difference between the two spatial patterns by a useful device we call a justified graph (figs. 3a and 3b). In this we imagine that we are in a space that we call the root or base of the graph, and represent as a circle with a cross. Then, representing spaces as circles, and relations of access as lines connecting them, we align immediately above the root all spaces that are directly connected to the root. Then above the first row we align the spaces that connect directly to first-row spaces, and so on. The result is a picture of the *depth* of all spaces in a pattern from a particular point in it.

We can see that one is a deep tree form, and the other a shallow tree form. By tree we mean that the patterns lack any rings of circulation. All trees, even those as different as the two in figures 3a and 3b, share the characteristic that there is only one route from each space to the other—a property that is highly relevant to how building layouts function.

However, where rings are found, the justified graph makes them clear as depth properties (figs. 4a, 4b, and 4c). Using justified graphs, then, we can begin to make visible two of the most fundamental properties of spatial configurations: how much depth they have from each space (how many other spaces must be passed through to get to others); and how each space relates to the pattern of circulation rings in the configuration (how it relates to the choices of route available).

More significantly, we can now take the crucial step in understanding spatial configuration as a product of culture. The key to spatial configuration in buildings and cities is that within the same building or urban system, space has different configurational properties when looked at from different points of view. This can be shown by drawing justified graphs, because the differences have mainly to do with the way in which depth and rings are distributed in the spatial configuration when seen from different points of view (figs. 5a and 5b).

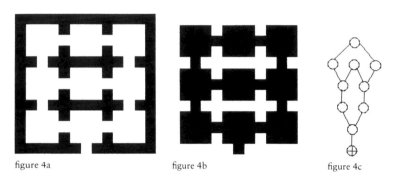

figures 4a-c
"Ring" Spatial configuration and its justified graph representation

figure 4a   figure 4b   figure 4c

The depth and ring properties could hardly appear more different if they were different configurations. It is through the creation and distribution of such differences by the arrangement of physical constructions that space becomes such a powerful raw material for the transmission of culture through buildings and settlement forms, and also such a potent means of architectural discovery and creation.

SOCIETY IN THE FORM OF THE OBJECT

Let me now show how buildings can transmit cultural ideas through this aspect of spatial patterning. Figure 6 shows ground floor plans of three French houses, and their justified graphs drawn initially from the outside, treating it as a single space, then from three different internal spaces. Looking at the first graph (drawn from the outside), we see that in spite of the geometrical differences in the houses there are strong similarities in the configurations. We see this most easily by concentrating on the space marked sc, or *salle commune*. In each case, the *salle commune* lies on all nontrivial rings (a trivial ring is one that links the same pair of spaces twice), links directly to an exterior space, and acts as a link between the living spaces and the spaces associated in that culture with the domestic work of women.

The *salle commune* also has a more fundamental property, one that arises from its relation to the spatial configuration of the house as a whole. If we count the number of spaces we must pass through to go from the *salle commune* to all other spaces, we find that it comes to a total that is less than for any other space—that is, it has less depth than any other space in the complex. The general form of this measure is called *integration*, and can be applied to any space in any configuration: the less depth from the complex as a whole, the more integrating the space.[9] This means that every space in the three complexes can be assigned an *integration value*. Other measures express how strong these differences are.[10]

Now once we have done this we can ask questions about the distribution of functions in the house. In the three French houses, for example, we find that there is a certain order of integration among the spaces where different functions are carried out, always with the *salle commune* as the most integrated. In other words, we can say with quantitative rigor that there is a common pattern to the way in which different functions are spatialised in the house. We call such common patterns *genotypes*, because they refer not to the surface appearances of forms but to deep structures underlying spatial configurations and their relation to living patterns.

These results flow from an analysis of space-to-space permeability. But what about the relation of visibility, which passes through spaces? Figures 7 and 8 show what we call the convex isovists (that is, all that can be seen from a space in which all points are mutually visible, in this case drawn to omit the corners of rooms in a consistent way) from the *salle commune* and another space labelled *salle*. In each case the *salle commune* has a far more powerful visual field than the *salle*. These differences provide a basis for quantitative and statistical analysis and subsequent exploration of genotypical cultural patterns that lie embedded in the material and spatial objectivity of buildings.

This method allows us to retrieve what we might call Glassie properties from house plans, and to formalize the notion of cultural types. We have thus shown both how buildings can transmit social knowledge through their spatial form and how this can be retrieved by analysis. This is clearly useful knowledge for an architect to have. But it is not yet architecture, according to my definition, and certainly not a theory of architecture, even a partial one.

So how does this relate to the definition of architecture proposed earlier? Let me begin by referring to a study of selected houses by Adolf Loos and Le Corbusier by Dickon Irwin.[11] I cannot do justice to the subtlety and complexity of Irwin's argument in this brief text, but I would like to review some of his conclusions. Irwin's analysis of five houses by each of the two architects showed that although in each house there was configurational differentiation of functions, there was no consistent pattern within either architect's work. It was as though each recognized the principle that functions should be spatially differentiated, but regarded it as a matter of experiment and innovation, rather than as the reproduction of a culturally approved genotype.

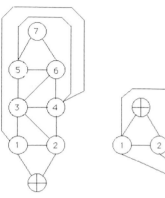
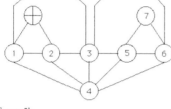

figure 5a   figure 5b

figures 5a and 5b
Justified graphs of the same spatial configuration
justified from different points.

However, Irwin was able to show that each architect had a distinctive spatial style, in that whatever each was doing with the functional pattern, distinctive spatial means were used to achieve the ends. For example, in the Loos houses, adding visibility relations to permeability relations increased the intelligibility of the space pattern (for a discussion of intelligibility see page 17), whereas in the Le Corbusier houses it did not. Similarly, in the Loos houses, the geometry of the plan reinforced aspects of the spatial structure of the plan, in that major lines of spatial integration coincided with focuses of geometric order, whereas again in the Le Corbusier houses it did not. Some of these differences were captured by Irwin in diagrams he called *line isovists*, where he took the most integrated lines in the axial map of the house (see below) and drew all the space that could be seen from them. Figures 9 (Loos: Tristan Tzara House) and 10 (Le Corbusier: Villa Stein) show in order the isovists from the two most integrated lines from the point of view of the permeability pattern in each house, followed by the visibility isovists of the two most visibly integrating lines. If we imagine each isovist as an episode in the spatial experience of moving through the houses, we can see that in Loos the isovists are very rich, but relatively uniform, whereas in Le Corbusier the isovists are more selective in the spatial relations they show from the line, but each episode is dramatically different from the others.

In this respect, Irwin argues, the two architects are adumbrating different fundamental—almost philosophical—programs through architecture: Loos creates a house that is a novel expression of cultural habitability, Le Corbusier creates a less habitable, more idealized domain of rigorous abstraction. Neither Le Corbusier nor Loos is denying the social and cultural nature of the domestic interior. But each, by satisfying the need to give space cultural meaning through functional differentiation—first one way then another, but with a consistent spatial style—is giving priority not to the functional ends of building but to the architectural means of expressing those functional ends. The genotype of these houses lies, we might suggest, not in the functional ends, as in the vernacular cases, but in the way architectural means are used to express the ends. The means modify the ends by reexpressing them as part of a richer cultural realm.

This distinction between ends and means is, I believe, fundamental to the definition of architecture offered earlier. It suggests that we can make a useful distinction, in architecture as elsewhere, between the realm of social meaning and the realm of the aesthetic—in this case the spatial aesthetic. The cultural and functional differentiation of space is the social meaning, the spatial means is the spatial aesthetic. The former conveys a clear social intention, the latter an architectural experience that recontextualizes the social intention. Meaning is the realm of constraint, the spatial aesthetic the realm of freedom. The spatial meaning of form expresses what architecture must be to fulfill its purpose as a social object, the spatial aesthetic expresses what it can be to fulfill its purpose as architecture.

But although space moves outside the realm of specific codes of social knowledge, it does not lose its social dimension. The relation between spatial and social forms is not contingent, but follows patterns that are so consistent we can hardly doubt that they have the nature of laws.[12] The spatial aesthetic carries social potential through these laws. The autonomy of architectural means thus finds itself in a realm governed by general principles, with its freedom restricted not by the specific spatial demands of a culture but by the laws of space themselves.

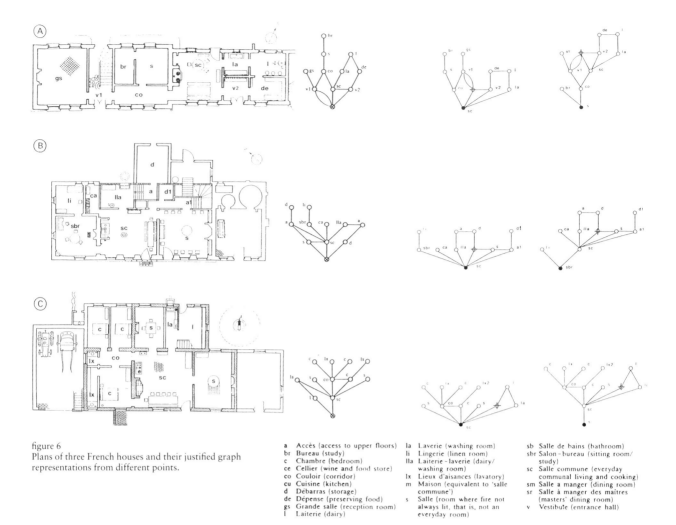

figure 6
Plans of three French houses and their justified graph representations from different points.

a	Accès (access to upper floors)	la Laverie (washing room)
br	Bureau (study)	li Lingerie (linen room)
c	Chambre (bedroom)	lla Laiterie-laverie (dairy/
ce	Cellier (wine and food store)	washing room)
co	Couloir (corridor)	lx Lieux d'aisances (lavatory)
cu	Cuisine (kitchen)	m Maison (equivalent to 'salle
d	Débarras (storage)	commune')
de	Dépense (preserving food)	s Salle (room where fire not
gs	Grande salle (reception room)	always lit, that is, not an
l	Laiterie (dairy)	everyday room)

sb	Salle de bains (bathroom)
sbr	Salon-bureau (sitting room/ study)
sc	Salle commune (everyday communal living and cooking)
sm	Salle a manger (dining room)
sr	Salle à manger des maîtres (masters' dining room)
v	Vestibule (entrance hall)

These laws find one of their strongest expressions in urban space, where the social programming of space is much less closely defined than in building interiors. However, in looking for the operations and effects of these laws, we will find that certain attributes of urban space believed by many to be aesthetic in origin in fact arise from functional laws.[13] What these functional laws of space might be like is the theme of the next part of my argument.

THE URBAN GRID AS AN OBJECT OF ARCHITECTURAL THOUGHT

There are two factors that make the analysis of urban space especially difficult for configurational analysis. First, urban space is continuous. There is no obvious division into elements. Second, with obvious exceptions, urban space usually has a good deal of irregularity. Most towns and cities have deformed grids, with no obvious geometry. Both factors are

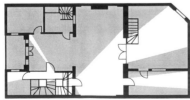

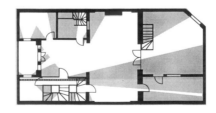

figure 9
Adolf Loos. Tristan Tzara House.
Fourth floor: permeability isovist from the most integrated line.

Fourth floor: permeability isovist from the second most integrated line.

Fourth floor: isovist from the visibly most integrated line.

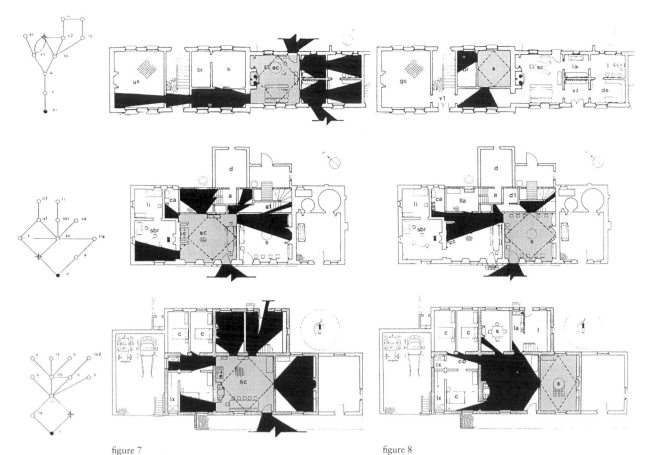

figure 7
Diagrams of the houses from figure 6 showing convex isovists from the salle commune.

figure 8
Diagrams of the houses from figure 6 showing convex isovists from the salle.

aspects of the problem of representation: how do we define an element of urban space so that we can subject it to configurational analysis?

It will be useful to begin by looking at a familiar case and considering how we might think of urban grids as spatial patterns. Figure 11a shows in black the plan forms of all the open spaces and public squares in Rome, respecting orientation but not location. Figure 11b shows their location. Figure 11c shows the shapes, orientations, and locations, and adds a further element: the full spatial shape visible from each square, its isovist. From this we see that some subsets of the isovists of the spaces form interconnected clumps with more or less continuous visibility and permeability, while others do not. These are pattern properties, arising from the interrelationships of many distinct entities.

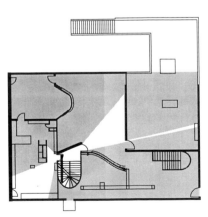

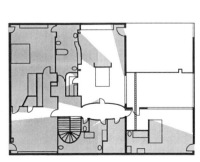

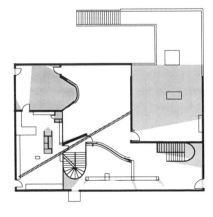

figure 10
Le Corbusier. Villa Stein.
First floor: permeability isovist from the most integrated line.

First floor: Permeability isovist from the second most integrated line.

Second floor: visibility isovist from the visibly most integrated line.

How shall we analyze these Roman properties? The complexity of the situation is such that we must recruit the computer, and begin with some simple experiments. Figure 12 is a hypothetical arrangement of built urban blocks, that create by their disposition an arbitrary deformed grid with a major, squarelike space. Although deformed, it has a degree of continuity of space, which gives it an approximately urban look, unlike figure 13, where the same blocks have been re-arranged to create a pattern that is manifestly not urban. The difference is instructive. It tells us that the deformed grids we recognize as urban may have a good deal of internal order to them.

Like other deformed grids, however, neither hypothetical figure has obvious spatial parts or elements. What, then, does it have that can be modelled? The answer is that as we move about a deformed grid, it exhibits everywhere local properties that continually change. Just as the shapes of space that were experienced locally in the Le Corbusier or Loos houses changed as we moved through the house, so the shape of space we see as we move from point to point in an urban grid also changes.

The question is, how does it change? And can these changes be captured in a representation? The Roman case established several concepts that may be of use. For example, wherever we are in a deformed grid we are in some maximal convex element of space defined by the surfaces of building blocks. The property of convexity means that any two points that can be seen from a point can also see each other. Figure 14 is a computer analysis of figure 12 in which all such convex elements have been identified, allowing them to overlap as much as necessary, and then analyzed and coded in terms of how *deep* each is from all the others: the darker, the less depth, the lighter, the more depth.[14] In other words, figure 14 shows the distribution of *integration* (as defined above) in the convex representation of the deformed grid of figure 12, with the darkest elements making up what we call the *integration core*.

figure 11a
Open spaces and public squares in Rome.

figure 11b
Location of open spaces and public squares
in Rome

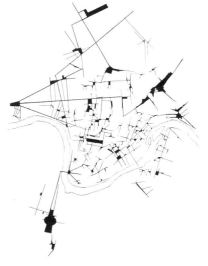

figure 11c
Map of open spaces and public squares
in Rome. (From a study by Marios Pelekanos, a
student in the Advanced Architectural Studies
Programme at the Bartlett School, University
College London, 1989.)

Now let us carry out the same analysis on figure 13. We find that the pattern of integration has changed completely, with the core moving to the edge and much weaker integration in the central areas (fig. 15). The integration core, one feels, has a much less powerful effect in creating an intelligible pattern to the space structure.

This property of intelligibility can in fact be demonstrated quite formally. If we go back to imagining that we are moving around in the spaces of these two configurations, then we can easily see that the field we see from points in figure 15 will on the whole be a good deal less rich than the field in figure 14. It will be a great deal harder to learn about the space structure as a whole because we get much poorer information form the localized parts. Few points in the pattern give much clue to the overall structure of the pattern, and even less to its distribution of integration. In figure 14, in contrast, we get a good deal of global information from local parts, and what we can see from points gives a good indication of how each space fits into the overall system.

This in fact reflects one of the most important pattern characteristics of deformed grid urban space. The information you get locally from the visual field you experience as you move around gives plenty of clues about how the overall spatial system is structured. In intelligible urban space, one might say, you get global information at the same time as you get local information about spaces, as we saw with the Roman squares.

Intelligibility can be quantified by a simple statistical trick. Figure 16 is scattergram in which each point represents one of the overlapping convex elements of figure 12. The number of convex elements each point overlaps with is indicated by its position on the vertical axis, and its degree of integration in the overall pattern on the horizontal axis. The more the points form a straight line from bottom left to top right, then the more connections an element has, which can be seen from each line. This is a reliable guide to its integration in the system as a whole, a property that cannot be seen from a line.

The tight scatter in figure 16 shows that the first configuration has a high degree of intelligibility, which can be expressed as a number by taking the correlation coefficient of the scatter. A value of 1 would indicate a perfect straight line of points, and 0 a random scatter. If we now look at the scatter for the second configuration, shown in figure 17, we can see that the scatter is much less tight, meaning that it has a lower value and therefore a lower degree of intelligibility. This expresses formally what intuition suggests: that the visual fields you see locally as you move around are a poorer guide to the system as a whole. The space structure is too labyrinthine.

This analysis of the convex organization of urban space is more than a formal game. It relates to important functional aspects of how space is used. For example, studies have shown that the choices that people make in selecting urban spaces for informal activities, such as eating, drinking, talking and sitting, reflect proximity or adjacency to areas with strong visual fields that are well integrated into the system as a whole.[15] Such spaces are ideally suited to what seems to be the favorite occupation of those using urban space informally: watching other people.

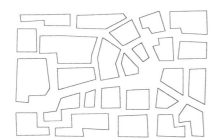

figure 12
Hypothetical arrangement of built urban blocks.

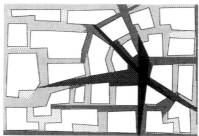

figure 14
Computer analysis of figure 12 showing distribution of integration.

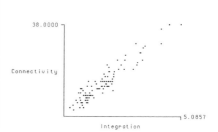

figure 16
Intelligibility scattergram of figure 12.

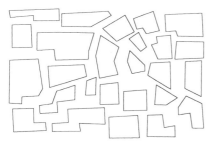

figure 13
Hypothetical arrangement of built urban blocks.

figure 15
Computer analysis showing total convex visual field of figure 13

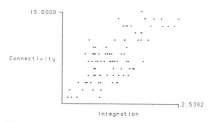

figure 17
Intelligibility scattergram of figure 13.

However, the most important and consistent functional effect of urban space follows from the configurational analysis of a different representation of its structure: one based on its one-dimensional, or axial, structure. We can again use the computer to explore the basics. The tangled skein of lines in figure 18 represents the maximal linear visibility available within the open space structure of figure 12, namely the set of all straight lines that are tangent to pairs of vertices of building blocks. That is, each line just passes by at least two such vertices, thus drawing a limit of a line of sight. Once the computer has found this set of lines, it can then subject them to integration analysis and code the results as before, with the darkest lines the most integrating, and showing the integration core of the pattern, and the lightest lines the most segregated (fig. 19).

Figures 18 and 19 thus represent different configurational views of the block arrangement in figure 12. Each says: seen in terms of this type of local element, and analyzed by that pattern parameter, the global structure of space looks like this. This is the essence of *space syntax* modelling. It is not a single technique but a set of techniques that allows two questions to be posed: how is the spatial system of interest to be represented as relatively localized elements, and how are the interrelationships to be analyzed to identify global patterns, so that we may understand the system's underlying structure.

Once we have this understanding of structure, we can begin to ask questions about function in a new way. Because syntactic analysis assigns to each spatial element in a system numbers that index its pattern relations, we can investigate the relation between these patterns and function simply by seeing how far the syntactic numbers assigned to spaces correlate with numbers describing aspects of function in those spaces: movement rates, informal use, rents, land uses, plot ratios, and so on. We can thus pose questions about space and function in a new way. In the case of urban space, we can ask: what does function mean when space is universally public and more or less unrestricted? We will receive a resounding answer: urban space is about movement. Urban space creates a field of movement and thus copresence and potential encounters among people.

We can show this by using again the scattergram technique. Figures 20-23 analyze the pedestrian and vehicular movement for the Barnsbury area of North London. The high degree of correlation in figure 22 (the correlation coefficient is .85 on a scale of 0 to 1) shows that the number of people passing along each line is largely a function of the spatial pattern itself. The same is true of vehicular movement, whose scattergram shows a correlation of .81 in spite of the existence of a number of one-way systems (fig. 23). The fundamental result is that the pattern of movement in an urban system is determined in the main by the spatial configuration itself, and in particular by the distribution of spatial integration in the axial map of the system.[16]

These results are quite fundamental to our understanding of urban space, since they show that it is the *architecture* of the urban grid itself that is chiefly responsible for the pattern of movement, not the positioning of attractors and mag-

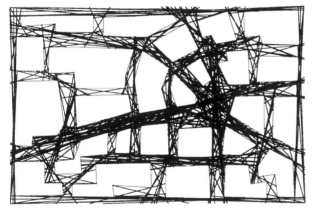

figure 18
Diagram of maximal linear visibility available within the open space structure of figure 12.

figure 19
Computer analysis coding the diagram of maximal linear visibility shown in figure 18.

nets, as has commonly been believed. These results have been repeated so often that we have little doubt that they are something like a law. However, the law does not simply say that movement in a grid is a function of the distribution of spatial integration in the grid. The relationship, it turns out, is subject to the degree to which the grid has the property of intelligibility, as defined earlier. If you make urban space unintelligible, then you are also likely to make it unpredictable. We call this the theory of natural movement. Natural movement is the proportion of movement determined by the architecture of the grid itself. Where there is no natural movement, then most space will be empty for most of the time, leading almost inevitably to one aspect or another of urban malfunction. This is the reason why we must once again learn to make the urban grid an object of architectural thought.

Because natural movement is fundamental, it is also reasonable to suppose that it accounts to a great extent for the way in which urban grids evolve. It is likely that over time a dynamic relation develops between the evolving urban grid, its natural movement patterns, and the developing pattern of land use. Certain types of use, for example retailing, survive best in locations that are accessible and have through-movement—that is, in locations that have both the spatial properties and functional effects of integration. The result is that over time, urban grids evolve not only to optimize patterns of mutual accessibility, but also to optimize the usefulness of the by-product of movement from place to place—that is, the spaces that must be passed through on journeys from all origins to all destinations. Through this mechanism, spaces that are accessible for to-movement also become those with strong through-movement, and these spaces then become the busy focuses of urban life. We call this the theory of the movement economy. If the theory is correct, it means that the architecture of the urban grid is of far greater significance in urban evolution than has been allowed in planning theory, and provides further reason for bringing back the urban grid as an object of architectural analysis and creativity.[17]

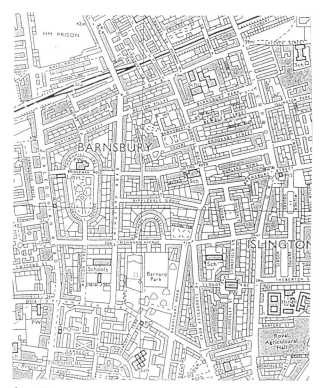

figure 20
Map of the Barnsbury area of inner London.

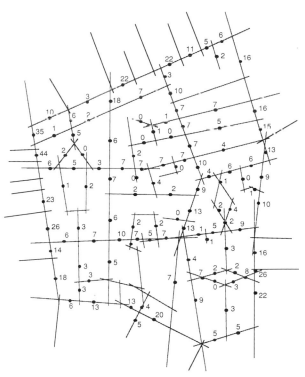

figure 21
Axial map of the Barnsbury area. Numbers represent pedestrian movement rates per five minutes.

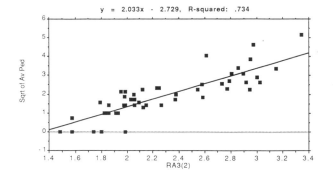

figure 22
Scattergram plotting pedestrian movement against degree of integration. Degree of correlation is .85.

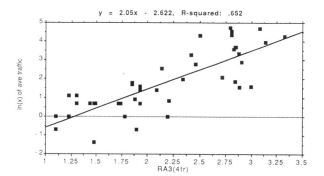

figure 23
Scattergram plotting vehicular movement against degree of integration. Degree of correlation is .81.

DESIGNING WITH SPACE SYNTAX: THE KING'S CROSS MASTERPLAN

What does all this imply for design? Let us proceed through a real case study: the design by Norman Foster Associates of the master plan for the King's Cross development in inner London for the London Regeneration Consortium. King's Cross is currently the biggest urban development project in Europe. Our published research using space syntax to predict pedestrian movement patterns, and the involvement of space syntax in public inquiries on major urban redevelopment schemes, had alerted first the community groups, then the planners and developers to the potential of using space syntax to help solve the fundamental problem of the King's Cross site: how to design the development in such a way that it continued and joined the urban structures of Islington to the east of the site and Camden to the west. Natural pedestrian movement to and through the site was seen as essential to this aim. Foster Associates, backed by the developers, asked us to make a study, and work with the design team in trying to build these relationships into the master plan.

The first step was to study the spatial structure, space use, and movement patterns in the existing contextual area. This study is documented in figures 24-30. From a design point of view, the key product of the study is a spatial model of the contextual areas of the site, verified by its power to "post-dict" the existing pattern of movement around the site. This allows us to add design proposals to the model, and to re-analyze in order to see how each proposal is likely to work within, and affect, the urban context.

We can therefore begin to explore intuitions as to what kind of master plan will most successfully adapt the existing structure of the area and create the levels of natural pedestrian movement requested by the designers. This will depend on the achievement of two spatial objectives: bringing adequate levels of integration into the site in a way that reflects and adapts the existing natural movement patterns in the area, and maintaining or if possible improving the grid's intelligibility.

figure 24
Block plan of part of the 15 km sq area of north London surrounding the site studied for the King's Cross project. Because natural movement is most strongly affected by the large-scale spatial pattern of an area, the contextual study area for a new development must be large enough to cover the likely pedestrian catchment area of the development, but it must also cover the catchment area of the catchment area, in order to ensure accuracy in the investigation of the catchment area. These two levels are modelled independently as the "small area"—usually about 5-6 km sq— and the "large area"—up to 20 km sq—to check that both levels are giv- ing the same story (large cities have no natural internal boundaries) and also to ensure that any "edge effect"—that is distortion in the analysis resulting from the fact that some parts are close to the edge of the area modelled—is kept to the edge of the large area, and does not affect the immediate contextual area of the site.

figure 25
Black-on-white representation of figure 24, showing the space of public access in black. The small-scale complexes around the site are public housing estates.

There is, however, a technical problem with the formal definition of intelligibility. Because intelligibility measures the degree of agreement between the local and global properties of space, a small system is, other things being equal, more likely to be intelligible than a larger one. We can overcome this by bringing in a database of established London areas of different sizes to compare with King's Cross as it is now and as it will be when it is developed (fig. 31). Figure 31 shows that not only is the King's Cross area less intelligible than London areas in general, but also the small area is rel- atively less intelligible than the large. This is probably because the "urban hole" created by the King's Cross site has a stronger impact on the area immediately around it than it does on the larger surrounding area.

We can now use the area axial map as a basis for design simulation and experimentation. In fact, what we will be doing in this text is conducting a number of experiments that explore the limits of possibility for the site.[18]

Let us first suppose that we impose a regular grid on the site, so that it has a local appearance of being ordered but makes no attempt to take advantage of the existing, rather disorderly pattern of integration in the area (fig. 32). In spite of its high degree of internal connection, the scheme acts as a substantial lump of relatively segregated spaces, rather like one of the local housing estates shown in figure 25, which freezes out virtually all natural movement and creates a quite unnerving sense of emptiness.

In other words, the grid scheme completely fails to integrate itself into the area or to contribute to the overall integra- tion of the area. The effect on intelligibility is no better. We can see this by plotting the intelligibility scattergram and using the space syntax software to locate the spaces of the scheme on the scatter. Figure 33 shows that the scheme's spaces form a lump (within the box) well off the line of intelligibility, occupying the segregated and rather poorly con- nected part of the scatter. We conclude not only that the scheme is far too segregated to achieve good levels of natural movement, but that its spaces are insufficiently integrated for their degree of connection and therefore worsen the intel- ligibility of the area as a whole.

Still in the spirit of experimentation, let us now try the opposite and simply extend integrating lines in the area into the site, and then complete the grid with minor lines more or less at will. This means that instead of imposing a new con- ceptual order onto the site regardless of the area, we are now using the area to determine the structure of space on the

figure 26
An axial map of figure 25, showing the least set of longest straight lines of sight and direct access that pass through all the public space shown in the previous figure, omitting housing estates for simplicity. The axial map is the model of the area analysed by the computer to establish its underlying patterns. Of these the most important is integration, that is the mean depth of each line from all others in the system. The integration value of a line (or an intersection) is in effect the number of other lines that must be used to go from that line to all others in the system.

figure 27
Axial map of figure 26 analyzed in terms of its distribution of integration, with the most integrating lines shown darkest, graded towards the least integrating shown lightest. Since integration predicts natural movement, one can think of the blackness (i.e. dot density) of the line as predicting the amount of movement down that line.

site. We must stress that this design is impossible, since it would require, among other things, a ground-level train crossing at the exit of St. Pancras station!

In spite of its unrealism, the experiment is instructive. Figure 34 shows the integration structure that would result from such a scheme. In effect it shows that certain lines extended across the site would become the most integrating lines in the whole area, stronger even than Euston Road—the major east-west trunk road passing south of the site, which would be the major integrator with respect to an area expanded to the south and west. We also find a substantially greater range of integration values in the development, in contrast to the much greater uniformity of the grid scheme.

This is a "good" urban property. Mixing adjacent integration values means a mix of busy and quiet spaces in close association with each other, with the kind of rapid transitions in urban character that are very typical of London. Figure 35 shows a much improved intelligibility scattergram, with the lines of the scheme picked out in bold, showing that they not only improve the intelligibility of the area, but make a linear—and therefore intelligible—scatter themselves.

Now if we plot these two hypothetical solutions on the London Intelligibility Index (fig. 36), we find that whereas the grid leaves the area as poor in intelligibility as it was, still lying in more or less the same position below the regression line, the "super-integrated" scheme moves well above the regression line, and would even be above the line formed by Islington and the City. We might even conclude that we have overdone things, and have created too strong a focus on the site for the mixture of commercial and residential development that is envisaged.

The final Foster Associates master plan, working as it does within the concept of a central park to bring democratic uses into the heart of the site, is a much more subtle and complex design than either of these crude illustrative experiments. In developing the design, a protracted process of design conjecture and constructive evaluation through space syntax modelling took place, much of it around the drawing board. The final master plan (figs. 37-40) draws integration in and through the different parts of the site to a degree that matches the intended land-use mix, which goes from urban office and shopping areas, where levels of natural movement need to be high, to quieter residential streets, where levels of movement will be lower.

The intelligibility scattergram shown in figure 38, again with the master plan lines picked out in bold, shows that the scheme improves the intelligibility of the area, and also has high internal intelligibility, seen in the linear scatter of the master plan lines. But the scheme also has more continuous variation from integrated to segregated than the super-integrated scheme, with its markedly more lumpy scatter. This indicates that the local variation in the syntactic quality of spaces, arising from mixing integrated and segregated lines in close proximity, is also better achieved. This is confirmed by the overall intelligibility index, which shows that the scheme falls very slightly above the regression line, meaning that it continues the established level of intelligibility in the London grid (fig. 36).

Thus the design team may not only use space syntax to experiment with design in a functionally intelligent way, they may also use the system to bring to bear on the design task both detailed contextual knowledge and a relevant database of precedent. We think of this as a prototype *graphical knowledge interface* for designers—meaning a graphically manipulable representation that also accesses contextual knowledge and precedent databases relevant to both the spatial structure and functional outcomes of designs. The experience of using space syntax on King's Cross and other urban master plans has convinced us that what designers need from research is theoretical knowledge, coupled to technique, not information or data or constraint. Furthermore, with theory and technique, much more of the living complexity of urban patterns can be brought within the scope of architectural intuition and architectural intent, without subjecting them to the geometrical and hierarchical simplification that have become the commonplaces of urban design.

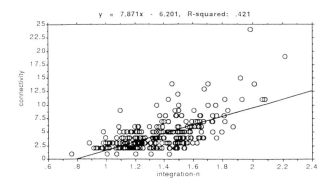

figure 28
Iintelligibility scattergram of the area as it stands, in which each line in figure 27 is represented as a dot and located on the horizontal axis according to its degree of integration (a global property that cannot be seen from the line) and on the vertical axis according to its degree of connectivity (a local property that can be seen from the line). The index of intelligibility is the square root of the number at the top right. The scattergram shows a rather poor level of intelligibility, partly due to the hole in the system formed by the King's Cross site.

figure 29
Map showing 239 line segments in ten areas around the site (including three housing estates adjacent to the site that are not shown on the axial map) where pedestrian space use and movement was observed using a simple moving observer technique, and distinguishing only between moving and static pedestrians, and between men, women, and children.

SPACE SYNTAX AS A PARTIAL THEORY OF ARCHITECTURE

If these are the implications for design, what then are the implications for specifically architectural knowledge and specifically architectural theory? There are two issues here. One concerns the forms that architectural theories and architectural knowledge take, the second how we conceptualize the relation of knowledge to design.

Regarding the first issues, it seems to me vital that space syntax theories are expressed in architectural form. By this I mean that theoretical knowledge is brought to bear on the design through a form of representation that is directly architectural, not only in the sense that it actually copies, and allows manipulation of, aspects of architectural forms, but also in the sense that it carries within itself, through theory, knowledge of functional consequences. Syntactic representations are *theoretical descriptions*[19], in that like buildings themselves, they are spatial forms with functional implications. Syntactic theories are architectural not only in the sense that they are *about* architecture, but also in the sense that they are in the language *of* architecture.

As for the second issue, the relation of knowledge to design, let us review the ascent from the vernacular to architecture. What we have seen is a series of levels at which we find theorylike entities in architecture. There is the level of the abstract social knowledge built into the "architectural competences" that underlie the vernacular. Next is the level of the abstract typological comparison of forms. Then there is the level of general theoretical propositions, such as the theory of natural movement.

What is clear from the design application is that the most useful form of abstraction for design is the third level, that of general theoretical propositions. It is only at this level that strategic design thinking takes place—for example, about how a socially desirable functional outcome of design, such as the integration of a new neighborhood, might be achieved. It is also clear that theories generated by space syntax do not enter a theoretical void, but challenge theoretical ideas that already hold the field. Thus, in different ways, space syntax theory challenges notions like territoriality, defensible space, spatial enclosure, legibility through landmarks, geometrical theories, and a whole panoply of ideas about cities that currently play the role of theory in urban design.

Space syntax even challenges how design questions are defined. For example, a current topic of debate in Europe is the degree to which future development should be based on the past. In historic centers, for example, there is a widespread fear of doing anything except keeping the old street system, in spite of the obvious criticism that the street system to be conserved was created by a dynamic process of growth and change as each generation modified what it inherited to meet its needs and passed it on to the next generation. Conservation leads to the paradox that to freeze this process at one point in time to conserve a specific form would be antihistorical, since it would conserve a product but violate the process that gave rise to the product.

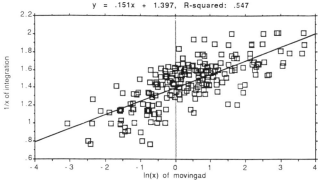

figure 30
Scattergram showing each observed line in figure 27 as a dot located on the vertical axis according to its degree of integration and on the horizontal axis according to the observed rate of pedestrian movement along the line. The correlation coefficient is .74 on a scale between 0 (no relation between the degree of integration and pedestrian movement) and 1 (a perfect relation between the two), showing how strongly the pattern of the urban grid itself influences the pattern of pedestrian movement.

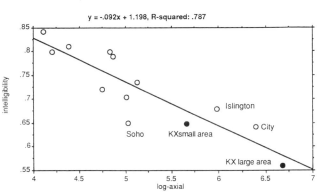

figure 31
Intelligibility index plotting intelligibility against the size of system for selected areas of London. The regression line represents the established degree of intelligibility for an area of a given size. Of the four areas at the bottom right, the farthest right, and below the line, is the King's Cross area shown in figure 24; next and above the line is the City; next, also above the line, is Islington; next following that, and below the line, is a smaller area around the King's Cross site.

Space syntax redefines this question by making the issue one of genotype rather than phenotype. We can now ask not whether we should preserve specific forms, but whether we should preserve the underlying principles of specific forms in the light of present needs, or adapt them in the direction of a new genotype. History is replete with examples of both, in that, as cities evolve they can change their genotypes as well as their phenotypes.[20] What history does not offer is a precedent for the current fashion of phenotype conservation.

By showing how we can understand urban space genotypes, space syntax does allow the genuine continuation of a historical tradition without necessarily copying its surface forms. It does so by suggesting what is essential and what is inessential in the structures of the past. The King's Cross master plan is a genotypical continuation of the logic of London. Yet it resembles no known part of London. It extends the deep structure of the existing grid, not its surface structure.

The tighter forms of reasoning permitted by space syntax thus have a liberating effect, precisely because they allow us to oppose the superstitious following of an established vernacular with abstract reason about forms and their functional consequences within an evolving structure. The intervention of theory in effect permits us to set the argument about history at the level of the evolutionary processes that generate the architecture of the city, rather than at the level of its

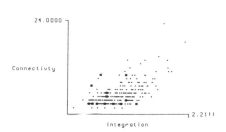

figure 33
Intelligibility scattergram of grid scheme shown in figure 32.

figure 32
Grid scheme analyzed in urban context to show how it affects the pattern of integration.

specific products. The theoretical ascent from the vernacular as social reproduction to architecture as the knowledge-able exploration of form through theory—even partial theory—is thus also an ascent from social constraint to libera-tion. Design can seek its goals not within the stultifying constraints of particular forms of social knowledge (which nev-ertheless can be and must be understood) but within the limits posed by the laws of architectural and urban space, and their realization within a particular context.

ARCHITECTURE AS SCIENCE

This redefinition of theory in terms of liberation is not obvious. At first sight, theories seem to be abstract schemes of thought that constrain rather than liberate. They appear to fix the mind in a certain way of looking rather than opening up new possibilities. However, this is to misunderstand the nature of theories, and their potential in architecture.

For a scientist, a theory means an abstract model through which the phenomena available to experience can be related to each other in such a way that their nature and behavior as phenomena seem to have been accounted for. But scien-tific theories only count if they have two kinds of clarity: the internal structure of the theory must be clear, and the ref-erence to phenomena must be clear. These two conditions create the possibility of refutation, and refutability is the morality of science. If a theory does not predict what can be seen to be the case, or fails to predict what is the case, then we must eventually give up the theory and try another. We must also give up a theory if a simpler one explains the same phenomena. There is an aesthetics as well as a morality in science.

At first sight, architectural theories appear to be rather different. An architectural theory is usually presented as a set of precepts that, if followed, lead to architectural success. The prime aim of an architectural theory thus seems not to be to explain architectural phenomena, but to guide design. We might therefore be tempted to conclude that architectural theories are normative rather than analytic—that is, they tell us how the world should be rather than how the world is—and are therefore not subject to the strict rules that govern scientific theories.

Although architectural theories do come in a normative mode, this by no means implies that they are not also analytic. On the contrary, it implies that they are. The only possible justification for a normative architectural theory is that the theory will work because this is the nature of architectural phenomena. Theories from Alberti to Le Corbusier in fact make profound and far-reaching assumptions about human nature, about perception, about behavior, as well as about the nature of architectural order. It cannot be otherwise. All normative architectural theories are also, perhaps covert-ly, analytic theories.

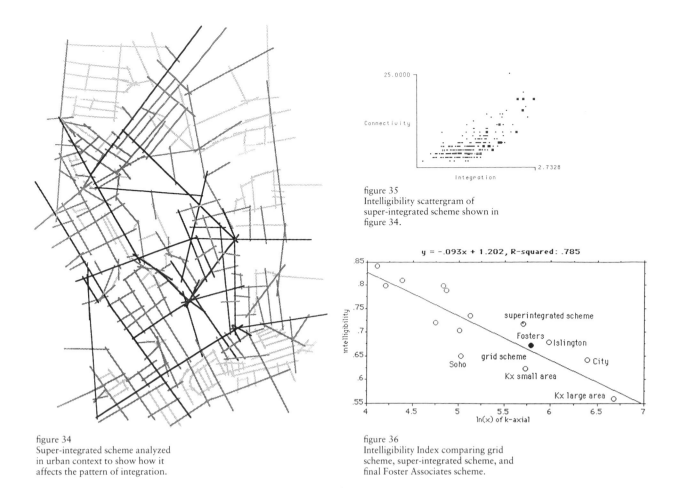

figure 34
Super-integrated scheme analyzed
in urban context to show how it
affects the pattern of integration.

figure 35
Intelligibility scattergram of
super-integrated scheme shown in
figure 34.

figure 36
Intelligibility Index comparing grid
scheme, super-integrated scheme, and
final Foster Associates scheme.

The difference between scientific theories and architectural theories, then, is not a difference in type but a difference in clarity. It has never been possible to have architectural theories that have the two kinds of clarity—of internal structure and of reference to phenomena—that are the precondition for refutability. This is why architectural theories can be refuted by life, but not by analysis. One useful effect of space syntax is that it takes certain aspects of architectural theory a little way in the direction of the two kinds of clarity. The structure of reasoning is clear, and the reference to phenomena is clear. The propositions of space syntax can therefore be shown to be wrong—and theoretically wrong—by reference to evidence. Life is right, of course, and only life can eventually decide. But it is possible that with theories that have the two kinds of clarity, more of life can be brought to bear on our theorizing at the design stage.

ARCHITECTURE AS ART—THAT IS, AS THEORETICAL CONCRETION

Does this mean, then, that the line between architecture as science and architecture as art needs to be redrawn closer to science? I do not believe so. We can call on the beautiful ideas of Ernst Cassirer on the relation between art and science:

Language and science are the two main processes by which we ascertain and determine our concepts of the external world. We must classify our sense perceptions and bring them under general notions and general rules in order to give them an objective meaning. Such classification is the result of a persistent effort towards simplification. The work of art in like manner implies such an act of condensation and concentration. . . . But in the two cases there is a difference of stress. Language and science are abbreviations of reality; art is an intensification of reality. Language and science depend on one and the same process of abstraction; art may be described as a continuous process of concretion . . . art does not admit of . . . conceptual simplification and deductive generalization. It does not inquire into the qualities or causes of things; it gives the intuition of the form of things. . . . The artist is just as much the discoverer of the forms of nature as the scientist is the discoverer of facts or natural laws.[21]

Those of us who believe, as I do, that science is on the whole a good thing, accept that science is in one sense an impoverishment—though in others an enhancement—of our experience of the world, in that it cannot cope with the density of situational experience. It has to be so. It is not in the nature of science to seek to explain the richness of particular realities, since these are invariably so diverse as to be beyond the useful grasp of theoretical simplifications.

Science is about the dimensions of structure and order that underlie complexity. Here the abstract simplifications of science can be the most powerful source of greater insight. Every moment of our experience is dense, and, as such, unanalyzable as a complete experience. But this does not mean that some of its constituent dimensions are not analyzable, and that deeper insight may not be gained from such analysis.

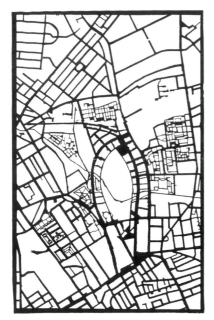

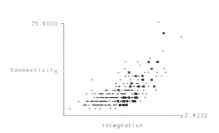

figure 37
Final scheme for King's Cross masterplan shown in urban context.

figure 38
Final scheme for King's Cross masterplan analyzed in urban context to show how it affects the pattern of integration.

figure 39
Intelligibility scattergram of final scheme shown in figure 37

This distinction is crucial to our understanding of architecture. Architectural realities are dense, and as wholes unanalyzable, but that does not mean that the role of spatial configuration, for example, in architectural realities cannot be analyzed and even generalized. The idea that science is to be rejected because it does not give an account of the richness of experience is a persistent but elementary error. Science gives us quite a different experience of reality, one that is partial and analytic rather than whole and intuitive. As such it is in itself valuable. It needs to be accepted or rejected on its own terms, not in terms of its failure to be like life or like art.

It is in any case clear that the dependence of architecture on theories, covert or explicit, does not diminish its participation in Cassirer's definition of art. This is true both in the sense that architecture is, like art, a continuous process of concretion, and also in the sense that, like art, "its aspects are innumerable." But there are also differences. The thing "whose aspects are innumerable" is not a representation but a reality, and a very special kind of reality, one through which our forms of social being are transformed and put at risk. The pervasive involvement of theory in architecture, and the fact that architecture's continuous concretion involves our social existence, define the peculiar status and nature of systematic intent of the architectural kind: architecture is theoretical concretion. Architects are enjoined both to create the new, since that is the nature of their task, and to clarify and improve the theories that tie their creation to our social existence. It is this dichotomoy that makes architecture distinct and unique. It is as impossible to reduce architecture to theory as it is to eliminate theory from architecture.

Architecture is thus both art and science, not in that it has both technical and aesthetic aspects, but in that it requires both the processes of abstraction by which we know science and the processes of concretion by which we know art. The difficulty and the glory of architecture lie in the realization of both: in the creation of a theoretical realm through building, and in the creation of an experienced reality "whose aspects are innumerable." This is the difficulty of architecture. And this is why we acclaim it.

1. Roger Scruton, *The Aesthetics of Architecture* (London: Methuen, 1979), 234; Bill Hillier, "Quite Unlike the Pleasures of Scratching," *9H* (London) 7 (1985): 66-72.

2. Julienne Hanson, *Encyclopaedia of Architecture* (New York: McGraw-Hill, forthcoming).

3. Henry Glassie, *Folk Housing in Middle Virginia* (Nashville: University of Tennessee Press, 1975), 4: 19-40.

4. Margaret Mead, "The Transmission of Culture through Artefacts," in *Continuities in Cultural Evolution* (New Haven: Yale University Press, 1966), 83-106.

5. Scruton, *The Aesthetics of Architecture*, 43.

6. To which, incidentally, he has written the best introduction. See Roger Scruton, *A Short History of Modern Philosophy: From Descartes to Wittgenstein* (London: ARK Paperbacks, 1984).

7. René Descartes, "The Principles of Philosophy," Part 2, Principle 10, *The Philosophical Works of Descartes*, CUP ed., 13:259.

8. Bill Hillier and Julienne Hanson, *The Social Logic of Space* (Cambridge: Cambridge University Press, 1984).

9. See Hillier and Hanson, *The Social Logic of Space*, for mathematical development of this concept.

10. Bill Hillier, Julienne Hanson, and H. Graham, "Ideas are in Things," *Environment & Planning B: Planning & Design* 14 (1987): 363-85.

11. Dickon Irwin, *The House the Architect Built* (M.Sc. thesis, Bartlett School of Architecture and Planning, University College London, 1989).

12. See Bill Hillier, "The Nature of the Artificial: The Contingent and the Necessary in Spatial Form in Architecture," *Geoforum* 16, no. 3, special issue on links between the natural and social sciences (1986): 163-78; and Bill Hillier, "The Architecture of the Urban Object," *Ekistics* 56, nos. 334/5, special double issue on space syntax urban research, ed. John Peponis: 5-21. It is suggested in these papers that there are three types of spatial law: type 1 are limiting laws that govern the constructibility of usable spatial patterns, and give rise to the fundamental analytic properties, such as depth and rings; type 2 are laws through which social forms express themselves in space, for example through the integration of certain types of function and the segregation of others, as seen in the French houses; and type 3 are laws through which spatial forms produce specific social effects, for example, the effect of axial patterns on movement and thus on patterns of the natural copresence of people in space, as set out in the next section.

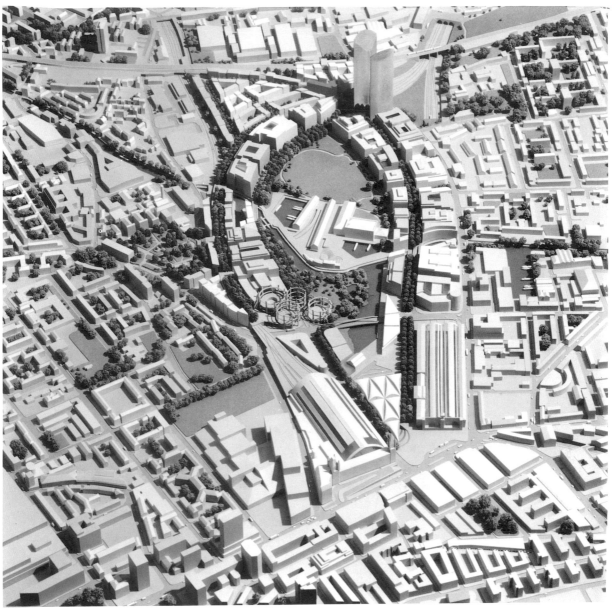

Foster Associates. Photograph: Richard Davies

figure 40
Norman Foster Associates. King's Cross masterplan, photograph of the model

13. For example, Camillo Sitte and Gordon Cullen. Even the Krier brothers are strongly influenced by this tradition.

14. All the computer programs used here form part of the Space Syntax software developed by N. Dalton of the Unit for Architectural Studies at the Bartlett School of Architecture and Planning, University College London, with funding from the Science and Engineering Research Council and our industrial partner, t² Solutions Ltd.

15. A full study of all open spaces in London was made for the Mansion House Square Project in 1984, and reported in "A Proof of Evidence of the Public Inquiry." A second study of open spaces in London, including some new ones, was made in connection with the Broadgate Development and made available in a report called "The Broadgate Spaces." (Both reports by Unit for Architectural Studies, Bartlett School of Architecture and Planning, University College London, 1989.)

16. An axial map is defined as the smallest set of straight lines that cover the open space of the area. See Hillier, "The Nature of the Artificial"; and Bill Hillier, Julienne Hanson, John Peponis, J. Hudson, and Richard Burdett, "Space Syntax," Architects Journal (November 30, 1983): 47-63.

17. These issues are dealt with at greater length in a series of recent papers. For an examination of natural movement, see Bill Hillier et al., "Natural Movement:

Or, Biggish is Beautiful," Environment & Planning B: Planning & Design (forthcoming). See also Bill Hillier and A. Penn, "Is Dense Civilization Possible: The Shape of Cities in the Twenty-first Century," in Proceedings of Watt Committee Conference on the Rational Use of Energy (London: Elsevier, forthcoming), for a discussion of the movement economy; and Bill Hillier and P. O'Sullivan, "Urban Design and Climate Change," in Proceedings of Solar Energy Society Conference on Architecture in Climate Change (forthcoming), on the urban design implications of both.

18. In the real situation, the experimentation took a rather different form, and was more oriented to pragmatic design ideas and constraints. The experiments here are therefore illustrative, not historical.

19. Bill Hillier, "Theory Liberates: Intelligent Representations and Theoretical Descriptions in Architecture and Urban Design" (inaugural lecture presented at University College London, June 13, 1990; forthcoming in The Bartlett Review).

20. Julienne Hanson, Order and Structure in Urban Space: A Morphological History of the City of London (Ph.D. diss., Bartlett School of Architecture and Planning, University College London, 1991; Cambridge: Cambridge University Press, forthcoming).

21. Ernst Cassirer, An Essay on Man (New Haven: Yale University Press, 1944; New York: Bantam Books, 1970), 152-88.

PERSPECTIVE, ITS EPISTEMIC GROUNDING, AND THE SKY

An Outline for a Research Project

Hashim Sarkis with Pegor Papazian

1. The research for this paper was begun during a fellowship at the Chicago Institute for Architecture and Urbanism, 1989-90. I have benefited from discussions with other fellows at the foundation and from the environment which it provided. I wish to thank John Whiteman, Catherine Ingraham, Michael Markham, Jennifer Bloomer, and Jerry Cohen, as well as Sonia Cooke, Ricky Burdett, Mika Hadidian, and Jane Allen. I owe many clarifications to Yehuda Safran and to the generosity of his intellect. I also wish to thank Peter Rowe for his comments on the Harvard GSD presentation draft. The students of the courses I have been teaching at MIT continue to engage this research with wonderful insight.

This research continues under the areas specified in the presentation, in the form of classes that I am teaching at MIT, Department of Architecture, and in a project, in collaboration with Pegor Papazian, on the problem of components through computer aided design models. The material presented here does not take on the shape of a self-contained argument, as much as an outline for a research project that is already branching out in several directions. I have elaborated, in footnotes, on each part of this research with material that I did not include in the oral presentation.

2. *The Concise Oxford English Dictionary,* 7th Ed., s.v. "recognition."

3. Recognition necessarily involves the study of a sign-structure within which it takes place; thus the need to study the social constructs of seeing in which it takes place. This presentation does not cover the aspect of my research that discusses this problem of visuality. (I refer the reader to the work of Norman Bryson for an extensive discussion of visuality.) I find it important to note, however, despite the fact that the bulk of this material is absent from the presentation, that my discussion of

INTRODUCTION[1]

I want to address the problem of recognizing in an architectural product the initial concepts of its design, concepts according to which design decisions are made. I will call this the problem of *recognition*. Recognition is distinguished from *cognition*, the act of looking and constructing significance within a construct of seeing. In this essay, I will not address the problem of recognition in design directly, but will concentrate on the problem of recognition in perspective. By recognition in perspective, I mean the more literal sense of recognition, "to perceive something that is previously known."[2] I will be using the term *return* to suggest the movement of recognition in the process of representation.[3]

Three terms: recognition, cognition, return.

Let me briefly attempt to relate the problem of recognition in perspective to the problem of recognition in architecture. In speaking of initial concepts and their recognition, I am evoking intentionality, or *aboutness*. In the design studio I have been taught that a concept or a coherent set of ideas has to guide the design process in order that I may construct rigorous and consistent justifications for the built product. Once the building is carried back or returned to the initial concepts, the building is considered a successful design. Rigor and consistency become the qualities of the building. A person experiencing the building would therefore be able to relate, through this rigor and consistency, the thoughts behind the building to what the building is about.

Because of the problems it raises in the study of mental processes—in the definition of experience, meaning, and representation—intentionality has been important to both the analytic and the poststructuralist schools in philosophy, albeit through emphasis or denial. It has also made its way to recent architectural theory, where related issues such as authorship, totalization, and representation have been isolated and criticized. Denial has led many architects to try to work without intentions, as if that in itself were not an intention.

The premise of my larger project lies here: because critical architectural practices have relied on classical means of representation, means that maintain conventional postulates, these means must subvert and fail the attempted criticisms.[4] An examination of intentionality's workings requires an examination of the whole process of production, not just the problems (such as authority) that it entails. In other words, revisions of theory fall short insofar as the very problems they expose at the level of the first use of the term recognition continue to operate in the means of production being used to ask such questions at the level of the second use of the term recognition.

It is for these reasons that I would like to examine the workings of intentionality in the means of production of architecture, and it is also for these reasons that although my research concerns perspective and visual cognition, this discussion is implicitly about methodology. By methodology, I refer not to the repeatable procedure by which a building is made, but to the *meta-hodos*, the second order passage of things—not the path from decision A to decision B, which can secure my return from B to A, but the operational circumstances within which such a move is undertaken. By calling both the reading of the author's intentions and the identification of the represented scene in perspective *recognition*, I not only desire to see a continuity between the two, but also to show how architecture, through its means of production, is already inadvertently grounded in acquired references and meaning—operational circumstances that traditionally have been considered to be either innocent, or extradisciplinary.

When discussing perspective, I will not make problematic issues of subject/object relations, or of natural and artificial seeing in perspective, for these issues, as Gilles Deleuze says, no longer correspond to our problems, nor do

the question of recognition attempts to find the social constructs of seeing latent within what is sometimes considered external to the process of recognition, in other words, outside the domain of visuality, and closer to the perceptual processes of cognitive science. It is for this purpose that I accept in the beginning the term *cognition* and set it in contrast with *recognition*, only to find pure cognition impossible and recognition operating as a function of itself rather than as an advanced stage of cognition.

4. I prefer to locate myself within a tradition that has come to say, with Hilary Putnam, that if "intentionality is intractable that does not mean it will go away." The problem cannot be discarded nor can it be reduced to its aspects of authority and totalization. However, and before being able to engage this position, it is important for this project, I believe, to ask questions about reference and meaning at levels where they are assumed to be non-existent, levels that are taken over by the study of perception.

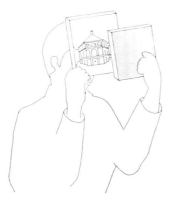

figure 1. Brunelleschi's first experiment.

5. See Hilary Putnam, *The Many Faces of Realism* (La Salle, Ill.: Open Court, 1987), 20-21.

6. See Erwin Panofsky, *Perspective as Symbolic Form*, trans. Christopher S. Wood (New York: Zone Books, 1991), 27.

they bring out any wondrous qualities through the architecture, nor do they benefit from (or even inform) the problems in vision and cognition that confront researchers and artists today. I will not dismiss perspective as simply a means of representation, or as a technique. Because I maintain that to look at the world differently is to see a different world, I do not want to question the distinction between a world and its representations, its versions.[5] Rather, I want to look *through* perspective and see how the world is a perspectival world. Thus we can begin to understand Albrecht Dürer's definition of perspective as "seeing through," and perhaps suggest a way out of perspective's exhausted and restricted discourse of oppositions.[6]

Like its title, this essay is divided into three parts. I will start with the sky, to show how even if one were to accept (or dismiss) perspective as a simply representational construct, it would still not fully return to experience what it represents. The second part will discuss the modern epistemic grounding of perspective, as well as our misconceptions of what perspective can and cannot represent. This will expose certain meanings that perspective has wrongly acquired. The third part concerns operations for constructing perspective and the confounding of its components with the components of architecture. This section will also explore possible links between perspective and related disciplines that perspectivists have excluded from their domain. I will conclude with an attempt to redefine recognition.

Evidence from the Sky

I start at an acknowledged beginning. It is said that Filippo Brunelleschi, in his first attempt to verify the operations of perspective, had to silver over the sky in his painting of the Florence Baptistry. When seen reflected in a mirror that Brunelleschi held facing the painting, the image of the Baptistry included an already-once-reflected patch of real sky from above (fig. 1). Within the construct of perspective that he mastered so well, Brunelleschi seemed unable to accommodate for the sky.

In the experiment described above, the depiction of the sky in the painting was

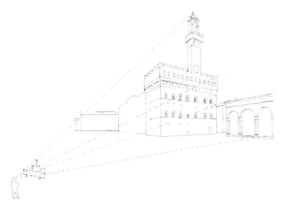

figure 2. Brunelleschi's second experiment.

replaced by a reflective silver; the image of the sky was deferred But seen reflected in the mirror, the painting's silver "sky" presented the viewer with a piece from the sky above, which even though it might have completed the cycle of deferrals, could not have appeared the same as the sky behind the baptistry when seen with the unimpeded eye (for instance, clouds would have appeared smaller and farther away). I will more carefully examine this deferral, what Hubert Damisch calls the "phase effect," later on.

In Brunelleschi's second experiment, according to Damisch, he excluded the sky completely. He held a cut-out drawing of the Castelvecchio up against the sky without using a mirror. The skyline marked the border at which his perspective stopped being operative (fig. 2).

But what is it in the construct of perspective to which the sky does not adhere? Two major phenomena that perspective explains cannot be detected in the sky, namely occlusion and foreshortening. In the sky, the effect of one figure hiding another, occlusion, does not work; there is nothing to hide in the sky. Neither does the sky foreshorten; it does not undergo any diminution, neither in depth nor laterally, that would indicate the relative placement of one body to another. If the sky does not occlude and does not foreshorten, then, in the set-up construct of perspective, as it has come down to us today, it is not perspectival. But perspectivists quickly incorporated the sky and tried to identify properties that could make the sky perspectival. I need only mention the gradation of blues in a painting that renders the sky as if it were a solid and measurable sphere in perspective, or the following argument by the second perspectivist, Alberti. In his treatise *On Painting,* while discussing composition and proportion, Alberti refers to certain philosophers "who affirm that if the sky, the stars, the sea, mountains, and all bodies should become—should God so will—reduced by half, nothing would appear to be diminished in any part to us. All knowledge of large, small; long, short; high, low; broad, narrow; clear, dark; light and shadow and every single attribute is obtained by comparison."[7]

In Alberti's account, the halving of the sky is a necessary step in the halving of the rest of the picture. What is important for me here, and even though I am

7. Leon Battista Alberti, *On Painting,* trans. John R. Spencer (New Haven: Yale University Press, 1966), 54.

figure 3. Schinkel's stage backdrop for the
queen of the night in Mozart's *The Magic Flute*.

8. Perhaps this perplexity is acting as a premonition in the opera, that is, as a meaningful fault by a painter whose perspectives were known to be so accurately constructed to the extent that he refused to correct the optical distortions in them. This particular scene introduces to the audience the queen who appears to be a good, but victimized mother, in search of her daughter, but whose true evil nature is revealed at the end. Schinkel is known to have introduced the narrative into his stage designs. He not only drew the stage design but also the actors and the action. See Helmut Borsch-Supan, *Karl Friedrich Schinkel Stage Designs* (Berlin: Ernst and Sohn, 1990), 11. By relying on occlusion and foreshortening, but by confusing their order in the sky, Schinkel is perhaps also using the sky as a function of the narrative, effectively recreating the deferral of Brunelleschi's "phase effect." While in Brunelleschi's experiment the deferral is tied to the verification process, it could be seen here as linked to the narrative.

taking the statement out of its context, is that Alberti sought to attend to the sky from within the same system with which he described the rest of the world, despite its intangible attributes. Alberti's *costruzione legittima*, which, unlike Brunelleschi's perspective method, depicted nonexistent spaces and skies, did not need to project anything, was not concerned with producing geometrical verifications of perception, and therefore did not need to accommodate a real sky.

Although in this essay I am not concerned with determining once and for all if the sky is perspectival, I would like to illustrate further that even if the sky is contained in the perspective construct, it always performs a deferral not very different from Brunelleschi's first experiment. (And this is where my argument, I think, departs from that of Hubert Damisch.) For this purpose, I have in mind two examples. The first is an image of the sky, and only the sky, produced in perspective, namely Schinkel's stage backdrop for the queen of the night in Mozart's *The Magic Flute* (fig. 3).

Here, under a domelike arrangement of stars, and above low clouds that obscure the bottom edge of the scene where the figure of the queen centers and scales the celestial construction, the sky is subjected to rules of perspective. There is a gradual foreshortening of the stars, and the blue is shaded to accentuate the distribution of light and distance. When I identify the sky, when I try calling it "sky," this blue slips out from behind the stars as if it belongs to a different surface closer to the sky. But when I observe a gradation of blues, the sky slips out once again, this time from behind the blue, as if all the operations undertaken to capture the sky only managed to contain the night. In Schinkel's image, a few stars appear to be in front of some of the clouds at the bottom. By relying on occlusions and foreshortenings in order to represent the sky, and then by confusing their order, Schinkel is activating the presence of the sky in his picture.[8]

But the sky in Schinkel's backdrop is not outside the structure of the image. It is not a mirror. The sky does not transgress the structure of the perspective picture. Instead it allows the structure to exceed its role as a picture-making device—a device for recognition—becoming a device for consciously imagining, projecting, and cognitively *picturing* a sky. It exceeds, exhausts, and, for those very reasons, paradoxically maintains the construct that attempts to contain it. More important, it also exhibits the means of its making.

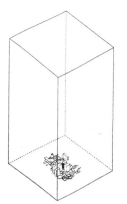

figure 4. The sky box.

figure 5. Elevation of the sky.

The second example of the sky's deferral in perspective comes from the tutorial for a computer-aided design system developed jointly by IBM and Skidmore, Owings and Merrill.[9] The tutorial recommends the following procedure for constructing the sky. A box 45 miles by 45 miles and 100 miles high is placed over the data of a project (fig. 4). Its sides are constructed out of overlapping rectangles, which foreshorten in a geometrical progression until they reach the bottom edge or the horizon (fig. 5). The rectangles change gradually from a dark blue at the top, at the zenith, to a much lighter blue at the horizon, where the sky meets the dark ground. The whole box is then put into perspective with the rest of the data. What is occurring here is that the sky in its upright representation of single flat surfaces is already feigning perspective. In other words, the foreshortening and the occlusions are first simulated on a flat surface and then put into perspective again. The sky is in perspective twice; it is excessively perspectival.

The above examples do not indicate an absence of perspective in the sky. The sky does not exclude perspective but is a *construction through* its operations and components. The sky entails that the act of seeing be performed consciously against what I identify and name, against simple recognition, and therefore allows, like in Brunelleschi's experiment, a constant displacement *within* the construct of seeing. Indeed, I can describe the sky in terms of the operations of perspective. The sky in perspective is where lines keep converging, where projections are exhausted, and where there are no secure returns. I can also describe the sky in terms of perspective's components. It is the picture plane behind everything else, or the horizon stretched to the zenith. The sky, while escaping measurement (orthogonal measures are key in a perspectival construction) no longer interrupts the homogeneity of the perspective scene, but it still suspends and stretches the operations of seeing through perspective and exposes projection, imagining and picturing. And while the sky is produced out of densities of air, graded blue shades, and shadows of clouds, its infinite attribute could be thought to be a result of this cognitive displacement. The Brunelleschi "phase effect" is, after all, a performance of a parallel cognitive activity that maintains perspective as a construct beyond the recognition of the scene.

Perspectivists, ever since Brunelleschi tried proving the validity of their craft, have been aware of the difficult presence of the sky in their pictures. They reduced its infinite attribute to a point and its countenance to a background against which their figures, drawn in perspective, would rise out of the perspec-

9. *Graphics Application Tutorial Three*, IBM Architecture and Engineering Series, 1988, 29-35.

10. By "picture making," I mean the act of achieving a representation in a fixed medium or format, whereas "picturing" is the act of constructing the image through certain reflexive resemblances to what it represents (although it only achieves a displaced representation). My terminology does not compare images and things, but rather the activity of producing images of things. I have omitted from this outline of "Evidence from the Sky" a discussion of the questions of evidence and redundancy in research methodology, and also some other examples that I am studying. Mainly, these include Pozzo's ceiling paintings, Buckminster Fuller's domes, and the auditorium perspectives by Mies van der Rohe, where the presence of the sky is produced through architectural means.

11. For an elaborate description of the origins of perspective and its uses in the Renaissance, see Hubert Damisch, *L'origine de la perspective* (Paris: Flammarion, 1987).

12. That is, a perspective whose filiation starts at Alberti's *costruzione legittima*.

13. See Maurice Merleau-Ponty, "Eye and Mind," in *The Primacy of Perception* (Evanston, Ill.: Northwestern University Press, 1964), 159-90.

tive order. Perspectivists have always desired a full and instantaneous recognition of the scene in perspective. All the activity described in the sky is encapsulated in an unobservable leap, in the brevity of "representation." No matter how difficult the sky was to render, it could no longer endanger the rigor and consistency of perspective , and was always to be simulated through perspectival means. Atmospheric perspective was assigned to take care of that. Their desire, as I will show in the following section, has fed into the discourse about perspective in design. By pointing to how the sky can be recognized *against* what constitutes it in perspective, I am preparing a route by which to return and reconsider perspective in architecture. It is not only the sky that reveals the cognitive activities of perspective, but because of the absence of recognizable tangible attributes, one can see these activities better against the sky.[10]

THE PROBLEM OF RECOGNITION

Perspective, as it has been handed down in design thinking, is most successful, as a picture-making device, when it can faithfully return to experience what it has undertaken to depict. Although verification might have been *one* of the early uses of perspective, a certain discourse has accumulated and solidified around it, as if it were the sole and original purpose of perspective.[11] In order to elaborate on this point, I will try to take the problem of recognition in this section through a consideration of perspective's representational and semantic tasks.

In architectural production, and because of a certain dubious similarity to retinal projections, perspective is assigned to illustrate what experiential effects other drawings like plans, sections, and elevations, will have. Perspective, since Brunelleschi, submits to and illustrates the precedence of orthographic forms of projection. When constructing a "legitimate" perspective[12], we tend to rely on the disposition of elements in plan and their composition vertically. This, in brief, is the verificational use of perspective in design. But this use, when considered with respect to received knowledge about the kinds of spaces that can be represented in perspective, discloses more limitations in how architectural design has been using perspective.

A philosophical distinction between geometrical space and experiential space, like Merleau-Ponty's for instance, questions whether perspective, because of its adherence to a geometric construct, can represent subjective experience.[13] In such an argument, because perspective is limited by the orthogonality of its means, it may be inferred that perspective is confined to illustrating the orthogonality of the architecture, not just that of the drawing itself.

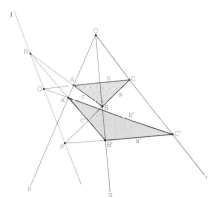

figure 6. Illustration of Desargues's theory.

Because of these epistemic fixations, perspective in architectural thinking and production is used to reaffirm the established distinctions, such as that of geometrical versus experiential space. However, this restriction does not come from a careful evaluation of what perspective can or cannot do. The alleged link, forced on perspective, between orthography and experience is too fragile to be sustained. The return to orthogonality is too quick. A certain semantics, building on these attributes, has maintained perspective in these confines.

According to Panofsky's canonical essay "Perspective as 'Symbolic Form'," perspective, in its adherence to the geometric construct of the *costruzione legittima*, embodies a homogeneous, commensurable, and infinite space. Certain corollaries of such assumptions are now so grounded in the understanding of perspective that it is difficult to see them as anything but properties of the construct itself: the privileged viewpoint, subjective view, subject-based (rather than object-based) representation, pictorial space, infinite space, punctiform subject. Moreover, the security of perspective's scientific pretenses (in this case, that all the components function together systemically under a unifying projective geometry in a repeatable manner) prevents the image from expressing the heterogeneous, the incommensurable, and the finite, which are the properties ascribed to "natural perspective." Here again, the opposition between artificial space and natural space surreptitiously returns to this modern understanding of perspective as a visual convention, a habit of seeing. The same argument has also preconditioned our belief that the Renaissance viewer immediately indulged in what perspective was only much later used to signify.[14] Indeed, it is the space of projective geometry, not perspective, that is homogeneous, commensurable, and infinite.

According to Panofsky's argument, theories of linear perspective in painting have come to locate the moment of conformity of a depicted space—the moment of artificial perspective's realization and closure—as the vanishing point. When the picture adheres to Alberti's construct, it yields a homogeneous and infinite geometrical space. But this has not always been the case. Such components as a high horizon identifying a celestial scene, or a cone of vision extromitted from the medieval eye, evoked referents different from those of the coherent model or its symbolic form, even before the coherent model within which these components were orchestrated became known as perspective. Moreover, because there was not a coherent scheme by which to draw in perspective, the domain of the components' operation was much broader, ranging from religious to optical and even physiological considerations. A succession of perspective theorists sought to free the coherent construct from the discrepancies resulting from such associations. Alberti, for instance, made the claim that painters had no use of the study of physiology of the eye.

14. This last argument is thoroughly covered in Damisch, *L'origine de le perspective*, chapter 2.

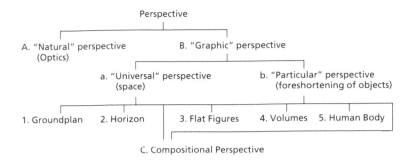

figure 7. Chart of Pomponius Gauricus's categories of perspective, after Robert Klein.

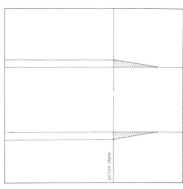

figure 8. The horizon refracted by the picture plane.

15. I will not deal with the "subjective view" attribute of perspective in this presentation. I just want to mention that Leibniz, who wrote after Desargues, described perspectivism as being "the truth of relativity rather than the relativity of truth." It could not have been with him, and perhaps not at his time, that perspective became known as a relative and subjective means of representation, even though the restriction of viewing to a point was, since the beginning, seen as a technical limitation. (See the discussion of Pomponius Gauricus in part three of this essay.) See Gilles Deleuze, *Le Pli, Leibniz et le Baroque* (Paris: Editions de Minuit, 1988), 27-30. Joel Snyder discusses this topic in a forthcoming book.

As scientists tried to explain how this curious construct owed its coherence to a point, a new geometry— "projective geometry"—arose. For one thing, this geometry accepted that parallel lines met at infinity and that the basic unit of geometry was not only the point, but the point and the line. When Gerard Desargues brought forward his theory in 1639, he was able to overlay fully the construction of perspective with the explanation of projective geometry: "If two triangles ABC and A'B'C' are placed in such a way that their lines AA', BB', and CC' intersect at one point, then the three points aa', bb', and cc' lie on the same straight line"(fig. 6).

It is difficult to explain this theory in planar geometry, but if you imagine for a moment that the two triangles are the faces of a solid body set in perspective, Desargues's explanation becomes obvious. Therefore, the way perspective explains foreshortenings, and overlaps—that is, the relationships of objects in space—can now be explained through this geometry. More importantly, projective geometry, because of its projection properties and the translation of points into lines, provides a homogeneous and regulated quality to the spaces and objects it describes. From here on and not before, the discourse of homogeneity and infinite space becomes attached to perspective.[15]

Perspective has therefore preceded and seems to be surviving its signification as a symbolic form. This is not because perspective is a natural way of seeing. Even if it is, I will have no use for perspective until I can make it problematic in architecture, as *trompe l'oeil*, for example. Nor does perspective survive because it is simply a pictorial convention that has been acquired by habit. As I will suggest in the following section, perspective, through its construction and components, indelibly marks the way things are seen, described, and made when our world is seen, described, and made through perspective.

I have one more observation to recall from the first section and to carry with me to the third. If we do not acknowledge from the beginning the cognitive activity necessary to put two lines together in perspective, then recognition will always repress the cognitive act, and the discourse on perspective will always remain tautological.

PERSPECTIVES AND COMPONENTS

Having made the closed round of recognition, I will now examine how perspective functions as an integrated system of rules and components. Here again, there are quick returns, and again, the task of recognition has been to overwhelm seeing and hide the fact that the components of perspective are doing more than represent, and that they are capable of informing architecture more contingently and individually than simply through the coherence of the construct. And here again, the modern epistemic grounding of perspective has restricted its uses in design.

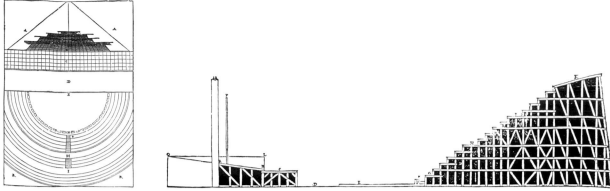

figure 9. Plan and section of Serlio's theater.

The Perspective of Pomponius Gauricus

In Robert Klein's *Form and Meaning*, a perspectival lineage from the early sixteenth-century treatise *De sculptura* by Pomponius Gauricus is explained in a diagram that begins with a raw and undefined general term, "perspective," and ends with "compositional perspective" as its culminating, artificial pole (fig.7). Compositional perspective is made from an uneasy assemblage of five components: groundplan, horizon, flat figures, volumes, and the human body.[16]

Klein's reading focuses on how Gauricus, writing almost a century after Alberti, tried to legitimate perspective as a liberal art. In this pyramidal list, the attempt to realize a homogeneous space, according to Klein, is impeded by a certain bifocal method of construction with which Gauricus was trying to solve for the singular point at infinity, but of whose rules he was ignorant. Gauricus had developed his perspective without knowing the *costruzione legittima*. Had he been aware of Alberti's method, Gauricus would have written otherwise. What is happening, Klein explains, is a misunderstanding, an awkwardness in construction that could have been, and indeed eventually was, worked out.[17] Klein then tries to justify and contextualize some of the discrepancies through a comparison between a bifocal construction method, like that of Gauricus, and one that relies on a single vanishing point for drawing the checkered floor, like Alberti's.[18]

The aspect of Klein's argument that attracts me is *where* he seems to find the inconsistency. It is found partly in the difference between images produced according to Gauricus and those produced through Alberti's system, but partly also in their components. Gauricus's subdivision of perspective's components into volumes, flat figures, and the human body on the "particular" or objects side, and horizon and groundplan on the "universal" or space side, according to Klein, had more to do with the construction of a narrative in painting, an *istoria*, than with pictorial depiction. Perspective, as we have come to know it, should not allow for such a specified usage, or for a distinction between things and the space of their containment.

Perhaps the problem can be posited differently. I do not want to equate the paradigmatic strength of the perspective model with the unification of its components at the vanishing point, nor do I want to equate the restriction of the verification act to a geometric point with the restriction of the subject of the painting to a point in space. Other possibilities can be inferred if I accept that a perspective is being produced and called perspective despite the unorthodoxy of the image. As Klein contends, "a picture executed according to the precepts of Gauricus would give a Trecento spatial depiction: the checkerboard would be correct, but of no help in placing objects; a central vanishing point would be lacking, and the foreshortenings would be anarchic, without consideration of the viewpoint. If Gauricus' checkerboard is interesting to the history of perspective, his instruction on foreshortening, with its strange anachronism, has worth only as a document in the sociology of art."[19]

16. Robert Klein, "Pomponius Gauricus on Perspective," in *Form and Meaning* (Princeton: Princeton University Press, 1979), 105.

17. While the problem of modernist readings of early perspective is an interesting topic, it is not my concern here to discuss the reasons behind the moderns' attitude toward Renaissance perspective. A very rigorous study of this topic can be found in James Elkins, "The Modern Understanding of Renaissance Perspective" (Ph.D. diss., University of Chicago, 1989).

18. Klein recalls Paolo Uccello's irritation with the restriction of viewing to a single point in Alberti's method. Uccello chose the bifocal method in order to expand the range for seeing the perspective image "as a protest against the arbitrary postulate of the perspectivists: that the eye of the spectator must be fixed." Is it not only for verification that it needs to be fixed?

19. Klein, "*Pomponius Gauricus on Perspective*," 123.

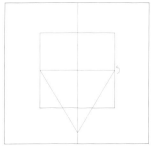

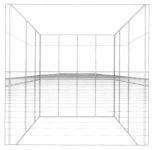

figure 10. Rotating the picture plane.   figure 11. A Miesian lobby.

20. There are several descriptions by art historians of perspective "incidents" that attest to the practicability of these breakdowns in making the construction of perspective a device for understanding the depicted scene. Damisch's description of Serlio's theater in *L'origine de la perspective* and Joel Snyder's description of Las Meninas are accounts that presume that the subject possesses a knowledge of the construction method of perspective, in order for the significance to be constructed. See Joel Snyder, "Las Meninas and the Mirror of the Prince," *Critical Inquiry* (Spring 1985).

21. This section was written with the assistance of Pegor Papazian.

22. See Damisch, *L'origine de la perspective.*

23. Hilary Putnam, *Reason, Truth, and History* (Cambridge: Cambridge University Press, 1981).

What separates the history of perspective from the history of its usage? Perhaps such a document in the "sociology of art" also refers to possible other perspectives that once existed alongside artificial perspective and the "symbolic form" we have come to know.

Gauricus produces a format to help him *narrate through* the construct of perspective. He confounds the components of perspective with the components of his narrative. His format confuses abstract and physical entities. He makes no clear distinction between what is represented and the devices used to construct their representation in perspective: for Gauricus's horizon, I can read horizon and vanishing points; and for his groundplan, I can read bifocal measuring points, plan, and ground. Picture plane, walls, as well as backdrops are read into the list under flat figures. It is also possible to put the viewing point, the viewers, and the actors all under human body, and to confound objects of his perspective with the props of the dramatic narrative.[20]

COMPONENTS[21]

Horizon and Picture Plane (figs. 8,9)

The horizon is said to be located four kilometers from an observer standing on a flat plane in Kansas on a clear April day. This distant horizon is inaccessible to the space of architecture. However, when a picture plane is introduced, a refraction of the line of sight or of the ground plane occurs (as in Serlio's theater), bringing the horizon into the immediate space.[22] It may even become an architectural element or a tool for measurement. In the case of Serlio's theater, the lines of refraction—from flat stage, to tilted plane, to backdrop—divide the stage into zones that correspond to the different activities on the stage. The perspectival organization of the space also reflects the divisions required by the dramas to be enacted.

Mechanisms for Constructing Perspective (figs. 10,11)

When a picture plane is rotated from its position in plan to elevation in order to reveal the constructed view, the rotation axis is usually the horizon, because it keeps the projection lines in place. This act of rotation can be seen captured in a Miesian lobby. The glass elevation is reflected in the marble floor, and the glass mullions align with the space between the marble tiles, producing the effect of rotation around a horizon. In this case the horizon is brought in close tension with the end of the ground plane.

I will not attempt any generalization about components. It is important not to return to a general perspective theory, but if anything, to make it a property of use-oriented and contingent constructs, and, as Hilary Putnam says, to "hold that *what objects does the world consist of?* is a question that only makes sense to ask within a theory or a description."[23] I want to continue to think through perspective *within* the above descriptions at the level of their operational circumstances and methodologies, in order to reposition the concerns about recognition in design that were raised at the beginning of this investigation. Clearly, there are as many perspectives as there are specific descriptions in perspective. A particular description, or use of perspective, relies on the

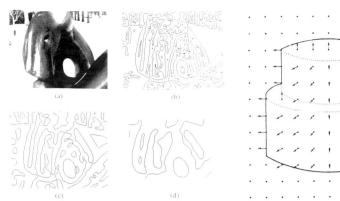

figure 12. David Marr's primal sketch.   figure 13. David Marr's 3-D model.

24. The theory is referred to as RBC, or recognition by components. It was elaborated by some of Marr's students. For an extensive account of this theory, see David Marr's *Visual Cognition*.

open configuration of its components, their ability to merge with the components of what is seen, and—as in the examples of the sky, or the Miesian lobby—to expose the cognitive activity behind the construct of perspective.

The difficulty with components becomes, then, how and where to fix them. The definition of an entity, of a component, is only pertinent to the range within which it can retain its identity, its fixedness. In turn, the question of how I can suspend the systemic unity of perspective, and the unengaged operation of its components, without losing the pertinence of the construct—so that I may, as in Gauricus's example, still call the construct "perspective"—is also contingent upon how much of perspective's use in a particular situation is determined by its components. This question does not serve as a new theory of perspective; it only defines an approach to its latent possible uses.

Another problem, tied to the definition of components, is the domain in which such a definition is possible. As I mentioned in the above discussion of perspective's epistemic grounding, the description of perspective can no longer be limited to projective geometry. Other disciplines that initially informed the definition of perspective's components have to be exposed, but we now move out from the closed pictorial language to the problem that the early perspectivists faced: how can one operate within such a large domain, not only of uncertainty but of conflicting descriptions of the same thing? Do we have to study all the related fields, such as optics and cognitive science, in order to be able to use perspective? One must question the reasons for the exclusion of optics and other fields from the perspectivist's area of competence, which has contributed to the reduction of perspective to a technique of representation. Perspective has not been able to confront the disciplines that initially informed it. In attempting to relearn the science of optics and to look at recent research in visual cognition, my aim is not to use the computational method in design, nor to generalize the problem of recognition—even though in both cases the possibilities are more than tempting—but to better understand the conditions of operation of a not-so-disciplined domain of knowledge.

In the work of the late David Marr on the computation of perceptual processes in vision, the following procedure takes place. Initially, a "primal sketch" is formed from an image (fig. 12). It consists of very faint impressions made up of hues, outlines, or shades depending on the information available. What is called a "2 1/2 dimensional sketch" is then intensified from this information. Even though it is vague and subject-based, the sketch begins to suggest a three-dimensional form, which becomes better sculpted in a following stage, the "3-D model" (fig. 13). In the last stage, the objects observed in the initial image are recognized. The viewer breaks down the perceived volumes into simple geometrical solids and then recognizes the object by identifying the composition of these solids.[24]

Notice that Marr's description of the act of recognition involves a series of intensification processes. At each stage there is a distinct set of operations or components: in the case of the primal sketch, for example, the operations involve the extraction of shades or contours from an image. The transition from one stage to another, however, relies on the predefined hierarchy among these different representations: from primal sketch, to 2 1/2-D, to 3-D, to recognition by components. Recognition of an object is only possible when its

25. See James Gibson, *The Ecological Approach to Visual Perception* (Hillsdale, N. J.: Lawrence Erlbaum Associates, 1986), 5-44.

26. Ibid., 36.

27. Ibid., 127.

components have been identified, and not at earlier levels. Marr is not interested in naming the shaded areas in the primal sketch, for they might not correspond to the outlines of the observed object. All the components of the resultant image, however, have to be named. What is not describable through components cannot be considered to be part of the observed object. There can be no excess or lack of information.

When Marr starts his experiment by looking at an image of a cup, the success of his experiment depends on whether he can—after a succession of preliminary images, sketches, and processes—find the right tools in order to perceive a cup. After all, the aim of Marr's research program is to find the right tools to achieve recognition. The world of objects has to be recognized by its components. The moment of return to the cup might also be problematic, even in cognitive studies. The task of vision and its constructs has been to inform the viewer that there is nothing to see (only confirmations of what the viewer had been taught to see). Recognition is the terminus and closure of a perceptual process. Its object, the cup, is predetermined. Perhaps it is time to start "unlearning," as Ponge says, and to explore the possibility of naming the components of the object after every representation—in effect, to imagine Marr walking away from his experiment saying, "This is not a cup."

It is not absurd to think of such an approach. After all, the approach of another cognitive scientist, James J. Gibson, names components—in his case "invariants" and "affordances"—in an unmediated description of the environment. This procedure allows a description of compositions that constitute the cup without necessarily calling it "cup." Gibson's definition of an unmediated description of the environment does not rely on a disciplinary account that is imbued with meaning from beyond the act of cognition, like that of physics or mathematics.[25] Invariants are the persistent attributes of the optic array. They range from geometric entities to intensities of light. Affordances are those "surfaces, layouts, objects, and events that are of special concern."[26] They are considered the graspable entities of the ungraspable ecological environment that a perceiver's activity can afford, thus they are called affordances. Gibson writes: "Perhaps the composition and layout of surfaces *constitute* what they afford. If so, to perceive them is to perceive what they afford. This is a radical hypothesis, for it implies that the 'values' and 'meaning' of things in the environment can be directly perceived. Moreover, it would explain the sense in which values and meanings are external to the perceiver."[27]

Gibson is able to jump to recognition at every stage of Marr's complete process. That is, he relies on the ability of one means of description, such as the primal sketch, to intensify information from within toward the moment of recognition. Gibson, however, maintains that the description of the environment as surfaces, shades, and planes is unmediated. It is the way the environment is. But if the perceiver walks into Gibson's environment and describes it using Gibson's very tools for description (planes, surfaces, shades, and textures), a certain tautology occurs in the production of meaning through already recognized elements. This support of a description against itself puts into question, from within Gibson's theory, the possibility of an unmediated description of the world, and the construction of meaning through perceptual processes alone. In that sense, Gibson's immediate environment is nostalgic for an originary setting, one that awaits its "discovery" by a meaning-emanating perceiver. He believes in a pure form of cognition. But cognition as a

figure 14. The eye according to Descartes in the *Dioptrics*.

means of constructing significance alone cannot be possible. Every description is a mediated description.

Recognition is imminent. And after taking the term through all the above arguments, I will attempt a redefinition that I hope will recall the cognitive activity in the sky, the role of components, and this inevitable return to, but displacement of, the processes of recognition.

Recognition could be redefined as the moment when the elements by means of which a process of representation progressed are displaced. That is, in the particular case of perspective, recognition could be the moment when, after some basic givens are identified as components in perspective, and after these basic components build up to the description and recognition of the scene or the design, their own artifice is exposed either through perspective, or through some other form of description. I do not want to set up a hierarchy, as David Marr does, between different methods of description or an originary description, as Gibson does.[28]

This redefinition, however primitive and premature, could suggest some changes in how means of representation are understood and used in design. An image might, for example, suggest the constructs that created it, and give them back to experience. Instead of maintaining that its means of representation are innocent, an image might perform them as ways of its seeing and its making. It might thereby reveal its configuration in design and extend it into experience. If we are confronted with the possibility that an image of such qualities may not be reached, I suggest that this unattainability could itself become a quality of the image. It would not engage in its own specificity, and would perhaps blur at the details. It would be an inarticulate form, preceding and then constructing its own significance, but doing so anew every time it is encountered. It is not by coincidence, I think, that these observations about perspective were prompted by looking at the sky.

In every act of "looking through" perspective there is admittedly a recognition, a return to Brunelleschi's first experiment. It is a conscious return, following from the moment of recognition, like that of Sisyphus to his rock at the base of the mound. In a famous drawing from Descartes's *Dioptrics* , there is a little man behind the eye (fig. 14). He looks out from a deep darkness at projections on the retina. According to Descartes, this is a metaphor for the mind looking at the retinal image. But in the science of optics, the little man creates a difficulty known as the homunculus problem. The man looks at the retinal image with his own two eyes, and behind each of his eyes there must be another little man looking at retinal projections, and so on without end.

The science of optics is scared of this endless proliferation. It tries to break down the little man's actions. This does not mean, however, that the homunculus needs to be excluded from the domain of perspective, for every time the outline of an object is drawn through the operations and components of perspective, it builds up to the recognition of the object, only to displace against the specificity of its definition. This displacement does not occur because there is no correct explanation for seeing, or because we are simply caught up with a wrong metaphor for seeing.[29] It occurs because the little man *sees* and *sees how* perspective's components are composed as he draws the image again and again with the same or different means, in effect performing the infinite other possibilities that the image might be.

28. See George Lakoff, *Women, Fire, and Dangerous Things* (Chicago, Ill.: University of Chicago Press, 1987).

29. See John Hyman, *The Imitation of Nature* (Oxford: Basil Blackwell, 1989), 16-18.

Credits:
Figs. 1, 2: Hubert Damisch, *L'Origine de la Perspective* (Paris: Flammarion, 1987).
Fig. 3: Helmut Borsch-Supan, *Karl Friedrich Schinkel Stage Designs* (Berlin: Ernst und Sohn, 1990).
Figs. 4, 5: Graphics Application Tutorial Three, *IBM Architecture and Engineering Series*, 1988.
Fig. 9: Sebastiano Serlio, *The Five Books of Architecture* (New York: Dover Publications, 1982).
Fig. 12: David Marr and Hildreth, "Theory of Edge Detection," *Proc. R. Soc. Lond.* B 207: 187-217.
Fig. 13: David Marr, *Vision* (New York: W. H. Freeman and Company, 1982).
Fig. 14: René Descartes, *The Philosphical Writings of Descartes*, Volume 1 (Cambridge: Cambridge University Press, 1985).

EX LIBRIS ARCHITECTURE

Lars Lerup

So I have erected one
of [the Collector's] dwellings,
with books as the building stones,
before you,
and now he is going to disappear inside,
as is only fitting.

1. In the Margin[2]

In the Derridian universe, Deconstruction is the mode of analysis, while writing is the mode of composition.[3] Design as composition is a form of writing that lies beyond the analytical concerns of deconstruction. The reader may see no relationship between the work discussed here and work of the architects of Deconstruction; however, the basic concern of Derrida's project—to unsettle the way we think by radically displacing the underpinnings of our thought processes—is shared by both Deconstruction and grammatology.

The formal difference between my work and theirs may be due to the apparent preoccupation on the part of the architects of Deconstruction with the representation of the analysis implied by Deconstruction, its decenteredness and fragmentation. I am instead preoccupied with grammatology and its "interrogation of the relationship between knowledge and metaphor."[4]

My concern is with the process of modern composition,[5] and with Derrida's suggestion that writing is no longer the representation of what we say. In architectural terms: form is no longer the representation of what we do (what the user or occupant does as represented by the program), but is rather a somewhat independent process that weaves new webs of potential meaning with its own history and metaphorical parallels. This suggestion undermines the very basis for design as we have known it, opening the door to a new play of form and meaning.

Now on to the scene of writing.

2. Firewood

While driving through the Alps to see an old house, site of a new library extension, I notice stacks of firewood in the periphery of my vision. The stacks, on closer inspection, lean against exterior walls of houses, protected by the overhanging eaves, or sometimes form entire houses of firewood. Piled like bricks, they are like a building material: the selection of a tree, the sawing, the felling, the cutting, the transport, the chopping, and the piling.

Mesmerizing in their persistent monotony, under each of the eaves, next to each house, each stack of firewood is pure production, beyond both style and representation. Added to a house's walls, a stack gives thickness and weight. When a stack fills an entire wall, the roof of the house belongs to the stack and—reduced, elemental, mute, compact, yet loose in its rudimentary stack-construction—the pile of wood becomes a house without an interior, a nonhouse, as a model of a house is more like a house than the house itself.

When held up as a Neanderthal comparison with the thousands of books in the old house, firewood surreptitiously moves into the Ur-realm of writing, next to Derrida's *gramme* or trace—wood, paper, books, texts, words, and the spaces in between.

3. Books

The old house stands Palladian and villa-like, against the surrounding Alps. The books that its owner obsessively and painstakingly collects and stacks against the walls and in little piles on the floor are his fuel. He loves them. They are an integral part of the house. Thus pochéed by the great and ever present multitude of books and their contents, the house become thicker, more protected against the chill of the winter (and the times), while the rooms become smaller and cozier. Books, too, take their place as building material.

There is a striking parallel between the stored physical heat of the neatly stacked firewood outside the house and the stored intellectual heat of the neatly stacked books inside the house.

Books, like firewood, are hand-held, hand-shaped, and hand-sized, ready to be lifted, shifted, and stored away for a rainy day. Such knowledge, hovering in the analogical fold between books and firewood, induced me to respond enthusiastically to the book collector's request for drawings for a private library adjacent to his house.

4. Bookhouse

Returning to America, I am haunted by the plans, the books, the firewood, the thickened wall (stone, books, and firewood), and the mysterious light that dominates the interior of the house. This is no ordinary house. This is no ordinary light, created by the unusual thickness of the wall, the wall openings with layers of draperies, solid shutters, the windows themselves, the outer slatted wood shutters, and the odd rakish angle of the alp that soars to the sky just

House / Firewood

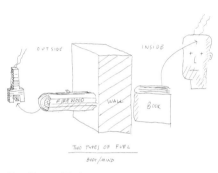

Two Types of Fuel

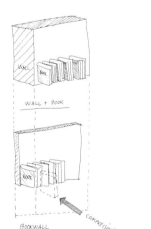

Beginning: Compression of Wall

behind the house, shoveling light down its slopes into the rooms. Here it intertwines with the thousands of fires lit by the books.

Architecture, like alchemy, engenders in me a desire to forge an alloy of form and content. Until the project is finished I play with rules that may be set, but whose destiny is sheer desire. When the collector adds his books to the walls of his house, he (unknowingly) gives them to architecture. The metaphorical and actual proximity between wood, book, and wall produces a smoldering fire that fuses them into one material in the new library.

More obliquely, when the collector gives his books away, his personal needs and desires are set aside in favor of the books and architecture. Now he must work for architecture as I do.

5. TRANSFORMATION

If the present villa is a house with space for books and their collector, the new library addition must (in the spirit of fusion) transform this triad, so that book and house become inseparable, and the collector (the reading subject) becomes but an uneasy visitor. The displacement of the reader in favor of the book becomes my obsession, part of a general strategy to overthrow the hegemony of the subject, architecturally and economically speaking, as well as to explore the potential relationship between subject and object.

The severance of subject and object is not intended to demonstrate some quotidian malaise, but rather to free them both from dependency. Curiously, this may allow the subject to inhabit the previously inaccessible solid of the surrounding woodpiles, however briefly and fleetingly. He may become like Sir John Soane, who gladly removed himself to the attic of his house in Lincoln's Inn Fields because his collection of fragments left no more

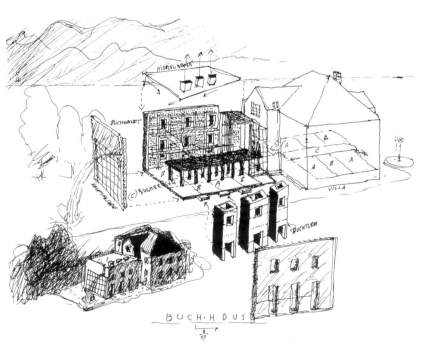

Bookhouse Transformation

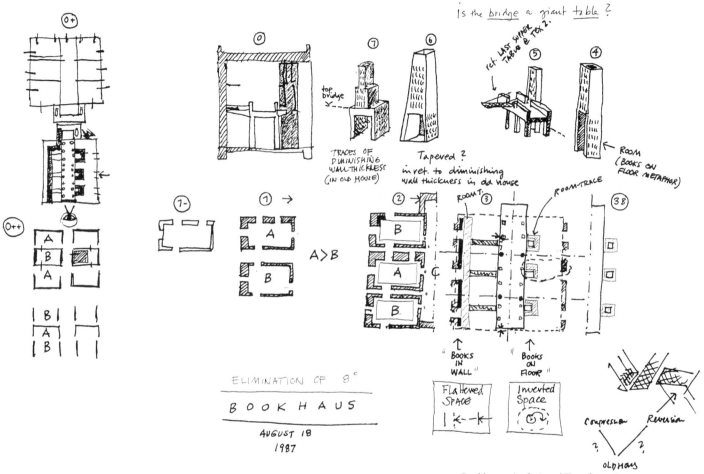

Is the bridge a giant table?

0+

0++

| A |
| B |
| A |

| B |
| A |
| B |

0

7

top bridge

TRACES OF
DIMINISHING
WALL THICKNESS
(IN OLD HOUSE)

6

ret. LAST SUPPER
TABLE & TEX 2.

5

4

ROOM
(BOOKS ON
FLOOR METAPHOR)

Tapered?
in ret. to diminishing
wall thickness in old house

7-

1 →

A
B

A > B

2 →

B
A
B

ROOM T.

3

ROOM-TRACE

3B

↑ BOOKS
IN
WALL

↑ BOOKS
ON
FLOOR

Flattened
Space

Inverted
Space

ELIMINATION CF 8°

BOOK HAUS

AUGUST 18
1987

Compression ?   Reversion ?

OLD HAUS

Bookhouse: Analysis and Transformation

space in which to live. The house and the books are no longer an expression and extension of the subject, they are a world by themselves.

5.1 Compression

The first strategy in transforming the villa is to make a new compound wall of concrete (thinner but as strong as stone) and books within the thickness of the existing wall. Compression is one of the powerful signs of modernity—what Karl Popper called "the ephemeralization of technology"—and becomes the leading theme of the project. The old villa is squeezed like a lemon, and its subject, like the pip, is expelled to the outside.

5.2 Rotation and Shuffle

The villa, with its central hall (the Palladian *sala*) and surrounding *enfilades* of rooms, holds another secret that leads to a second compression. The A-B-A array of rooms reveals that the As are larger than the Bs. When the plan is rotated to provide the ground for the Bookhouse, it is also shuffled (the card trick!) to produce a new enfilade B-A-B, a compressed version of the old plan.

Rotating the plan (turning the page) reveals a desire to see the old villa as the manna and source of the new. Turning the page on the old villa allows the new to emerge. The Bookhouse is a shadow of—or a direct quotation from—the old villa, since I have deliberately taken a bite out of its fabric. This bite, with its quotation-marks-cum-teeth, is a morsel that is now in the process of digestion.

5.3 Flattening and Squeezing

Rotated and shuffled, the basis of the new plan is established, but the symmetry bothers me. It suggests closure, finality, and a simple repetition of the old.

Beneath this symmetrical ground lie more complex, open,

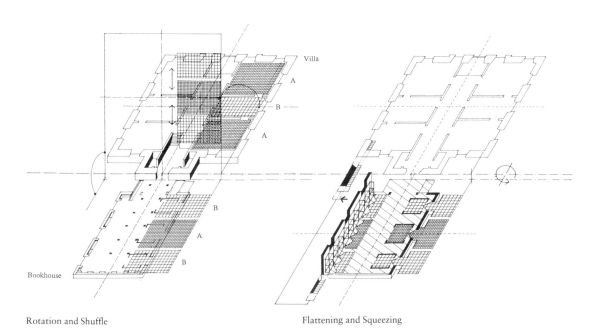

Rotation and Shuffle

Flattening and Squeezing

and yet ambiguous architectonic strata. They can be likened to a menu of figures (of space) that more or less obscurely outline a whole geology of potential space and associated strategies. Two strategies are selected: flattening (to make a book wall) and squeezing (to make book towers).

A series of realizations occurs at this point. First, I begin to see the interior of the Bookhouse as a geography—the artificial double of the landscape that itself is a virtual interior because of its enveloping quality; the sky is its ceiling.

Secondly, I realize that manhandling the architectonic substance is much like cutting, chopping, and stacking firewood. The stacks of firewood present in the landscape's "interior" run parallel (in more than one way) to the book wall within the interior of the Bookhouse; the book towers become the Alps.

The symmetrical plan of the old villa, once rotated, is put under compression: the enfilade of rooms to the right is flattened into a thick book wall, while the rooms to the left are gathered and individually squeezed into three book towers—a symmetry without likeness. The air, the atmosphere of the old villa, is compressed into the new containers of wall and tower, and the old voided walls become the uneasy space of the subject, leading to the last transformation.

5.4 Transfiguration

The great hall in the old villa is the central communication core, organizing the enfilades of rooms as vertebrae organize the organs; the hall offers up the villa to its visitors. This serving quality (as in served and serving space in Kahn's vocabulary) becomes the metaphorical conduit for its transfiguration into the great "table" in the new library.

Entering from the stair tower of the villa, the potential

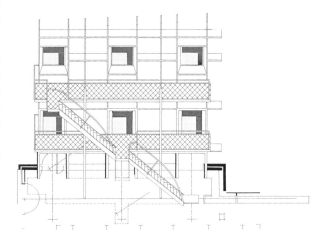

Bookwall: Axonometric/View

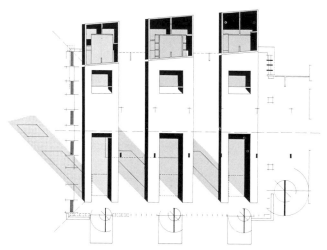

Booktower: Axonometric/View

Southeast Elevation

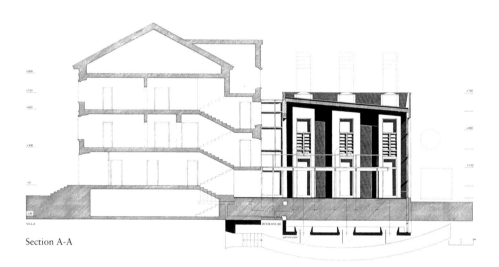

Section A-A

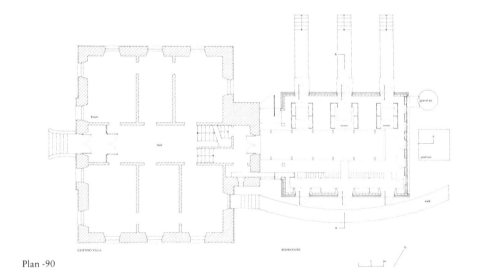

Plan -90

reader steps onto the giant table that stands in the center of the new space: the reader is literally served up to the mouth of the space. Thus made smaller, the reader encounters the compressed space of the villa that floats inside the new, large, boxlike open space. The old space and mass, packed into wall and towers, and the uneasy subject all swim in the aquarium of modern space.

The best view of this play of space and subject is from outside, in the garden, in front of the giant picture window, looking in.

6. FINALLY

Other transformations of the stair tower, facades, and roof are performed. However, the dominating image of the Bookhouse is the catachresis subjected to the sign of the Book by corrosively substituting it for firewood. This thought foregrounds the book as object, as stackable unit, as subject, rather than as book.

A giant closet, the Bookhouse will swallow the books, which, like hats, shoes, and coats, will find their suitable resting place at the top, in the thickness of the wall reached by ladder only, or in the depths of the tower, lit by the sickle moon hovering in the ceiling of the outer space, the Alpenraum.

The collector will not build the Bookhouse. The fire engines of Truffaut's *Fahrenheit 451* roar onto my scene of writing. Books are burning. Like another catachresis the Bookhouse remains a "blind mouth" of space.

7. AFTERTHOUGHTS

For me, architecture is a branch of philosophy in its oldest and widest sense: the pursuit of wisdom. Architecture has played this role as one discipline within another, living more or less clandestinely in the shadow of the profession and the business.

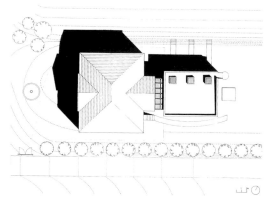

Site Plan

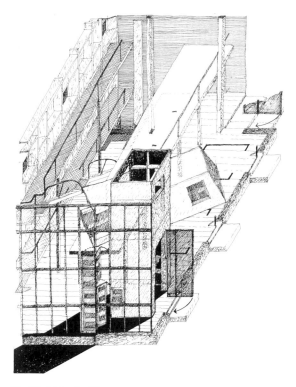

The Blind Mouth of Space

For better or worse, architecture for me is always driven by reason. I have come to see reason and rationality in architecture as a branch of rhetoric rather than of truth. In this sense, the Bookhouse is a system of persuasion. The architectural transformations of compression, rotation, shuffling, flattening, and squeezing are similar to the transformations in figures of speech—addition, subtraction, omission, and rearrangement—thus the possibility for "figures of space." Figures of space can be traced to Palladio and his "geography of villas," which I have hinted at elsewhere.[6] The Bookhouse claims a place in this geography.

This overt gesture of belonging to a geography has been underscored by recent work of the Italian philosopher Gianni Vattimo.[7] Vattimo's claim that everything is interpretation radically displaces truth and has helped me to cope with my own innocent desire to interpret rather than invent. His writing has also reinforced my skepticism of the new. My difficulty has been to find a course between what is new and what is nostalgic, for I am equally skeptical of the recourse to nostalgia.

The Bookhouse is thus to a great extent "about" villas. Philosophically, it is an attempt not to overcome but to get used to the history and weight of villas as present in the old house. It is a *Verwindung*—Heidegger's term—which in Vattimo's interpretation suggests a going beyond that is both an acceptance (resignation) and a deepening, also suggesting a convalescence, a cure, the healing, and distortion or twisting of the old house-cum-villa. The Bookhouse is an attempt to remember, to think about—*Andenken*—and to interpret the old and to use it as material for the new.

This gesture to the villa and its history is ironic, mocking the symmetry of the old plan, flaunting asymmetry as the necessary other, and displacing the human subject in

Interior View from the Giant Table

favor of the book. It is also constructive, signaling the production of a new library out of the old, questioning the value and the possibility of what is truly new.

For those of us who are steeped in the delirium of the new, this step is a very difficult one. It is an attempt to erase the Modern architect's ego, while sidestepping the neoclassical architect's, as we try to turn Truth into momentary truth and use-value. The Bookhouse is therefore not simply a failed project but also a chapter in my moving scene of writing.

What is new is contaminated not only by the old house but by firewood, books, the art of rhetoric, movies, philosophy, and so on, which threaten the autonomy of architecture—"it ceases to be a specific fact."[8] The Bookhouse is polemical, since it attempts to persuade you, the spectator, to participate in a fiction in which architecture is a branch of writing, in which the Bookhouse writes itself via figures of space (the death of the architect), in which the books have become building blocks (the death of the book), and in which the reader is no longer in the center but propelled to a place just outside. For me the Bookhouse is at best a funerary monument; like a tombstone, it is here to "bear the traces and the memory" of the geography of villas "across time, for others."[9]

These reflections on the writing of the project—on the technique as well as on the footnotes that cloud the field of meaning in the form of metaphors—ultimately disappear once the project is drawn. All commentary fades to the background, becoming a curious aberration, while the object itself stands massively mute, leaving the viewer to his or her own ruminations.

It would come as no surprise to me if the curtain remained completely drawn on the scene of writing, and the object, like the phoenix, emerged immaculate, open to the next interpretation.

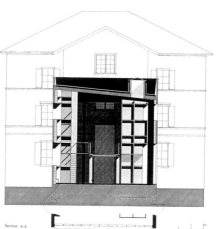

Section B-B

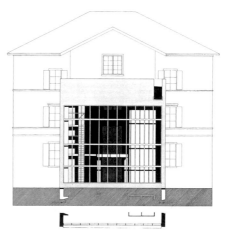

East Elevation

1. Walter Benjamin, "Unpacking my Library," *Illuminations*, ed. Hannah Arendt (New York: Schocken Books, 1969), 67.

2. This project was designed with the assistance of Michael Bell and Antonio Lao, Berkeley, 1987-88. An earlier version of this text has been published in German: "Das Bücherhaus," *Archithese* 2 (1989):18-23.

3. Gregory L. Ulmer, *Applied Grammatology* (Baltimore: Johns Hopkins University Press, 1985), xi.

4. Ibid., 11.

5. "Composition" is extremely loaded with its classical history. It is therefore put into question and made subject to a *Verwindung*. See note 7.

6. Lars Lerup, "Villa Meyer: Dolf Schnebli + Tobias Amman," *Architecture and Urbanism* 2 (1989):59-74.

7. Gianni Vattimo, *The End of Modernity*, trans. Jon Snyder (Baltimore: Johns Hopkins University Press, 1988).

8. Ibid., xxvii.

9. Ibid., 73.

DYING IN THE THRILL OF SONG

I guess you had to be there:

it was a philosophical two step,

an architectural syncopation on the idea of

RESEARCHING RESEARCH

For Ann Bergren with thanks and admiration
for showing me how ancient are my own contemporary concerns

John Whiteman

I am remembering two scenes from Woody Allen's film *Annie Hall*. In the first an especially degenerate character, played by Tony Roberts, is speculating on a particular form of the triad, a form in which two of the three terms are identical, literally twinned, that is: twins. The third term is the character himself, the speaking subject. While driving in an open car, to increase contact with the worldly effects of mechanical movement, Max, the character in question, asks Woody Allen, whose character is always in question, to imagine, if he can (which he can't), the doubling of sexual experience.

The scene is followed a little later in the movie by another scene, in which an especially pretentious character, a mental degenerate, is explaining alternately to Annie and the camera both[1] that he has just finished a piece of research, funded by the National Endowment for the Arts, in which he has taken a notion and turned it into a concept. He further explains, with unashamed seriousness, that he will now apply for a second grant with which he will take his new concept and turn it into an idea. The precise meanings of his notion, concept, and idea are withheld from us, the viewers, the audience, deliberately creating the impression that the individual speaking is content free, or, as my students would say, an air-head. Annie is bored; her eyes glaze over, and she moves on in the form of the camera, or at least in the form of its seeing but unseen eye. For a while, the movie adopts her own searching attitude, her researching attitude. We, the audience, move on with her, and I have

[1] A switch that, when taken literally, can be very confusing.

now cut and spliced you into another reference, this time a text, a passage in the writing of Jacques Derrida, in which he points out

that the opening pleasantries and the scene setting and switching of Plato's dialogues ("One, two, three,—but where, my dear

Timaeus, is the fourth of our guests of yesterday, our hosts of today?")[2] are far from incidental or irrelevant to the form and the

content of the ensuing arguments. Thus Derrida points out that in the *Phaedrus* Plato has the main character (for whom the dia-

logue is named) take Socrates out of the city in order to engage him in a dialogue on, among other things, the origins of writing.

Leaving the city is something that Socrates is said only to have done very rarely,[3] and so to set the dialogue outside the city walls,

after the previous day's performance of a famous speaker, Lysias, is to introduce the theme of the familiar and the estranged with

respect to the relation, yet to be announced, between writing and speaking. Plato manipulates, puppeteers his characters, Phaedrus

and Socrates, among the meadows down by the river Ilissus, where the chorus of insects, cicadas, can be heard and where by the

"diaphanous purity of the waters . . . it was, while playing with Pharmacia [*sun Pharmakeiai paizousan*] that the boreal wind

[*pneuma Boreou*] caught [the virgin] Orithyia up and blew her into the abyss, 'down from the rocks hard by,' . . . 'and having thus

met her death [she] was said to have been seized by Boreas.'"[4] Socrates (or is it Plato?) is both quick and careful to point out that

one cannot ascertain the truth of such stories or references.

Later in the *Phaedrus*, we, the readers, come to learn that writing, in its estrangements from speech, possesses something of the

structure of the drug. The writer engages in something of the activities of the pharmacist, in that writing finds itself in some strange

alternation between itself, its own form marked out in death upon the page, and the supposedly innocent and fluid life of the spon-

taneous voice in time. (Do not forget the fresh and lively incident of the song of the insects, the cicadas: "How welcome and sweet

the fresh air is, resounding with the chirping of the cicadas' chorus.")[5] Writing alternately initiates and rescues the living voice

from its necessary fading into an otherwise deadly silence. Remember also, dear reader, that the physical document that you are0

now handling expresses but the deadweight in transcription of a once spontaneous talk.

Plato, Timaeus, in *Plato in Twelve Volumes*, trans. Rev. R. G. Bury, Loeb Classical Library, vol. 9 (Cambridge, Mass.: Harvard University Press, 1929, 1981), 17A.

"Phaedrus: 'Whereas you, my excellent friend, strike me as the oddest of men. Anyone would take you for a stranger being shown the country by a guide instead of a native—never leaving town to cross the frontier nor even, I believe, so much as setting a foot outside the walls.'" See Plato, Phaedrus, trans. R. Hackforth, in *Plato: Collected Dialogues*, ed. Edith Hamilton and Huntington Cairns, 12th ed. (Princeton: Princeton University Press, 1985), 230D.

See Jacques Derrida, "Plato's Pharmacy," in *Dissemination*, trans. Barbara Johnson (Chicago: University of Chicago Press, 1981), 69-70. Derrida is referring to section 229D of the Phaedrus.

Plato "quoting" or rather giving voice to Socrates, quoted in turn by Derrida, "Plato's Pharmacy," 69.

Similarly, the opening to the *Timaeus*, to which I have already referred, but which is more relevant in certain ways to what I am about to do, if you will permit the line of my ideas, presents an opening scene that echoes the structure of the ensuing arguments. In it Socrates asks after a person who, although invited from the day before, is missing. Socrates is told that this person will not be present for the day's discussions. The individual remains unnamed in the dialogue, allowing us only to speculate on his identity. Some say it was Plato himself.[6] Timaeus, the individual for whom this second dialogue is obviously named, then proceeds to give an account of the origin of the cosmos from chaos, in the justly famous second section of this dialogue. But, as he expounds his ideas, Timaeus reveals to us that he too has a missing character in his ideas, a character that is necessarily missing and who eclipses all logic and reality. This is perhaps the third kind, which up until this point in the middle section of the dialogue has not been introduced. Or perhaps there is implied an analogy with the fourth character of the introduction, who is never announced, and who is only weakly implied by the announcement of the third kind itself, the so-called *triton genos*, the *chora*, the space of all spaces, the form of all forms, the living cosmos, the form that lives without export from or import to its self, the perfect self-sustaining entity. The fact that this character cannot be well thought or described rings with the faded echoes of the introduction, its seemingly irrelevant pleasantries, the mild distress of an absence too quickly passed over and forgotten. It is also significant that this passage follows an extraordinary section on the numerology of the cosmos, recalling Socrates' counting out the number of those present for the discussion and his observation that one is missing.

See R. G. Bury's footnote to this effect in his edition of the Timaeus, 16.

Ibid.

"One, two, three,—but where . . . ?"[7] By starting my talk along these lines, in faintly teasing you into accepting that Woody Allen is involved consciously, perhaps self-consciously, in certain Platonic themes and dramatic structures, impishly suggesting that he might be a Platonic scholar in disguise, I intend in turn to make you aware of certain themes that I shall be treating, and also to make you alive to the manner in which I shall be, perhaps already am treating them. By my references to *Annie Hall* I intend to make you aware that I shall deal with the problem of the double, the doubling of research, the *re* in research, the looking, and the looking again. And I shall further deal with the movement that this double ironically initiates by arresting the fleeting and passing notion, catching and setting it within the stable construct of the concept, and using the idea, the process of ideation, the construction of a protopicture in order to do this.[8] That this is, or rather will be, an implicit reflection on Allen's character gen(i)us who concerns himself with notions, concepts, and ideas is already obvious, as, I should imagine, will be the suspicion of an erotics of architectural power.

Literally: to do this in order.

I hope also that you will already know, given my references to Plato in general and to Derrida's elucidation of the structure of the Pharmakon in writing in particular, that I shall be attending to the rhetoric of research itself, the technique of its adopted stance toward architecture, its relation to and its strategies within its own medium. This revolving attention will be the means by which I shall say in turn something about architectural research, my declared topic. And perhaps you will have sensed also that I shall attend reflexively to the structure of my own rhetoric as I treat these now clearly announced themes.

By my reference to missing persons in the Timaeus **I intend to forewarn you that my story too shall have a missing character, that** what I am telling you now about what I shall be doing is not, indeed cannot be the whole story. How else, why else should I continue to speak? Thus we have something of a mystery story on our hands, but one that has been rendered suspicious by the fact that I declare it so overtly to be as much, and thus one that may go unsolved, perhaps even unnoticed.

I have a friend (cut) who lives in New York, the originating scene of Annie Hall. **This friend owns a painting, which shows an** image of a studio primitive, about to head off into the landscape to hunt. It is not clear what he is hunting, other than another picture within the picture. The image is taken from a movie, but set within the picture as if it were on television, thus evoking the contemporary originations that arise in Los Angeles, and also their transmission within the culture.[9] The technical reflection in this

The painting is by Christian Hubert and is reproduced in B. J. Archer, Follies: Architecture for the Late Twentieth Century Landscape (New York: Rizzoli, 1983).

image, rather than its content, which is too obviously relevant to the idea of research, introduces a geographical alternation to my story, a spatial back and forth, a flip-flop, a form of movement that I hope you will later see as being very important to my ideas on research in architecture.

In the lower part of this image is written, "This may seem like an extraordinarily circuitous way of getting into our subject."[10]

Indeed, it may seem that in dealing with such extraordinarily irrelevant scenes and ideas, that I have done little more than put the entire line of my argument at risk. So, let me take another tack, and, by delimiting all content from my own speaking, try to talk about nothing. Or rather let me write only about talking, and do this as if I were talking, and see whether that will get us some way toward the problems of architectural research.

Imagine then the following sounds: "The words that are coming out of my mouth follow one upon the other as a sequence in time." Each fades as the next is announced, first into and then from memory. This reflects the necessary habit that speaking has a forward flow in time. In speaking I draw on and return words to their accumulation, their dictionary, their thesaurus. What I make of them, with them, exists but for a brief moment and then is gone." Following Lessing's *Laokoon*, and the unfortunate alliteration thereof, I might remark on the irresistible fact that speaking is a temporal art.[11] But I do not. Instead, I displace your attention to the fact that writing, as opposed to speaking, is something other than a temporal art, even though its words are read in time. This is so, because writing is written out upon a page, and the page introduces an element of spatiality. Thus I draw your attention, as I have in my reference to Plato's *Phaedrus*, to the strange alternation, a certain stopping and starting, that goes on between speaking and writing. For example, when originally I delivered this lecture, the audience was unable to know if it had been written out beforehand as a text, which it had not. I teased them by saying that they could not know if I was actually reading the end before the beginning.

Ibid.

G. E. Lessing, Laocoon: An Essay upon the Limits of Poetry and Painting, trans. Ellen Frothingham (New York: Farrar, Straus & Giroux, 1969). Translation of *Laokoon: oder über die Grenzen der Malerie und Poesie* (1766).

In the soliloquy of your mind, however, you are, in the absence of speech, listening to the transfigured movement of phatic material, of spoken signs in time. That is what these dead letters are standing for, the remnants of my having spoken. However it has happened, I have initiated a line and a movement for you. And as my words wing their way across the distance between this page and the silent voice that they initiate in your head, one after the other announcing themselves in the vocal silence of reading, reverberating in the accumulation of your references and memories, you are expecting something. Specifically, you are expecting that, as the rhythm of each word and sentence rises and falls, the one coming taking over the assigned temporal space of the one preceding, you are expecting that an argument be made. Given the specific signs under which my argument is announced, "Architectural Research," and under which I am now writing, formerly speaking,[12] it would be fair to assume that you are expecting a residue or reverberation in your head that somehow will constitute a set of ideas on architectural research.

When delivering the lecture, I could not say "under which I am now writing." Instead, to be more literal and careful, I was forced to say "after which."

However, early on it may seem in the line or sequence of the game that I am playing . . . out, this would seem an opportune moment to stop . . . my argument by asking just exactly how either you or I expect this to be done. How is either one of us expecting that through this sequential froth of forever faded sounds, a stable set of ideas concerning architecture, architectural thought, or architectural research can be transmitted from my head to yours?

Before I answer this question, I want to stop the argument again, this time drawing your attention to the kind of play involved in stopping an argument, as I have just done, twice in fact, a return to the theme of the double that in turn is redoubled in my reflexive indication of it. Clearly I have not stopped writing, and, if you are reading this in the sequence of its transcription, the strict line of my once having spoken it, the silent voice inside your head is still annunciating these very words to you. Something is still going on: and what is going on is the creation in sequential time of a kind of reserve, a space of emptiness, filled only by the silence of faded talk about talk. This space is not literal, at least it was not originally literal in phonic terms, and in making this transcription I wish to avoid making it literal in the graphic terms of this page. That would be too easy, too trivial a reflexion. But I am, even, indeed

only as I write out these words, marking out a space elsewhere, a space in which the cumulation of my argument is held back. So,

if it is the case, that I am still sending out signals, which you may be fantasizing phonically in your head, are

presently marking a stoppage in the argument that I am making.[13]

Well, not quite. And it is the "not-quiteness" of my claim of a stoppage, the fact that I have had to continue not just my words, but

also my argument, even as I claim to have stopped it, that will allow me to continue by showing that what may seem like an ellipti-

cal excursion, if indeed you think I have got anything going at all, is in fact a central point in my argument on architectural

research.

In drawing your attention to the fact that a stoppage in my argument can be sustained not just in the continuation of my speech but

also in the continuation of my argument, I am in fact drawing your attention to a play in speech, which when played out in the

game between architecture (one medium) and architectural research (another, say the materials of words, sketches, or calculations)

is going to plague all of what I mean by architectural research. This is the play, formerly in speech, now in writing, between move-

ment and stasis, between the moving and the stopped.

Naturally, I am repeating myself, but not always, and each time with a slight difference. Indeed I have drawn your attention before

to the play between the moving and the still, as I have remarked continually on the difference between the spoken and the written,

especially in the incident when I drew my listeners' attention to the fact of the discrepancy between my notes and what I was say-

And there, look, listen, I have done it again.

ing.[14] I have also drawn your attention to this play, creating a deliberately faltering movement in my argument, when recording a

passage from the lecture in which I "slipped" in saying that my speaking was occurring "under," for which I immediately substi-

See note 12 above.

tuted the word "after" the announcement of the words, the title "Architectural Research."[15]

Note, parenthetically for the moment, that because of the spatiality of its written form, the word "presently" in my phrase "are presently marking a stoppage" is performing a triple operation n referring first to the time of my speaking, when I originally said these things, and also to the time of transcribing, in which through earphones I am now receiving back the signals I once sent, and finally to the time of your reading, which is now. And note further that I have already remarked, albeit somewhat formally, on the necessary double present of the word "now" in this text in making the word itself indicate a break between paragraphs in the introduction. This occurred in a sentence that, in being continuous, did not terminate as it should have at the point of rupture between two thoughts well and roundly expressed in their own paragraphical statement. "We, the audience, move on with her, and I have//now cut and spliced you into another reference."

Both these instances perform a rhetorical figure, a syncopation, a movement that ironically plays between the moving and the still.

The figure, its rhetoric, was in effect during the lecture when in speaking I passed through the words. Remember that I had then to keep talking, as you must now keep reading, in order to keep my argument on stopping going. But, then, remember also that I have already told you that I shall work my way to certain issues and arguments in architectural research by putting at risk the medium of research itself, then speech, now writing. The risk I courted then and still court now, but the risk that I turn on with a certain reflection and fluency, is the risk of stopping, of faltering. Hence the figure that I have introduced, the figure of a syncopation.

Here, now, is an interjection from the *Oxford Universal Dictionary on Historical Principles*:[16]

Oxford Universal Dictionary on Historical Principles, rev. ed., s.v. "syncopation," "syncope."

Syncopation (siˈnkopeˌfon). 1532. [ad. med.L. *syncopatio*, *-onem*, f. *syncopare*.] 1. *Gram.* Contraction of a word by omission of one or more syllables or letters in the middle; *transf.* a word so contracted (*rare*). 2. *Mus.* The action of beginning a note on a normally unaccented part of the bar and sustaining it into the normally accented part, so as to produce the effect of shifting back or anticipating the accent; the shifting of accent so produced 1597.
Syncope (siˈnkopí). late ME. [ad. late L.,a. Gr. συγκοπή, f. SYN- + κοπ stem of κοπτειν to strike, beat, cut off, weary.] 1. *Gram.* = prec. 1. Now *rare* 1530. 2. *Mus.* = prec. 2. -1795. 3. A cutting short; abbreviation, contraction; sudden cessation or interruption (*rare*) 1658. 4. *Path.* Failure of the heart's action, resulting in loss of consciousness, and sometimes in death.

The reference in the term syncopation to the heart attack, the potential that the figure induces for a real loss of consciousness, the risk even of death, originally fueled my concern for overt risk in the reflective, the continual, and the relentless winding down of my own argument in its own medium of speech. A syncopation is not mere rhetoric, for, when adjusted, it can indeed play out a set of disjunctive shifts between its own movement and the pulses of the body. The rhythm of the rhetoric may induce a physical resonance in the body, arousing an impulse via a syncopated beat. In certain forms of music this can be intoxicating, mind blowing, even deathly if not deadly.

As recorded now, of course, in its new form, in dead letters upon a dry page, the figure takes on a different, inverted profile. Do I bring it back to life by returning you to the beginning, reminding you of Plato's concern for the relation of writing to the fluid life of speech? I should say not. And indeed, the things of which I spoke can only come to you, the reader of this dead remnant, if you are one of those who supplies a phantom voice to the text which you read in silence. You must become the performer of this text.

Be your own pharmacist.

In which case it may seem that as yet I am saying too much about too little. But it is the fact, I claim, that I am bringing you closer

and closer, as I said that I would, to the central point of my argument.

Consider now what is at work in a syncopation: the play that it moves (ironically) between the moving and the still. Perhaps this contrast of movement and stoppage throws us back to those near-Kantian arguments in Lessing.[17] The reference to the *Laocoon* can be elaborated as follows: the moving is associated with the temporal, the stopped with the spatial. Thus, speaking and the performance of music, which move in time, are said by Lessing to be temporal arts. Drawing and painting, which lie still upon the paper or the canvas, are said to be spatial arts. Dance and architecture, the former occurring in movement, the latter in a massive stoppage, are said to be both spatial and temporal arts, space-time arts: dance because it is performed in both space and time, architecture because it eclipses any structure of reception that is spatially constrained. One must move through a building in order to appreciate it, and this requires time to do.[18]

In fact Lessing's arguments on the temporal and spatial modalities of the arts predate Kant's famous arguments on space and time as a transcendental aesthetic by some thirty years. It is important to remember that Lessing treats the space/time terms as modalities. He does not, so far as I know, deal with the problem of their implied essentialism in his arguments. That Kant's arguments could be used to acknowledge and treat this problem for him is obvious enough. Since we live after the writing of both individuals it is too easy, perhaps unavoidable for us to read Lessing through Kantian eyes.

See Lessing, *Laocoon*.

Now, I can avoid the space-time essentialism, or in Kant's terms the transcendence of the space-time terms, an essentialism upon which I am teetering and of which I find Lessing guilty, by pointing to the inextricability of the two terms in any specific form. Space and time are always involved in each other. One just needs to remember that the moving, while temporal, needs space in which to move, else nothing can be said to be moving. The still, while stopped, needs time in which to be maintained as a stoppage. Thus, each of the terms, space and time, when referenced to the existence of an object, however fleeting or durable its existence, implies the operations of the other.

This subtle inflection and dependency of the space-time terms effectively disarms any Kantian argument on the transcendental or essentialist grounding of forms in space and time themselves. To treat these terms, even at their limit, as absolute and autonomous categories is to cross a limit in the understanding beyond which the terms are no longer useful. This limit is the site of what Wittgenstein would have called a seduction in language.

So, for example, while I have continually drawn your attention to the movement of speech in time, its froth and bubble, not to say its babble in time, I have avoided saying after Lessing that speaking is irreducibly a temporal art. You see, or rather you could have seen if only you had been there, that I can always point to the space of speaking itself, the vessel of its resounding. Using my references to Plato, and turning on Derrida's idea of the scene of writing, I spoke into and about the scene of speaking. This gesture, pointing in the form of a reflexive index to the scene of speaking, took me then, as it takes us here, back to the initiation of the setup, by rendering the scene all too vividly, making the spatiality of speech all too visible and noticeable.

But this gesture gives me a problem, for in drawing your attention at this moment to the spatiality, either of speech or writing, I border on admitting my main concern, architecture, at a point that is too early for my own argument, too early in time, before I am prepared for it, before I can account for what has already happened. I am warning both myself and you that architecture always occurs in the past tense, and suggesting that research into architecture is better understood as a form of recognition.

Notice then my own stopping point in logic: the way I shy away from the essentialist statement of defining speaking in terms of the absolute, the absolute temporal. Notice further that I do not use the idea of speech as an absolute or essential temporality to play out a contrast by which to establish the nature of other art forms. Thus I am not saying, as in fact Lessing has said, that either drawing or painting is irreducibly spatial in logical contrast to the temporal modality of, say, song.[19] Ibid.

Instead of pushing past a limit to a statement of seeming clarity and simplicity (say, "Speaking *is* a temporal art"), a clarity and simplicity that I regard as false security, leading only to absurdity, I would have you notice that my stopping point in logic is actually the acknowledgement of a practice or habit, a linguistic or rhetorical gambit in which moving forms such as speaking are presented or formed in such a way as not to exclude but to repress their spatiality. The trick, of course, is not to be taken in by the trick of this repression. So, a temporal form is not, I emphasize, devoid of spatiality, it is merely formed and practiced in such a way as to render the spatial irrelevant. The temporal form is carved out of the spatial, as much as, even if more obliquely than, it is carved out of time.

In directing and turning the flow of my words, in analyzing their sequences, I have started to introduce spatial terms. While I have delimited (itself a spatial term) or forestalled (a temporal one) any absolute disjunction between the two, I have nevertheless opened out a certain space of play between them, and am now forcing my argument to occupy this space. Indeed this space, the space between signs with different spatial and temporal patterns and habits, say between architecture and speaking, or between architecture and writing, is, I claim, the kind of space into which architectural research must always play. That is to say, architectural research, occurring in one medium, must operate a transaction between its own form and the form of architecture itself. These forms may or may not have similar habits, and thus similar patterns of timing and spacing.[20]

In lecturing I implied a transaction between architecture and speaking, largely because that was what I was doing. Hence my rhetorical strategy for the introduction of architecture to the research material to hand (i.e., spoken sound) was one of a contrast between the moving and the stopped. This contrast, if you can grasp it in written form, is what allowed me to work open a space between the temporal and the spatial, providing a potential opening for a reflection between architecture and speech.

Thus, with a colleague at Harvard University, Peter Rowe, I once had a student mime a building when he found himself in difficulties with the verbal explanation of his design. The explanation, if that's what you would call it, was strikingly clear to all of those present: we knew immediately what he was "talking" about.

And clearly (or perhaps not so clearly) I am now slowly meeting your expectation that I should be saying something about archi-tecture, and I am doing this by opening out the possibility of a frame of reference for it within the structure of temporal continua-tion that passes for verbal sense. Through the category of the stopped, the unmoving, the still, the spatial is creeping in.

However, even though I announce it as such, I am anxious to resist the temptation of a certain mapping between a number of paired terms in my discussion: a transaction between the moving and the still that maps too readily onto a transaction between the temporal and the spatial, which in turn maps easily onto a transaction between the verbal and the architectural. And yet, my claim is that architectural research must work some such space or difference in order to produce its results.

I have drawn out this distinction, perhaps rather slowly and painfully, creating an operative space between the medium of archi-tectural research and architecture itself, and I have done this in implicit contrast to the habit of assuming that speaking, say, and architecture are autonomous practices, fully independent of one another in space and time.

I do this, create the distinction between the time either of speech or writing, because I want to characterize the space between the medium of architectural research and architecture itself as something other than an unfathomable void. So, while I acknowledge the distinction of speaking and architecture or of writing and architecture, I also wish to be able to point to their conjoint and reci-Hilary Putnam once pointed out to me, while we were walking through a gate in Harvard Yard, the distinction between a distinction and a dichotomy. procal operations.[21] I am hoping to express the idea that our world is formed by a family of different signs working in formation as well as in opposition. I imagine, subsequently, that within the faint residual rustle of speaking, within these unmoving letters, you might hear the silent and massive stoppage that is architecture. (Is this a threat, a promise, or a plea?)

I have elaborated the distinction between architectural research and its object in terms of a distinction between the strategies of

their respective media, characterizing that space of distinction with a certain tension of inextricability, for two reasons, which in their turn form a pair, a syncopated reciprocal. First, I wish to cast suspicion on the idea of the rhetorical as excess or superfluity. Instead, by the massive redundancy of my own reflexive remarks on what I am saying literally, I want to suggest that an overt rhetoric is a way of carrying forward in an argument, not just the plain and the simple (it can do that), but also a fuller amplitude and plethora of strategies, constructs, and qualities without reducing their crosscurrents to a naive linear construction.

Second, and a naive linear construction would count for me as a good example for my second reason, I want to claim that, without attending to the rhetorical strategy of the space between architectural research and its object, the contemporary individual tends only to assume that space to be void and intransigent. This assumption of an absolute disjunction between research and its object constructs the problem of research itself in a particular way. Specifically, one seemingly has the temptation, if not always the problem, of reconstructing the object of research, but on the strange, the estranged, and estranging grounds of the research medium, be it words or diagrams or whatever. The problem of an estranged reproduction, duplicating architecture off-site in the medium of research, leads in turn to the fantasy of the mimic, the double. This remark throws me back to the introduction, my opening remarks or solicitations, and the associated problem of an erotics of architectural power. But I shall not deal with this yet, so hold that thought, as they say. Book it.

Not to do this, not to develop the distinction between research and its object internally, as I am doing, trying to uncover the rhetoric of research, is to assume forthrightly that the distance between research and its object is directly negotiable and easily overcome. It is to assume that space to be without any clues or traces that form an intermediate and intermediating domain.

This means that research and its object can only be constructed as autonomous and independent of each other, and that each is imi-

tiated in a distinct medium or habit within a medium. Furthermore, the denial of any transactional rhetoric already in place between research and its object implies that research itself must start from a ground zero and cumulate from there. This sets up a peculiarly doubled structure of inferiority and superiority of the researcher over the object of the researcher's attention, but suggests that the task of research will only be carried out on the reduced and abstract terms of its initial reduction. The initial reduction of the research object is contrasted with the polyvalent and replete object of its attention, the building. The curious subordination of this estrangement suggests that the research object will never be fully elaborated. Like Hegel's figure of the slave, it will never be able to understand the terms of its master.

The implicit strategy of building back from reduction is how colloquially research has come to be understood as a term of progress. The very word research seems to hold out a promise of going from a state of ignorance to a state of knowledge and ability. This would seem to be its purpose and also its legitimation as a form of activity. Who could argue with that? But this is to restrict oneself to the positive and overt sense and operations of the term, to the way that it presents itself in language.

Perhaps this is the time that I must confess, if I have not inadvertently done so already, that I am a skeptic as concerns the hard core of what passes for architectural research, especially the pretense that it is, can, or should be a science. Or, if it is to be a science, then there is, I believe, more to it than current models of science can handle. Too often the subject matter of architecture[22] is force-fitted into an a priori conception of method and result. When talking of architectural inquiry I prefer the terms and the activities of *conversation* and *rehearsal* in preference to the production of codified results that are then labeled as the products of architectural research.

I mean to delimit the term architectural research provisionally to exclude those technical disciplines that, when treated as formal and autonomous concerns, are necessary to but insufficient for the production of a building as architecture.[23] Thus, by the term

This is the problem: that the subject matters, or rather somehow figures, or is inscribed in and so is underwritten by architecture.

By the term architecture I mean a habitable object or culture of predominantly but not exclusively habitable objects that contains within itself a reflection on its own instruments and purposes, both overt and covert, direct and indirect, and also contains a further, more difficult and elusive internal reformation, engendered as a consequence of this initial reflection.

architectural research I do not mean for the moment to include a reference to purely technical research, such as research into construction technology or lighting or building hazards, or the economy of building, or other physical stresses or material(-ist) creature comforts. Whether I can avoid such references is another question—one that will become (a little) clearer when I speak about the automatic contemporary association of rigor and reduction. By intending to exclude technical research from my meaning, I do not mean to denigrate this kind of activity. Indeed I intend quite the reverse: when restricted to its own self-appointed domains, it does, I believe, produce the right kind of results. However, while the methods and results of technically construed research appear to be the more secure, at least when compared to more slippery subjects such as architecture's rhetorical effects upon the (human) being, I shall later be casting doubt on the architectural validity of this restricted rigor.

Instead I have reserved my meaning of architectural research for those activities that have adopted the pretense of researching that little bit of excess that is called "the architectural." I am thinking of the now popular concern of devising architectural languages, whether for the so-called science of urban and architectural space or for the morphology and the representations that architecture may achieve in buildings, and whether for historical analysis, for the purposes of (risk-voided) production, or for the simulations of the computer. Or again, I am thinking of efforts to understand the rhetorical effects of architecture upon those who become subject to it by the adoption and adaptation of the techniques of psychoanalysis or literary criticism or both.

While it must be obvious that this kind of subject matter is my own greater interest, over and above the technical question of whether a structure will stand up, for instance, and whether I can calculate and predict as much in advance, I should emphasize also that my reserved subject matter also arouses greater suspicions within me concerning method and result. I believe that the philosophical basis and the methodological problems of architectural research, so reserved, are extremely difficult, leading those who undertake such activities to the most severe assumptions and shortcuts in the name of a false rigor. It is these short-circuiting strategies of architectural research that I am out to undermine.

More subtly, another two-step, I do not maintain in the final instance the distinction I have just drawn between those activities of technical research that are necessary but insufficient to architecture, say "the calculation of structures," and those that constitute its excess over this restricted material, say "the logic (?) of architectural design." I am at pains to point out that, despite the pretense and appearance of rigor and precision, a discipline such as structural calculation, is in fact architecturally vague and far from precise. I justify this claim by the observation, or you might say the counterclaim, that in analytical reasoning we have the habit of associating rigor with reduction. That is to say, the objects of objective analysis must be rendered as simples in order for the construction of the argument to proceed and for conclusions to be reached: they must not appear as repletes with complex internal structures.[24]

If the objects of (objective) analysis are not rendered as simples, and possess complex internal structures and cross relations with other objects, it is not possible to construct an unambiguous, linear or reductive account of the phenomena under scrutiny. One cannot build back to reality from the position of the reduction. In the wake of analysis one will always be able to point to instances that are counterfactual to the account presented by that analysis. Further, if the reductive account is used subsequently as a production command, the objects fabricated under its instruction can only be made under the force of a reduction that refuses to allow the full play of material qualities. The produced objects will therefore be plagued with the interference of what might be called material suppression.

Against this procedure I shall present my intuition, I prefer to call it an acknowledgement, that architectural skill is skill with replete form, and that the reason why analytical pretensions seem to miss the point of architecture so badly is that we lack a conception of rigor in repleteness.[25] The precise object of replete artifice is what, for lack of a better, if any, understanding, we have come as a culture (if that's the right word) to call and canonize as art, which gesture of nomination precludes any further possibility of understanding.

It is symptomatic that objective analysis does not deal with objects as such but with reductive representations of them, that is, diagrams. To my knowledge it was Wittgenstein who first noticed that, in the name of simplicity, the logical atomism common to most analytical philosophy requires the simplification, if not the elimination, of the internal structure of its constituent elements, its objects. Wittgenstein further observed that these elements were implicitly depicted in their elemental simplicity by means of a proto-picture. This idea has a long lineage. Indeed one form of it can be found in Plato's *Philebus*. (See note 27.) The same idea is also behind the analytical notion of the primal sketch in David Marr's information processing analysis of vision. See David Marr, *Vision* (New York: W. H. Freeman, 1982), 54 ff.

For a careful account and analysis of these ideas in Wittgenstein, see David Pears's tracing of Wittgenstein's understanding of objects in the Tractatus, in "The Basic Realism of the Tractatus," in *The False Prison: A Study of the Development of Wittgenstein's Philosophy* (Oxford: Clarendon Press, 1987), 89-114. Wittgenstein's later appreciation of this issue is much altered by his rejection of elemental simplicity, this revision being prompted in part by the difficulties presented by color predicates to such a system and his experience of having designed and supervised the construction of a building. See L. Wittgenstein, *Philosophical Remarks* (Chicago: University of Chicago Press, 1975), remark no. 83. It is as symptomatic for this argument, as it was for Wittgenstein's realization of the necessity to rethink his philosophy, that buildings and color predicates are especially ticklish problems for the analytical mind that has absorbed without reflection an implicit constructional model of itself.

The concept of repleteness as applied to the philosophy of art belongs originally to Nelson Goodman. See Nelson Goodman, *Languages of Art* (Cambridge, Mass.: Hackett Publishing, 1976), 229-30. I am modifying Goodman's idea by seeking a concept of rigor in repleteness as opposed to the concept of repleteness seen from the position of rigor in reduction.

Architectural research is characterized for me by the invention of large linear predicate machines of bewildering seriousness that, when put through their cumbersome paces, produce nothing but the most stunning platitudes, devoid of any reflection on the thundering force of their own redundancy. The initiation of research most commonly involves a reduction of and a distancing from the practices of architecture, whether in building or in the activity of design. This process, in the name of a clear understanding of the ordinary, removes the ordinary from experience by making it the object of an inquiry that subsequently is incapable of overcoming the reductions and distances upon which it is predicated. And yet, because research needs to determine the object of its inquiry, producing a stable conclusion (a reflection of its common and hidden ambition to remove the risk from production), there is a sense in which research activity is distrustful of the kind of mischievous play initiated by the activity of architectural design. Consequent upon becoming the object of research, and despite the best will and human politics in the world, the ordinary (as the construction of the real) is neither returned, nor elaborated, nor reflected.[26]

Some examples. One sober-minded researcher, the recipient of a large quantity of taxpayer money, recently has reached the important conclusion that "all cul-de-sacs are bad . . . that all streets must form an open weave with one another." This is a simple example of the confusion, induced by the linear and cumulative model of analysis, that inconstancy is inconsistency. (Against such a conclusion it should be recognized that one can be inconstant yet still consistent.) Another researcher has set himself the task of rendering all that is significant in architectural composition within the language of a "first order predicate calculus of primal sketches." Now I can imagine (up to a point) doing this in order to make a machine for architectural designing, in other words to produce a design tool, and I do not denigrate this activity. But I become suspicious when such "knowledge" is passed off as knowledge about architecture itself, as knowledge of the architectural.

Consider the similarity of the research promise with the promises made by realism: "Realism with a capital 'R' doesn't always deliver what the innocent expect of it." Hilary Putnam, *The Many Faces Of Realism* (Lasalle, Ill.: Open Court, 1987), 3–4. The realist, Putnam goes on to say, promises common sense, a rescue from idealists, Kantians, pragmatists, and irrealists, but after a short time "breaks the news" that after all the ordinary world is not going to be returned to the innocent, that "all there really is is what finished science says there is—whatever that may be." The innocent is left with only "a promissory note."

A final absurd platitude that I have heard announced with all solemn seriousness, this one by a researcher who has spent ten years or so researching musical ability and appreciation in children and adults, is that "artists tend to reflex on what they know." What irritates me especially about this last example is the presentation of this sentence as a conclusion. Any artist worthy of the appellation knows this immediately: for the production, the reception, and the analysis of artworks this is the most basic of premises, a recognition without which one simply cannot get started. To present it as the end of a course of inquiry is to leave all that is interesting and difficult about art untouched.

The main mechanism of this impoverishment is a constrained relay of signs that is designed to fix an ontology, to settle the score on reality, to make things clear, by telling and showing what words, when spoken, are really all about. It is a relay that runs from word to image to thing, and, above all, it is a stabilization strategy. The chief mischief at work here is a transaction between image and thing, which is called for, as it were, by the absent painting in the word.[27] This is precisely the problem (albeit unacknowledged) of our mental degenerate in *Annie Hall*, the problem of how a passing notion, some fleeting impression of reality, is fixed and given credence as a concept by the process of ideation.[28] A word, when announced, cannot by itself define its reference. Required is the supplement of an image, or what Wittgenstein called a proto-picture.[29] Within the rhetorical structure of everyday speech the conjoined function of word and image is capable of arresting the passing notion formed within sensation into an ideated construct.[30]

In architectural research such stabilization strategies meet a specific problem or impasse. The implied direction in the making of a position that is said to be something more than uncertainty and ignorance is one of cumulation and ascent through time.

Furthermore, in progressing from the simple to the complex on the basis of an assumed reduction, the analogy of this assumed accumulation and ascent, whether implicit or explicit, is nothing other than an analogy with building itself.[31] For a further and

[27] For an account of the figures of the writer and the painter implied in the construction of the imagination, see Plato, *Philebus*, trans. R. Hackforth, in *Plato: Collected Dialogues*, 38E-39E.

[28] See also the hierarchical stabilization account of the imagination given by G.W.F. Hegel in *Encyclopaedia: Philosophy of Mind* (Oxford: Clarendon Press, 1971), sec. 455ff. I have elaborated a detailed criticism of Hegel's account of the imagination in "Eye Sores: The Function of the Image in Deconstruction" (Chicago Institute for Architecture and Urbanism, 1989, Mimeo).

[29] See David Pears, "The Basic Realism of the Tractatus."

[30] Plato, *Philebus*: SOCRATES: It seems to me that at such times [during soliloquy] our soul is like a book. . . . It appears to me that the conjunction of memory with sensations, together with the feelings consequent upon memory and sensation, may be said, as it were to write words in our souls.
PROTARCHUS: That certainly seems to me right, and I approve of the way you put it.
SOCRATES: Then please give your approval of a second artist in our souls at such a time.
PROTARCHUS: Who is that?
SOCRATES: A painter who comes after the writer and paints in our souls pictures of the assertions that we make.

[31] For a more elaborate account of this analogy within a specific line of the history of philosophy, running from Kant to Hegel to Husserl to Heidegger to Derrida, see Mark Wigley's essay, "The Production of Babel, The Translation of Architecture," *Assemblage 8* (February 1989): 7-21.

specific example, remember that Immanuel Kant has famously analogized the structure of argument to the structure of a building in the opening passages of the *Critique of Pure Reason*.[32]

See Immanuel Kant's description of metaphysics as an edifice and his critique of prior philosophical systems as resting on unstable foundations. Immanuel Kant, *Critique of Pure Reason*, trans. F. Max Muller (New York: Meredith Editions, 1966). 47.

Commonly, the analogy of the configuration of the analytical structure of research to the structure of an edifice is made without recognition or irony. Yet, this is the analogy from which the ambition of architectural research, in its analytical mode, proceeds and toward which it strives, seeking a strange reification of its own initiation, the promise of its own fulfillment not just as an architecture of research but also as architecture out there, in the world.

Thus it is said that, as argument proceeds, its conclusions are built up, literally. That is, conclusions are literally built up into com- plex arguments, being formed in sentences, words and letters, sometimes with the aid of diagrams or computational schemata. The construction proceeds from simple, undisputed (though not indisputable) statements or facts to grand conclusions. Further, this edification is thought implicitly to be achieved by a method of analytical construction. It is this silent assumption of the architectural metaphor within the structure of analytical knowledge to which I direct the force of my skepticism. Why is the present object of analytical inquiry, architecture, already assumed, if not subsumed, and not merely as metaphor (it is something more than metaphor that is at work here) in the structure of analytical thought? Architecture in some estranged form (as a metaphor of philosophical underpinning) is being brought to bear back on itself. Such work teeters on the edge of an excruciating tautology that is neither acknowledged nor reflected.

Consider now the nightmare in which such a strategy of architectural thought is turned to a command over architectural produc- tion. I asked myself, as I ask you now, to consider what would happen if this project were to succeed, if its mappings were to be completed and made real? What kind of world would be in place were the tautology to be actualized?

My first observation is that there would be a kind of referential deadlock in place and in time operating between architecture and words.[33] This would occur because each, verbal thought or built architecture, would be fully implied and contained in the other.

This sounds a little like the present, although our present ineptitude springs from a different source.

Thus, we would be in an absurd world where architectural thought would be impossible in relation to the practice of building architecture, for each would be incapable of exercising any movement on or within the other.[34]

The fault in this argument is the philosophical conception of architecture, that it is a stable construction. There is nothing that prevents architecture from being as mischievous as a play of words. Ironically, this is most true of architecture at the very moment that it presents itself as a form of well-founded stability.

My second observation is that, while no one would ever see it as such, once released from this world, it would become apparent that architectural thought would have produced a specific architectural form or presentation of what Catherine Ingraham has called the "pornography of power."[35] If, being subject to this world, we had the wit to see (which we wouldn't, for as much is implied by the phrase "being subject to"), then we would see everywhere and in each and everything the horrifying evidence of our own intention completed according to the structure of its desires and expectations. To those transcendent to the world, there would be neither the possibility nor the appearance of chance in this world. Nor would any misapprehension of its presented reality be possible.

Catherine Ingraham, remarks made at "Looking for America, Part 2," Association of Collegiate Schools of Architecture conference, the Graham Foundation, Chicago, Fall 1988.

Taken together, these two observations imply that if we were subject to this world, which happily we are not, we would be at an end with our architecture. Architecture and thought would each have fulfilled their promises, and there would be nothing more to do and nothing more to say.

Thus, within the rhetoric of my own argument, I have now brought out, as I at one time promised, the full threat of a complete stoppage. This is the threat I introduced by the term syncopation, and reiterated along the way. It is the threat of a huge and massive silence that is everywhere present within architecture as it remains housed in its cold, unmoving stones.

However, I am still talking, talking after the end as it were, like a clown upon the stage after the play is over. I am still referring you back to specific themes in the introduction, even as in this sentence I show you the reflexive strategies of my reference. Given my declared intention to attend as far as possible to my own rhetorical practices, I must consider then the fact of my own contin-ued speaking.

Specifically, that my words can continue is a double index. First, the possibility of speech after such a (near) ending itself upends the idea that architecture is the simple stable construct that philosophy or analysis would make it out to be. While mechanically stable, its ways, its effects, and its songs are anything but obedient and traceable. Architecture is as mischievous as any rhetorical form that humans have invented. Second, such an observation suggests that, despite its obvious material presence, the elusiveness of architecture presents it as a worthy quarry for the hunt of the researcher. Neither on site nor off may its object be clearly defined.

Where then to go from here? Back to the beginning? Or, since I told you that I may have read the end already at the beginning, how will you or I know where we are or what I am now doing? What has taken place here in the name of truth? What kind of construc-tional model or map of rhetoric can serve as our guide now? Are we left alone with our memories? Can memory indeed bring us to the end?

Recall, then, the following once actual and once imagined passage: "The words that are coming out of my mouth follow one upon the other as a sequence in time. Each fades as the next is announced, first into and then from memory. This reflects the necessary habit that speaking has a forward flow in time. In speaking I draw on and return words to their accumulation, their dictionary, their thesaurus. What I make of them, with them, exists but for a brief moment and then is gone."

Panel 1   THEORETICAL AND EPISTEMOLOGICAL DIMENSIONS

October 6, 1990
Harvard University Graduate School of Design
Cambridge, Massachusetts

Panelists
Stanford Anderson, Massachusetts Institute of Technology
Alan Colquhoun, Princeton University, Colquhoun, Miller & Partners, London
Bill Hillier, University College London
Lars Lerup, University of California, Berkeley
Alberto Pérez-Gómez, McGill University
John Whiteman, Chicago Institute for Architecture and Urbanism

Moderator
Donald Schön, Massachusetts Institute of Technology

DONALD SCHÖN I want to congratulate the organizers of the symposium on the choice and ordering of the morning's speakers because, as I read them, we had four very different views of what some of the answers to some of the critical questions about architectural research and its epistemology might be. We had Bill Hillier quoting Aristotle at the beginning of his talk

Introduction

and then giving a very Aristotelian notion of what architectural knowledge is: the search for natural laws, illustrated by the law that connects the integration of paths through space with the patterns of what he called the natural movement through space. I was very interested in that portion of Bill Hillier's talk, where he made reference to the idea of "bringing natural movement into the site." A phrase like that catches the ear and indicates that here he makes what my colleague Martin Rein and I call the "normative leap"[1]—the leap from *is* to *ought*, the leap from fact to the way things ought to be, through this notion of "naturalness," which I think has pretty good antecedents to 400 B.C.

Then we had Hashim Sarkis, whose fascinating talk had as its main thrust a wish to rescue architecture from bondage to a particular privileged way of seeing—perspectivism—and to free up new possibilities of vision in architecture. That concept of the privileged and the other possibilities lying beyond it, was his way of making the normative leap. Lars Lerup was a sort of full-bodied, uninhibited romantic exponent of the joys of discovering surprise and the unexpected in phenomena, an anti-research researcher who saw architectural design as a form of invention and discovery. And finally John Whiteman's normative leap was made in a revealing passage in which he contrasted—what was it John?—"naive linear argumentation" with "the complex turbulence introduced by ironic simultaneous multiple self-commentary." These are all forms of making the normative leap that I thought I was detecting among my colleagues this morning.

ALAN COLQUHOUN The meaning of the word *research* used in relation to architecture is not at all clear. There is an inevitable connection with what is normally known as the scientific method. That is to say the assem-

Architecture and Science

bly of data for a specific known objective. I think everybody agrees that there is something peculiar with the application of this notion to architectural design. At this point I could make what Donald Schön calls the "normative leap" and say that the design of a building is only partly the solution of a problem; and, if I may use a literary analogy, the work of architecture is more like a novel than it is like a factual text. Architecture, therefore, is somehow involved with creating life, rather than merely facilitating life as something already given.

I don't want to take this normative leap now (although I believe it to be true) but instead look at the term *research* and the relation between science and architecture. Behind this is the unravelling of the humanist classical tradition between around 1750 and the beginning of the twentieth century, a tradition which was intimately bound up with a notion of imitation of good models. In other words,

classical humanism presupposed the preexistence of truth as an exemplar.

Now, among many other aspects, the modernist project seems to be an attempt to reveal and to fill the vacuum left by the disappearance of the humanist classical tradition by attempting to reveal the underlying structure of the artistic process without preconceived notions, and to establish art on a more fundamental and natural basis. In connection with this, I think there is an interesting connection to be made. It is made by Robert Klein in a book of essays[2] in which he compares Husserl's phenomenology with the projects of Schönberg, the Bauhaus, and the Constructivists in the 1920s. If his comparison is valid, I believe this kind of phenomenon, characteristic of the avant-garde at the turn of this century, attempts to arrive at a universal scientific way of approaching the problem of art; it is both similar to and different from the sort of scientific reductivism that both Hillier and Whiteman were talking about, although apparently from opposite points of view.

One way of looking at the project of the historical avant-garde in its search for these universals is as a substitution for the social meaning of architecture provided by the classical tradition. Kant proposed a paradoxical mod-

el of aesthetics, a nonconceptual practice which nonetheless has a universal truth value, and I think Modernism tried to convert Kant's free play of the imagination into a universal system. But I think after the Second World War, there was some confusion between the notion of a phenomenological reduction and positivism.

In architecture today, I think we are realizing after the simplistic models of the 1950s, that the changes being brought about by science and technology as a long-term result of the industrial revolution, do not lead to the order and coherence of the scientific reduction model; they lead, in fact, to freedom and chaos. The interest which we witness in this very conference in the idea of research is somehow symptomatic of a fear of this freedom and chaos; an attempt to get back to the safe order of a scientific model. I think it would be a pity if it did result in simply repeating the models which were so prevalent in the 1950s.

I think we should realize that the kind of phenomenological reductions of the 1920s lead to the opposite of the linear scientism that became its interpretation within the field of architecture. The closer we approach an understanding of the structure of artistic and architectural expression, the more we find ourselves in the unanalyzable wholeness of lived experience. The paradox of the need to create cognitive models of our discipline and the realization that these cognitive models are always false, is perhaps the fundamental question raised by the problem of research in architecture.

SCHÖN I'd like to pick up the tail of what you said, Alan, when you first talked about the dissolutions of the humanist classical tradition which left a kind of vacuum and produced both a sense of freedom and of anarchy. If we look at this morning from that point of view it makes an interesting picture. On the one hand, we have a sense of playfulness—John's celebrating playfulness and Lerup's illustrating playfulness—which becomes possible because of the feeling of being liberated from a clear-cut reality that can be imitated. On the other hand we have a sense of constraint and the importance of coming to terms with constraint, even discovering the lawlike characteristics of constraint, for which I felt Bill Hillier was really the spokesman. Sarkis I put in Whiteman's camp because he was trying to liberate us from a way of perceiving the world that seems natural but isn't; he left it open that there may be many possible ways of seeing in architecture of which perspectivism is only one. But opening up to multiple possibilities is also opening up to chaos and therefore, the function of research could be the production of multiple worlds, chaotic, each one in no relation to any other, not capable of communicating with each other.[3]

STANFORD ANDERSON I hope that I can find the time to put two issues before you and conduct a small defense relative to the jab that I perceived in John Whiteman's comments this morning. But these matters relate to one another, as my defense lays a theoretical base for the two comments on architectural research.

I have been devoted to a philosophical tradition which labels itself "fallibilist"—the conviction, that is, that human knowledge is not a matter of truth, but that we always work in a condition of error. Yet, isn't it the case that we have been able to make some progress, that we have learned some things, and are able to conduct ourselves in some ways that are valued despite that condition? If so, how does this take place?

On "Fallibilism"

the right direction; that the truth is to be found fragmentarily in different places. Then I sat here this morning thinking, well that seal is actually rather a nice symbol. We had three speakers—Hillier, Sarkis, and Whiteman—who offered texts that all perhaps have some partial truth and make up if not *Veritas* then some texts that fit into the three books and contribute to an eventual construction of knowledge that we might all be able to adopt, even from a fallibilist position. And of course Lars Lerup makes up the rest of the field. He is the one with the dynamics, the recollections, the inventions, the primary elements, and even the rubber stamps, the repetition of things that seem to appear some place in the field of that seal.

I've gradually come to terms with that symbol, but I feel that it is not as good as MIT's, which has the motto *Mens et manus*—"mind and hand." I would like to read into this motto a certain skepticism about all truth claims. (I say "read in" for I am told there is no record about the selection of the motto.) Surely "mind and hand" encompasses a generalized empiricism. It is significant that the "hand" of *Mens et manus* is proof against a thoroughgoing mentalist position. But, as the motto of an institution of research and education, I would like to read a stronger epistemological claim. The "hand" locates us in the world, and indeed in the artifice of the world of our time and place. It is in the reciprocities of mind and artifice that we gain not only our artifacts but also what we have of knowledge.

"Mind and hand" is for me a very good model; it evokes the epistemologies that I partially understand and which I endorse. It accords also with architecture as a product of both the mind and hand, and once again one could rather readily locate the work and presentation of Lars Lerup in this conjunction. But a conjunction is also something that marks the two parts it conjoins, and alongside the practice, production, synthesis, and enthusi-

If one is a fallibilist, one always feels a little nervous being at Harvard where the motto is *Veritas*. I'd like to think that Harvard was founded in a prefallibilist mode, but there is some ambiguity in Samuel Eliot Morrison's account:

We should miss the spirit of early Harvard if we supposed the founders' purpose to be secular . . . Veritas to them, as to Dante, meant the divine truth, although, more humble than he, they never hoped to attain it. The first college laws declared that every student was to be plainly instructed that the "maine end of his life and studies" was "to know God and Jesus Christ . . . and therefore to lay Christ in the bottome, as the only foundation of all sound knowledge and Learning.[4]

Whenever I come to this particular hall and observe that seal, I wonder if it was with some irony that *Veritas* has been fragmented and put into three books rather than being the possession of the Book. I take this as a step in

asm we saw with Lerup, it is appropriate also to entertain some of the more severe kind of inquiry exhibited by the other speakers.

Now to comment on where John took his jab at me. In his presentation he said that he was skeptical about architectural research as something that could be a science, or that architecture could be a science, and then he singled me out as the guilty party in this respect. I think there is recurrent in architectural discourse a division between science and architecture, and between science and the rest of the culture. And I want to suggest that drawing such firm boundaries is counterproductive and perhaps not even descriptive of the enterprise of science. Whenever such a rhetorical strategy is taken, science is immediately equated with positivism and reductivism, an equation that, despite its inadequacy, admittedly can be supported with some historical evidence.

Yet if you begin from a notion that human knowledge—including scientific knowledge—is fallible, then one immediately removes science from some austere realm that aspires to and succeeds in achieving a kind of knowledge that is radically different from what we have in other fields of human inquiry. Even Karl Popper's *The Logic of Scientific Discovery*[5] is not the positivist or reductionist account it is sometimes rhetorically asserted to be. Furthermore, in pointing to logical, epistemological, and historiographic problems with his construction, Popper's students and critics offered still more flexible interpretations of what scientific practice is. And with that comes the radical differentiation from Popper that is represented by Paul Feyerabend.[6]

But I would like to emphasize, however, the more limited criticism embodied in the work of Imre Lakatos. Relative to Popper's attention to theories and the defeat of theories, Lakatos shifts the unit of epistemological analysis from theories to research programs and the comparative analysis and judgment of these programs.[7] At the very core of the program as understood by Lakatos are metaphysical principles about which we have no certitude, but which we allow the scientist (or any other inquirer) to take by convention as a necessary ground for any research enterprise. Such constructed research programs are examined for logical consistency and empirical corroboration, but it is also important that there be competing research programs. Among these competing programs, we make judgments neither reductively nor by some absolute test, but rather by inquiring into the comparative strength and fruitfulness of the programs. Even if the relevant scientific (or other) community comes to the point of making a decision that one research program is preferable to another, it is not necessarily a final defeat; the seemingly less fruitful program has the opportunity to continue and may one day prove to be still superior.

My plea—not just as a response to John—is that we confront those who would claim that research or inquiry, or the attempt to take the "mind" side of "mind and hand" seriously, necessarily lapses into some kind of scientistic, positivistic, or reductivistic bent. Even in an attempt to learn from science, one does not have to come to that conclusion.

JOHN WHITEMAN My remarks were not intended as an insult. I actually understand fallibilism as one of the more sophisticated ways of pursuing a research program. But I want to point out two kinds of two-facedness, if that isn't to double my own double-talk. The first is that fallibilism, although it renders the structure of a research program contingent, nevertheless relies on that; it maintains it in a certain form. You can hold this structure in suspension, but the fact of holding it at all is a form of what Derrida would call a *maintenant* structure. If you were to look at the backside of fallibilism, look not at the way that fallibilism points towards doubt, but look to what it's actually maintaining; there is a kind of two-facedness going on there. Its structure has a double aspect. I think that however contingent one wants to render an accumulated body of knowledge, there is a kind of reliance there.

Now, my two-facedness comes in the fact that I'm doing that as well. Obviously, even as I denigrate certain terms like "linear thinking," it's clear that I'm relying on them, and the tensions that I've played out in my overly rhetorical performance are actually based on that kind of reduction being operative. My only excuse for that would be that it's

a tendency that seems to occur again and again in architectural thinking to make the world simple and clear so that we can go on. I'm reminded a little bit of Strauson's remarks about the skeptic, that the skeptic can only disbelieve the world because he believes it. If that's two-facedness, it isn't necessarily a bad one to live through.

ALBERTO PÉREZ-GÓMEZ It is certainly disturbing to me that we make a great effort to come together, with very good intentions, and we end up establishing these sorts of monologues with ourselves. Maybe we understand bits and pieces here and there, but always we end up with the feeling that we are speaking in a babble. I think this question of research—what is research in architecture?—would need long thought and the establishment of a basic language to understand what we are talking about.

I'm very sympathetic to John Whiteman's position, if I understood it correctly, which implies a criticism of the age-old notion that somehow we're going to accomplish something by adopting a model of research which is already very old and outmoded, which is the idea of a future-oriented search for something. I certainly feel that if we adopt that model—and it is my perception that this notion is implicit in Bill Hillier's presentation today—I think we are missing something which is essential to architecture now. The problem is to define what is central to architecture and what is marginal and how we can grasp it, establish a conversation, and how we can do something with it.

The first question I ask myself is how is this research, or perhaps what we do in school, different from what we do in practice? I've come up with a simple formulation—simplistic, perhaps—and it is to think that in school and in research, the question is of *possible realities*. It is ethical and appropriate for us to emphasize this question of possible **Real possibilities versus Possible realities** realities over other dimensions more present in practice, which I would articulate as *real possibilities*. Possible realities over real possibilities.

The endeavor of the architect moves in a subtle gamut between these two concepts. If I were to define what I could call research in architecture, it would be something like contemplating the possible realities, that which is appropriate in relation to the givenness of contemporary culture.

For me, the key is to learn how to speak. There again, I suppose that I'm close to John Whiteman's expressed position. I do believe that an exploration of possible realities goes hand in hand with the possibility of retrieving many things, one of them is the appropriate rhetoric, the appropriate way to speak. One thing that would immediately help to clarify what vehicles are open to us in this field is to see its limitations: first of all the nature of architectural theory through history; and eventually the limitations of any kind of architectural theory which is understood as a methodology.

Once one understands this problem, one ends up with different models for this appropriate speech. I would like to name this a "hermeneutics," in relation to the work of Gadamer and Ricoeur.[8] What we do in order to learn to speak properly (and this is what I would call research) is look at the traces of architecture in history without taking for granted that we know what architecture is—the danger being that we objectify architecture (as in the positive sciences) from the beginning. The first task, in my opinion, is to understand how this reality of architecture is fluid in history and to establish a discourse that is structured in relation to this understanding. As Ricoeur puts it, I must come to a self-understanding through distance, through that difference between the historical traces that I interpret (and I have to interpret it, that's the whole dilemma here, it's not a question of objective or fundamental knowledge) and my present lived situation.

Once one comes to terms with this hermeneutic task, one can position oneself in the present vis-à-vis a tradition without taking it for granted that somehow architecture is a natural phenomenon. Then, one is in a better position to contemplate the other possibility of narrative that Ricoeur calls fiction and that projects this self-understanding into the future.

For me this is a very interesting model where the theoretical discourse, becoming a narrative, has two vectors, if you like: a hermeneutic vector that allows me to understand myself in relation to traces of the past and that eventually serves as a vehicle for practice, and a fictional vector that allows me to understand the possibilities in the

A two-vector model for research in architecture

present for the future. Those two realms of discourse, those two narrative forms as Ricoeur calls them, are exemplified in projects that recover the understanding of program as a plot.

I admire John Hejduk's work in that regard; I also found Lars Lerup's stories very fascinating. I think that form of understanding, of research through making, which is not simply an exploration through materials, but which incorporates a narrative, which incorporates a vision of poetic inhabitation, is perhaps the aim of that exploration into possible realities.

ANDERSON I don't feel that something which fits under the general umbrella of the history of architecture necessarily engages architecture or architectural research. It is possible to conduct historical inquiry that incorporates information about architecture, without touching what is integral to the discipline of architecture. But such historical inquiry may serve in defining or criticizing the perceived boundaries of the discipline. Under a Lakatosian model, one would even be encouraged to push just a little bit further beyond conventional history to what he termed "rational reconstruction."

When we inquire into, for example, August Schmarsow's theory of architectural space[9], I think it is impossible to demarcate precisely the contribution that Schmarsow made at his historical moment from that which we—partially through hindsight—now can understand through his thought. The border between those, to me, is no longer definable. We may be projecting and learning something that is rationally present in his thought that he, himself, had not yet thought. For me the rational reconstruction of such research programs, while it may be pushing beyond a precise history of events, is even more important as architectural research and has a greater potential for the discipline of architecture.

SCHÖN I would like to open it up and to entertain questions from the floor.

ERIC FANG (Harvard Architecture Review 9): I wonder if anyone might like to comment on the issue of specific

modes of communication of architectural knowledge—among architects, in practice, and academia.

PÉREZ-GÓMEZ The problem I have with what Professor Anderson has put forward is that it seems to be a clear-headed and straightforward position, but in the end he is applying very implicit values about efficiency—the truth that functions better—which puts us back to the kinds of methodological reduction of theory of the early nineteenth century. The language of fallibilism itself is value-laden. Those implicit values are the ones that I would be very worried about. There is a difference between a language that purports a one-to-one relationship with the world, and a language that recognizes its necessarily metaphorical connection with the world of experience. That is why I talked about narrative—narratives that ultimately understand language in this way as opposed to scientific prose—that in the end carries its own values even though it may purport objectivity and neutrality.

COLQUHOUN I'd like to comment on that. I mentioned the question of the lived world and I suppose that most people will understand what set of concepts this refers to. But I still have a problem with what Alberto has just said, because it seems to me that if you suppose that the lived world contains everything that is already there, there is no guarantee that lived world doesn't contain precisely the kind of scientific or commonsense reductions that we are trying to get rid of. There is a paradox then.

BILL HILLIER I would like to make two points. One is about reductivism, which is one of those bad words—a pigeonholing word. Anyone who tries to analyze anything can be called a reductivist and that stops the show, and there is no more discussion because reductivism is a bad thing. I'm not trying to explain the richness of architectural experience; I live in the world, too. I'm not trying to control the whole of the variety and the richness of our day-to-day experience. What I'm trying to do is cut one particular dimension through that world which I think is capable of a more objective form of analysis than we've had before: the dimension of space organization. What I am saying, I believe, doesn't reduce experience; it activates experience because it makes us understand something more complicated about how buildings and places work.

A defense of rational analysis

Now I've never studied science. I'm not a trained scientist. What I am trying to do is to take an architectural idea, the idea of space as a pattern, and find a way of turning it into a rigorous form where one could actually apply it to buildings and let them tell us what they are like; so that the relative independence of the method allows buildings or places to answer back and say, "I as a place have this kind of spatial configuration."

I am also baffled by this idea of "lived experience," because I spend all of my time studying people as they live in buildings, observing them carefully and watching what they do and how they relate to these architectural patterns we create. I'm astonished to find these things related together. I'm fairly confident that what I am finding is that architecture is not meaningless. Architecture does communicate to human experience, even at the level of something like everyday movement around the city, which is important to people. Our work in design has some effect, consequences we should take note of. I'm not proposing any kind of ultimate truth or reduction. I am merely saying that we can learn more about a fundamental aspect of architecture by observing, and maybe sometimes by asking people how they experience the things we make for them. I see this not as something that's closing down architecture. It's something that is trying to enrich architecture and deepen the understanding of architects.

I am also puzzled by our discussion today—with the exception of Stanford Anderson, whose position on science I accept fully (I see myself as part of a Lakatosian research program). I am at a loss to understand the definition of science that so many nonscientists seem to have; it flies in the face of everything that real science seems to be about today. Science is an amazing, astonishing, and bizarre intellectual adventure with scarcely any rules except the old morality that if it doesn't work you eventually give it up. The objections raised today seem to have nothing to do with any form of scientific activity that I understand and nothing to do with the research that I do. What I do feel they do is stop the show. One tries to talk

collective patterns of movements. So what individuals experience as they move from point to point within a city is not of interest to you. What is of interest is the collective patterns that you're then able to correlate with the spatial properties of the aggregations of the city. As I listened to Lars Lerup's presentation this morning, there was nothing collective about it. It was all about individual encounters, about individual play and individual phenomena and therefore, the quality of experience that was talked about was exactly what's washed out when one gets to the collectivity. If I go from the one to the other, there is the possibility that as the subject matter changes, the way of researching also changes.

HILLIER I accept the collective argument, but that is because I'm trying to explain the form of the urban grid, which is one of the only collective things that emerges from what all of these individuals do. It is an emergent property. What interests me is that despite the merging of so much individual activity, there is a way of analyzing what a lot of individuals do, which is not obvious, but which yields interesting results.

about architecture analytically and what one is being told is: "No! There's no talk about architecture. It's not to be allowed! We must prevent this by labeling it as some kind of reductive or positivist activity."

So I'd like to try to reopen the debate, by being a little more humble about our discipline and being a bit more open-minded about the public out there, if you like, who live the experience of what we've made for them. I suggest we ought to be more interested in developing ways of complementing design creativity (which is the ultimate purpose of what I'm doing) with some better understanding of how what we do relates to these lived experiences. I think that trying to create methodologies which will allow one to interrogate the reality of architecture—not methodologies which one imposes on buildings—is rather different from the nineteenth-century project of trying to turn architecture into a sausage-machine kind of science. It seems to me that making methodologies into forms of inquiry is supporting just the kind of open-endedness that, for me, is the most valuable thing about architecture.

SCHÖN I was telling Bill Hillier at lunch that I wanted to confront the older Hillier with the younger, because of a piece he had written in the early 1970s where he talked about *prestructures* and presented our sense of physical and social reality as a transaction between our prestructures and the world that resists them.[10] This, of course, would lead us to be critical of the way of talking about the integration of paths and patterns of movement that he was presenting this morning. The order that you found in your studies is an order that you get to because of your integration of

The individual versus the collective

PÉREZ-GÓMEZ One could argue that the poetic language of Lars Lerup (if one is going to take fiction seriously) is much more about our collective aspirations than the reductive language of some applied—I don't even want to call it science, because I recognize that there is a very big difference between science and Science. The problem is again one of language. I would not take it for granted that because something is an architect's dream, it doesn't have collective value.

LARS LERUP The way Don characterized me this morning, as a sort of romantic exuberant, I think connects very nicely. I think that in the combination between the life of the hand and of the mind, Hillier and I probably would dance in the street. I will dance in his streets without any problem. I like his results much more than his process; it seems to me that those streets that he introduces in abundance work quite well. (Unfortunately, those buildings are probably going to be quite expensive to build because they have all those funny corners.) It is the process I am suspicious of.

Back to the collective. I like to think of myself as a kind of *bricoleur*, trying to take snippets out of all the books that are written in the world and spoken about, from engineering to psychology to sex, and trying to bring them together and fictionalize them in some interesting way not only for myself but for the world. It is all I can do as an individual.

Coming from a highly collective society like Sweden, I have a certain understanding—Americans have a tendency to see themselves as very lonely because they belong to a mass society. I'm still very *petit bourgeois;* I feel like I am part of a society and that when I speak, the whole society speaks through me.

WHITEMAN Which of course makes me very nervous. I found myself very sympathetic to Alberto Pérez-Gómez's remark on ethics; with a kind of lingering question in the back of my mind. When one uses terms like "properly" or "common" or "something shared," for whatever reason (maybe it's having spent ten years in America) red flags go up in my head. One is reminded of statements by Emerson—one doesn't need to go all the way to Paris to understand the logic of difference. Emerson once said that

"what is given is our separateness." And it seems to me that if we are to have an ethics one of the critical difficulties of the moment is not so much solving that problem as finessing it and understanding what structures we can either write or make around ourselves in which certain differences really don't have to be adjudicated. This was brought home very forcefully to me when I invited Carol Gilligan to a review at the GSD eight years ago. We went through this big snit about how you get over differences. I was arguing Alberto's position and she stopped me in my tracks when she said, "Look, there are some differences that can't be gotten over." You could think for example of the issue of race—that there is no real reason why the experience of one's life should be different given the color of one's skin. But she said this is different with the issue of gender because your body will not contain another person and that is a sufficient reason to think that your experience will be different and it might not be negotiable. And then another problem comes up: how do you design structures which operate across differences which are not negotiable and not understandable one to another? That to me is a kind of finesse; it's not looking for a commonality, it's not looking for a solution, it is, to use Wittgenstein's words, "finding a way to go on in some way."

The issue of the individual and the collective seems in some sense to be a red herring. I'd like to deal with the kind of difference in directionality which is brought to my mind when Donald Schön uses the term *prestructures*. The interesting thing about prestructures is whether architecture plays any role with respect to them, and whether it can bring to consciousness or experience "lived experience." It seems to me the role of these prestructures is not necessarily just that of the given. They are a kind of underwriting, if you like, of experience by architecture, and they play into or play out the differences that exist between individuals.

I am curious to know whether there is any role architectural research might play—in a sense of literally going backwards—in digging things up, exposing the machinery of assumptions, and so on. Architecture has been curiously locked out of an ability to be a sort of structure; it is always kept away as an object of thought, not seen as a form of thought itself.

SCHÖN Somehow, I'm still hearing Lars Lerup's words: "When I speak, the whole society speaks through me." I was associating this with James Joyce's statement that he was going to leave Ireland in order to "forge the consciousness of his race in the smithy of his soul"—remember? And I was thinking: if you have that sort of an attitude, what does architectural research look like? It looks like a kind of inward looking. To do architectural research is to find out what's inside yourself, with confidence that what you discover there is going to be true of the society as a whole. That can become the basis of a research program if you have enough ego strength to believe that what you reveal to yourself is what the society speaks through you. If I contrast that with social science—I don't suppose there is a single social scientist in the whole audience here—a social scientist would look for the reality outside himself or herself and find it in patterns that are out there.

I would like to thank the panelists for their—I thought—really exciting contributions this afternoon and to the speakers for coming back in and being self-commentators.

1. See Martin Rein and Donald Schön, "Problem Setting in Policy Research," in *Using Social Research in Public Policy Making*, ed. C. H. Weiss (Lexington, Mass.: Lexington Books, 1977).

2. See Robert Klein, *Form and Meaning* (Princeton: Princeton University Press, 1979).

3. See Jean François Lyotard, *The Post-Modern Condition: A Report on Knowledge* (Minneapolis: University of Minnesota Press, 1984).

4. Samuel Eliot Morrison, *The Founding of Harvard College* (Cambridge: Harvard University Press, 1935), 250-51.

5. See Karl Popper, *The Logic of Scientific Discovery*, rev. ed. (London: Hutchinson, 1959); Popper, *Conjectures and Refutations* (New York: Harper and Row, 1963).

6. See Paul Feyerabend, *Against Method* (London: New Left Books, 1975).

7. See Imre Lakatos, *The Methodology of Scientific Research Programmes* (New York: Cambridge University Press, 1978).

8. See Hans Georg Gadamer, *Philosophical Hermeneutics*, trans. David E. Liza (Berkeley and Los Angeles: University of California Press, 1976); see also, Gadamer, *Truth and Method*, trans. Garrett Borden and John Cumming (New York: Seabury Press, 1975). With reference to the work of Paul Ricoeur, see *Hermeneutics and the Human Sciences: essays on language, action and interpretation*, ed. John B. Thompson (New York: Cambridge University Press, 1981); see also, Ricoeur, *History and Truth*, trans. Charles A. Kelbley (Evanston, Ill.: Northwestern University Press, 1965).

9. See August Schmarsow, *Das Wesen der architektonischen Schöpfung* (Leipzig, 1893); and Mitchell W. Schwerzer, "The Emergence of Architectural Space: August Schmarsow's Theory of Raumgestaltung," *Assemblage* 15 (August 1991): 49-61.

10. See Bill Hillier and Adrian Leaman, "Is Design Possible," *Journal of Architectural Research and Teaching*, 3d ser., no. 1 (1974): 4-10.

William Adams

THE VALPARAISO SCHOOL

Fernando Pérez-Oyarzún

The word *research* is fairly new in the field of architecture. It first appeared in architectural discussions as a result of the incorporation of architecture schools into universities. During the last century, universities were increasingly dominated by the natural sciences, as these became a kind of paradigm of Western thought. Research, accepted as the most successful method of producing new knowledge in the sciences, has enjoyed a subsequent increase in prestige across a great many other fields as well. But while the notion of architectural research has indeed inspired much imaginative, experimental work, problems arise when one attempts to restrict its definition to cases that intend to produce verifiable, "scientific" results. In order to explore the possibility of truly architectural research, we are obliged to abandon conventional notions about research, and perhaps those about architecture as well.

François Jacob, in his autobiographical work *La statue intérieure*, describes scientific research as the result of two alternating processes. The first, which he calls "diurnal science," corresponds to the widespread notion of science as a clear process of connecting established principles with observable phenomena. But scientific research rarely follows the kind of perfect unchaining of thoughts found in say, bad mystery novels. Instead, a second process— "nocturnal science"—complements the orderly steps of logic, attempting to overleap the verifiable and to grasp intuitively some principles ruling the more mysterious, confused zones of our reality.[1]

Jacob's description not only enriches our concept of science, but allows us to perceive clear links between scientific and artistic activity. Art does not have an undisputed claim on creative intuition, nor science on reason and logic. By extending the boundaries of each of the two realms with Jacob's notion of nocturnal science, we can imagine a cultural setting in which the concept of research plays a significant role in artistic disciplines.

Architecture has always been something of a hybrid discipline, composed of both artistic and technological aspects. The study of architecture often borrows methods from related disciplines and applies them to architectural matters; technological research and historical research in particular have achieved a relatively accepted status in connection with architecture. Yet while properly oriented technical or historical research may enhance a design project—this is a task that has not been assumed with enough conviction by architects and scholars—the main core of architectural activity, namely the project itself, remains largely unconsidered from the point of view of research. Is it possible to consider project activity simultaneously as a subject and as a means of research?

This question lies at the root of a long-standing controversy in schools of architecture. Many professionals and academics maintain that any architectural project involves an effort of research; others contend that this kind of activity does not have enough rigor and universality to be considered research, *sensu stricto*. If one intends to get beyond those frequently sterile discussions that attempt to validate one kind of research and exclude others, the key attitude may be to consider research in a broad sense as the production of new knowledge, and perhaps also to enlarge the notion of knowledge itself.

The case of the Valparaíso School, referring at once to a formal school of architecture and to a group of architects working together for nearly forty years in Chile, addresses several of the most difficult issues raised by the idea of architectural research.

Led by Alberto Cruz and Godofredo Iommi, the Valparaíso School began with the explicit intention of refounding architectural education in modern thinking and modern art.

The school emerged in the early fifties, precisely the time when the Chilean professional universities began to promote scientific research. The personal connections of its faculty with several pioneers of Chilean science had a significant influence on the experimental orientation of the school; from the outset, research was seen as the proper basis for university teaching. Members of the school considered architecture not as a set of absolute principles applied to specific problems, but rather as a field of investigation that might produce new knowledge.

The Valparaíso School had its origin in the interaction of poetry and architecture; this interaction is the foundation stone of all building. Cruz and Iommi understood that modern poetry was not merely about writing verses; it involved a vision of reality intrinsically linked to questions of language and consciousness. In the original Greek sense of the word, *poiesis* was a concept underlying the most basic forms of production. Poetry was considered a privileged way of knowledge and therefore a kind of research about the human world and culture.

The complete task of the Valparaíso School was from the beginning considered experimental. This meant that the aim of the school was not to transmit a well-known body of subjects; instead, it fostered a search not only for new solutions but also for new problems. The production of architecture became itself the main subject of study.

Facing page: Palace of Dawn and Dusk. View of lateral addition.

1. François Jacob, *La estatua interior* (Barcelona: Tusquets editores, 1989), 299-300. Originally published as *La statue intérieure*, ed. Odile Jacob (1987).

By the middle of this century, Latin America was undergoing a great period of architectural change and renewal. With the publication of *Brazil Builds* by the Museum of Modern Art in 1943, and *The Work of Oscar Niemeyer* by Stamo Papadaki in 1950, Brazilian architecture received international attention and praise.[2]

It was the time of Cap Martin, Ronchamp and Chandigarh, the Lake Shore Drive Apartments, and the Guggenheim Museum. Le Corbusier was working on a small house for the Curutchet family in La Plata, Argentina, and was involved in the plan for the city of Bogotá with José Luis Sert and Paul Lester Wiener. The great building of university cities in Caracas and Mexico City had begun. Luis Barragán had built his house in Tacubaya, and Amancio Williams his Brook House in Mar del Plata.

It was during this time that a seemingly unimportant event took place in Santiago de Chile: the meeting of the Chilean architect Alberto Cruz Covarrubias and the Argentine poet Godofredo Iommi.[3]

Alberto Cruz was born in 1917. He studied architecture at the Catholic University of Santiago, traveled to Europe upon graduation, and later returned to Chile to begin a professional practice with Francisco Méndez and Jaime Errazuriz. At the time he met Iommi, he was thirty-three years old and had distinguished himself as an innovative teacher in the Catholic University's preliminary design studio.

Godofredo Iommi was born in Buenos Aires, also in 1917, and studied economics for two years before dedicating himself entirely to poetry. As a poet, he established connections with several members of the artistic avant-garde in Argentina and abroad. The outbreak of World War II caused him to abort plans for a European tour just as he was embarking. Stranded en route in Rio de Janeiro, Iommi instead set out to visit remote regions of Amazonia with a group of Brazilian poets; it was the first of many journeys he was to make into the South American interior. At the end of another of these journeys—this time an ill-fated trip to Juan Fernandez Island, curtailed by the war—he settled in Chile and married Ximena Amunategui.[4]

The meeting in 1950 of Cruz and Iommi, their intellectual affinity and growing friendship, must be seen as the origin of the Valparaíso School. It was not only a personal meeting, it was the meeting of poetry and architecture and the beginning of a common project.

Modern architecture in Chile had at that time some twenty years of history, beginning with Sergio Larrain's Oberpauer Building of 1930; yet Modernism still had not successfully penetrated the Chilean universities. This was especially true in the case of the Catholic University School of Architecture in Santiago. Dedicated to the education of professionals, particularly those involved in private commissions, the school remained attached to the old traditions of the École des Beaux-Arts, under whose direction it had been founded.

In 1949 a student movement took place in the school, demanding changes to the curriculum. It began with a symbolic ceremony: old books of Vignola, the basic text of the first-year students, were burned in a great pyre. The protest continued for two years and caused great public debate. In the aftermath of this discord, two important events in the history of Chilean architectural education took place. Sergio Larrain became the dean of the School of Architecture, a position in which he was to continue for for fifteen years; and Alberto Cruz left the school's faculty in order to accept a teaching position at the Catholic University School of Architecture in Valparaíso, 120 kilometers west of Santiago.

Cruz had accepted this invitation on the condition that he would come as part of a group, for he had become convinced that architecture had to be conceived as a collective work. Though initially refused, his proposition was eventually accepted, and in 1952 Cruz and Iommi moved from Santiago to Valparaíso with a group of young architects, including Jaime Bellata, Fabio Cruz, Miguel Eyquem, Arturo Baeza, Francisco Méndez, and José Vial. Some students in the later years of the Santiago School also joined them to finish their studies at Valparaíso. One year later, the Argentine sculptor Claudio Girola joined the faculty. Carlos Bresciani, a well known and widely respected professional, was named dean of the new faculty; his collaboration was considered a guarantee of success for their efforts.[5]

Within a short period, this group changed the school's orientation and pedagogic system completely. The idea of modernity as a particular way of understanding the universe formed the basis of this renewal. Modernity was conceived as a new state of consciousness, originating in the work of Baudelaire and the *poètes maudits*; it was therefore rather independent of the functional and technical determinism of mainstream Modernism.[6] Inspired by the words of Arthur Rimbaud, the school proposed that the greatest promise of the new age lay not in technology and its benefits of convenience, but rather in the spiritual liberation of mankind. The idea was, as Iommi stated it most succinctly, "no cambiar *la* vida sino cambiar *de* vida."[7] This meant that members of the school would not be content with the idea of making incremental improvements to an established way of life; they chose instead to address this way of life directly, intent on changing its parameters and values. Thus the innovations they were proposing for architecture had to begin with their own lives and not with general propositions for society and universe.

The faculty decided to share a common dwelling place, a group of houses near the school grounds. This situation allowed them to carry on research and debate at all hours of the day and night. They considered the university setting a place for classical *disputatio*, clearly more inclined toward research activity than professional education.[8] This classical concept of the university complemented the school's avant-garde position and reinforced their radical renewal with a sense of cultural continuity.

coduemos de Valparaíso :
coduemos de Valparaíso mirando el mar a traves de los arboles:
lo que tanto se buscaba.
el mar a traves de los arboles
la ola y la hoja

2. Phillip L. Goodwin, *Brazil Builds: Architecture New and Old*, 1652-1942 (New York: Museum of Modern Art, 1943); Stamo Papadaki, *The Work of Oscar Niemeyer* (New York: Rheinhold Publishing Co., 1950).

3. The casual meeting of Cruz and Iommi took place at an advertising agency, where a group of artists and poets were gathered. Cruz's studio was in the same building.

4. Ximena Amunategui, a charming, aristocratic woman, daughter of a famous politician and former mistress of the great Chilean poet Vicente Huidobro. Huidobro had introduced Amunategui to members of the European avant-garde, including artists Jacques Lipschitz, Man Ray, Tristan Tzara, Robert Delaunay, and Hans Arp.

5. Carlos Bresciani later became a partner in Bresciani, Valdes, Castillo & Huidobro, one of the most noteworthy architectural offices in Chile during the fifties and sixties; they designed several large-scale projects such as the Unidad Vecinal Portales and the Torres de Tajamar.

6. The vision of the world shaped by German Romantics such as Hölderlin and Novalis and interpreted by modern French poets, particularly Baudelaire, Mallarmé, Verlaine, and Rimbaud, has been fundamental to Iommi and the thinking of the Valparaíso School. Tightly linked to the reality of the industrial revolution and the development of the great European cities, the modern vision proposed by these poets does not embrace the unlimited faith in technological progress that so frequently appears in official modernist ideology. Rather, this poetry offers a critical view of culture, primarily centered on achieving new freedom for human life.

7. This proposition by Iommi is founded on the ideas of Arthur Rimbaud expressed in various letters of May 1871, particularly those to G. Izambard (May 13) and to P. Demeny (May 15); see Jean Marie Carre, *Lettres de la vie litteraire d'Arthur Rimbaud* (Paris: Librairie Gallimard, 1931). In these texts Rimbaud describes himself as being "another" ("Je est un autre"), and delineates the relationship between poetry and action. Iommi develops this issue of poetry and life in a later essay, arguing against Andre Breton's interpretation of Rimbaud: "Fracaso de la sustitución de Breton. Cambiar la vida no equivale a cambiar al mundo." See G. Iommi, "Hay que ser absolutamente moderno: Arthur Rimbaud," in Alberto Cruz et al., *Cuatro talleres de América en 1979* (Valparaiso: Instituto de Arte, Universidad Católica de Valparaíso, 1979).

8. In fact, members of the School of Architecture, both teachers and students, later played a fundamental role in the general reform process that occurred in the entire Catholic University of Valparaíso in 1967.

During the early fifties, the professional universities of Chile were developing their first scientific centers to promote basic research. Members of the Valparaíso group considered that their school of architecture, too, had to be grounded in university research; and so, with the reorganization of the school, an Institute of Architecture was founded.

The city of Valparaíso was considered a sort of laboratory for the institute. Professors went by themselves through the city, drawing, taking notes, studying its reality directly.

The methods used in teaching were the same as those used by professors in their research activity, with professors acting as role models for their students. Their method was an elaboration of Corbusier's way of sketching. The basic idea was to grasp quickly, directly from what was seen, some relations between place and human activity. These were not considered from a functional but rather from a phenomenological or poetic point of view.[9]

Through observation, the architect conceived an act—a kind of play of distances in space, a secret of human disposition under particular circumstances, open to a kind of transcendental meaning. Architecture was subsequently considered the coherent skin of this act.

Two projects—one for a small country chapel in a place called Pajaritos and another for the city of Viña del Mar's urban expansion into an area known as Achupallas—were published in the *Annals of the Catholic University of Valparaíso* in 1954.[10] Alberto Cruz authored these works, which both for their content and for their unorthodox presentation in the *Annals* became the first and possibly best-known products of the school's early research.

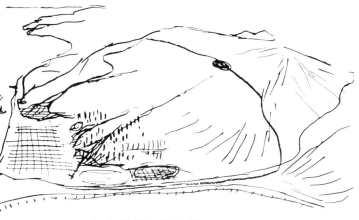

Achupallas site. Sketch by Alberto Cruz.

The Pajaritos Chapel of 1952 is a classic demonstration of Cruz's method of conceiving an act based on observation.[11] The long text that accompanies the project suggests an alternative conception of modernity, one that does not include technological progress as its main component. In the text, Cruz ponders the appropriate form for praying; he seeks a place where the body can pray in a natural, easy way, as when it lies on the sand by the sea. His answer is the cube—not a material cube, but a cube of light. This is a form without form, a form of absence. This cubic form is expected to embrace liturgical ceremonies, popular religious feasts, and religious images.

This chapel, which remained unbuilt, has often been cited as an example of Corbusier's influence over the Valparaíso School; but in comparing the work of Corbusier in the fifties (or even his purist works of the twenties) with the strict, minimal condition of the chapel's plan and the frontality of its main elevation, it is easy to establish significant differences. The geometric simplification of Corbusier's villas of the twenties is connected with problems of visual perception and with machine imagery. Both concerns are absent in the Pajaritos Chapel; instead the emphasis is on conditions of space, the lack of weight and materiality in the architectural body, and combinations of symmetrical and asymmetrical composition. Above all, the chapel is conceived as a poetic proposition.

The Achupallas project was a new working-class subdivision in Viña del Mar, a seaside resort near Valparaíso. The architects of Valparaíso envisioned a set of organizing rules and ideas for Achupallas. The work was published in the form of a set of manuscripts and ink drawings with a number of general propositions at the end.

The resulting project attempted, among other things, to redefine the social role of the architect. The text put forth the remarkable idea that the architect's role is not to make the lives of citizens easier, but rather to set in space the destiny of the city. This stance implied a complete rejection of functionalism and of conventional professional activity.[12] Only a few parameters of urban form were conventionally designed. The remaining discussions were left to particular projects or to the interventions of the dwellers. Seen in the context of dominant planning ideas of the time, this unorthodox attitude anticipated future developments in urban design theory. Again the project remained on paper.

9. The writings of Martin Heidegger provide a philosophical basis for this kind of research through observation; one of this central propositions is to base thought on the reality of things, excluding or bypassing the constructions of great philosophical systems. The early influence of Heidegger's thinking on Chilean architects can be traced to the presence of two of the philosopher's disciples, Ernesto Grassi and Francisco Soler, in Chile in the fifties and sixties. Both were in contact with the Valparaíso School through Godofredo Iommi.

10. *Anales de la Universidad Católica de Valparaíso* 1 (1954): 219; also *Fundamentos de la Escuela de Arquitectura* (Valparaíso: Universidad Católica de Valparaíso, 1971).

11. According to Alberto Cruz, this chapel is based on Le Corbusier's observation of the black cube on the Kaaba Stone in Mecca and is not directly influenced by his forms. Alberto Cruz and Godofredo Iommi, interview with author, May 30, 1991.

12. "El urbanista descubre el destino de la ciudad y lo coloca en el espacio, para que la ciudad y sus habitantes vivan su destino. Sea este suave o duro, heróico o no heróico. Pero no anda buscando medios para hacerle la vida agradable a nadie." *Anales*, 219.

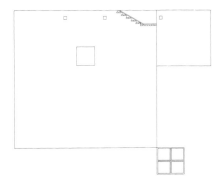

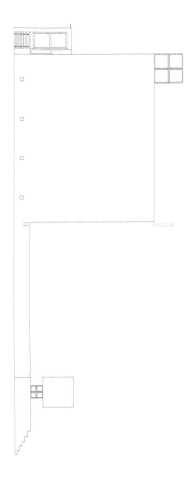

Pajaritos Chapel. Side elevation.

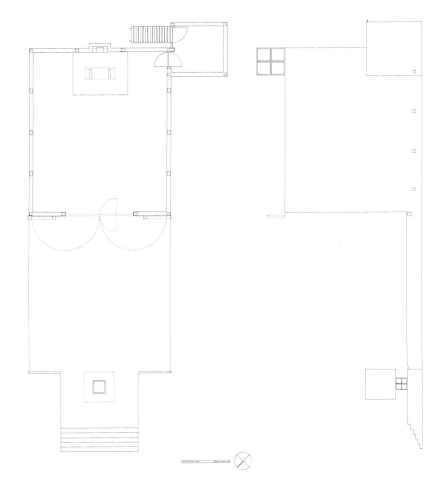

Pajaritos Chapel. Plan.

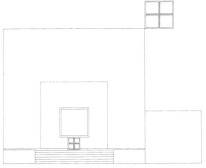

Front elevation.

THE PHALENE

Phalène is the French word for a kind of butterfly. It was chosen at random, by opening a page in the dictionary, to designate a special kind of poetic act.

The Phalène originated in contemporary art and poetry seminars given by the School of Architecture, particularly by Godofredo Iommi, and open to every student at the university. Students were encouraged as they learned modern and contemporary poetry to spread this knowledge to the public, to let common people know poetry in the streets, on trains and buses. Frequent public recitations by students and faculty freed poetry from the confined domain of books; poetry entered the life of the city.

Soon the idea arose of allowing people to participate in a poetic act as actors and not merely as spectators. The rules of the Phalène began to emerge. To play the game, people chose words following a set of prepared images in the form of playing cards. From the phrases suggested in the minds of the participants, the poet would improvise connections, giving birth to a sort of transient poem, a poem of a moment, conceived as a gift for the participants. Afterward it was to become an autonomous art form, which Iommi and other artists performed in European and American cities.[13]

The intention was to link art and life by exposing the poetic condition of all human beings, regardless of craft or profession. This condition was taken to lie at the deepest level of our understanding of reality as established in words.[14]

The idea of the Phalène (or in more general terms, of poetic acts) became essential to the thinking and the activity of the School of Architecture. The Phalène provided an opportunity for the interaction of different artists (painters, sculptors, and others) around the nucleus of poetry. It also brought up the possibility of linking art and place. Although the Phalène was conceived neither as a pedagogical tool nor in any specific connection to architectural teaching, the school's students were encouraged through it to adopt a critical attitude to the everyday, to rediscover beauty latent in the mundane. The desired union of architecture and poetry would come about only by achieving a certain liberated frame of mind. Within this framework, the students were to develop architectural responses that searched deeper than the neat functional solutions produced at the professional schools.

The Valparaíso School set forth the idea that once the basic, practical requirements of building are fulfilled, architecture, as a particular way of viewing the world, is something gratuitous; like the Phalène, it is a gift freely given, not forced or determined by circumstances. Seen in the context of the times, long before the eclipse of Functionalism as the dominant pedagogical philosophy in architectural schools, the Phalène represents a radically opposite way of understanding the aims and possibilities of Modernism. In later works of the Valparaíso School, the Phalène has come to play a significant role in providing a poetic basis for projects and in interpreting the poetic meaning of places—confirming the assumption that poetry may be considered a privileged way of knowledge.

Poetic act in Horcón, near Valparaíso, including the recitation of the epic poem *La Araucana* by Alonso de Ercilla.

13. "En 1952, persuadidos que el hacer de la poesía era de suyo lenguaje poético, abordamos la experiencia propuesta por Lautremont: 'La poesía debe ser hecha por todos y no por uno.' Involucramos el cuerpo entero, el gesto, la voz y el texto en un horizante libre de 'finalidades' políticas, psicológicas, religiosas, etc. Unidos a escultores, pintores, escritores, filósofos, improvisamos en actos poéticos irrumpiendo en las ciudades (Valparaíso, Paris, Rio, Londres, Munich, Atenas, etc.), abriendo el acto a la participación activa de 'público,' como en el campo abierto de un juego. El acto produjo y produce aún una pura catarsis poética desvalorizando toda duración de la obra." Iommi, "Hay que ser absolutamente moderno: Arthur Rimbaud."

14. Martin Heidegger, commenting on the poetry of Hölderlin, establishes the inherent poetic condition of human dwelling. See Martin Heidegger, "Holderlin y la esencia de la poesía," in *Arte y poesía*, ed. F. de C. E (Mexico, 1958). Heidegger refers to the same idea in "Die Frage nach der Technik," in *Vorträge und Aufsätze* (Pfullingen: Neske Verlag, 1967).

Example of a Phalène that took place at the entrance to a subway station in Santiago, November 1990. A group of students from the Pontifical Catholic University School of Architecture selected the subject ("the window"), drew up the cards, and led the Phalène, following instructions from Godofredo Iommi. The phrase "neither by day nor by night," taken from Amereida, determined the precise moment of the Phalène: sunset. Verbal reactions to cards were labeled 1 to 16, and connections were made by a student, José Quintanilla.

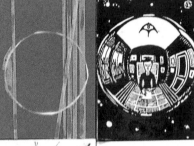

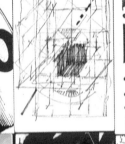
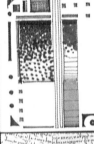

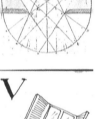

VERBAL REACTIONS OF PUBLIC PARTICIPANTS TO THE CARDS	REACCIONES VERBALES DEL PUBLICO A PARTIR DE LA LECTURA DE LAS CARTAS
1. centered cube	cubo centrado
2. red-painted window	ventana pintada de rojo
3. room in perspective	habitación en perspectiva
4. river of light	río de luz
5. a shadow	una sombra
6. star	estrella
7. eclipse	eclipse
8. face to water	cara al agua
9. penetrating eye	ojo penetrante
10. crowd in the window, paths in the grid	multitud en la ventana, huellas en la malla
11. cloistered starfish	estrella de mar enclaustrada
12. vitreaux	vitreaux
13. landed geometry	geometria aterrizada
14. contrasting picture	pintura en contraste
15. hue of black	matiz de negro
16. royal window	ventana real

THE WINDOW

(MALE VOICE) **(FEMALE VOICE)**

without a cube **centered?**

in the red-painted window
like some room in perspective
a river of light
within a shadow

the star!
even in eclipse

but **face to water?**

but a penetrating eye in crowds
and in the window among paths
**(or) in the grid
before a cloistered starfish?**

more vitreaux! . . . . more vitreaux!
from the landed geometry
by a contrasting picture!
**(ah!) from hue of black
to royal window**

LA VENTANA

(VOZ MASCULINA) **(VOZ FEMININA)**

sin un cubo **¿centrado?**

En la ventana pintada de rojo
Cual habitación en perspectiva
Un río de luz
Entre una sombra

la estrella!
aún en eclipse!

pero **¿cara al agua?**

mas un ojo penetrante en multitud
y en la ventana entre huellas
**¿(o) en la malla
de una estrella de mar enclaustrada?**

más vitreaux! . . . . más vitreaux!
desde la geometria aterrizada
por una pintura en contraste!
**(ah!) de matiz de negro
a ventana real.**

Amereida was to be a foundational journey: a new aeneid to America.

The *Aeneid* represented a sort of foundational myth of the Latin condition in Roman culture. The Latin condition is not a nationality but rather a status obtained simply by belonging to the world opened by Rome. Amereida wanted to establish a new and similar American status based on the idea of a "gift."

Amereida emerged from the work of the Mexican historian Edmundo O'Gorman[15] and from discussions held by the Valparaíso group with Mario Góngora, probably the greatest Chilean historian of this century. O'Gorman maintained in a book entitled *La invención de América* that the discovery of America constituted the world's completion in the mind of modern man.[16] America would complete the circle of the world, appearing as an obstacle in the path of Columbus, as a surprise, as a gift.

Columbus
>   never came to America
>   he searched for the Indies
>   amid his worries,
>   this land bursts forth as a gift.[17]

Góngora, on the other hand, had great doubts about the possibility of an American or Latin American culture, based on the lack of a constitutive sign or gesture to establish this culture. Without this sign, thought Góngora, Latin American culture was only one of imitation.[18]

Amereida was to constitute the foundational sign of an autonomous American culture. The idea was to make a journey, a poetic journey, from Punta Arenas in the extreme south of Chile to Santa Cruz de la Sierra in Bolivia, the "poetic" capital of America. The route was decided in an attempt to penetrate the interior of America—the unknown, the abandoned, the "interior sea," as they called it: "Santa Cruz de la Sierra, founded by Ñuflo de Chávez, we proclaim the poetic capital of America. Here the pampa ends and the forest begins as far as the caribbean, the union of two rhythms in the American interior sea. "[19]

The journey was intended as both a public declaration of America's condition as a gift to the modern world and an attempt to unveil the mystery of its interior. Among the participants were architects Alberto and Fabio Cruz, poets Godofredo Iommi, Edison Simonds, and Jonathan Boulting, sculptors Claudio Girola and Henry Tronquoy, philosopher François Fedier, and painter Jorge Pérez Román. During the journey many poetic acts took place, and a set of artworks (sculptures, paintings, signs) were improvised, interpreting the condition of a place or the meaning of an event.

August 12

At approximately 4 p.m. we see a mill near the road. We stop the car. We walk to it. The pampa is black in that region. Alberto, helped by Jorge, writes "AMEREIDA 1965" on the ground using some stones. Fabio takes a broken piece of the water trough, props it up with some stones, and makes a stele. Tumulus. I climb the mill and lay out some dry branches, and Godo hands me some twigs with a little flower or yellow grass. With a piece of wire found there I make a sign and put it in the water pipe that runs from the mill to the water tank. Fedier takes photos. Edy pronounces words about the place. The cloudy sky and the light suspended in the sunset. We continue the journey. We arrive at Marchand Station. We fill the fuel tank.[20]

Near Bolivia, in El Chaco, the political unrest caused by Che Guevara and his *Guerilla* ("Small War") made it impossible to end the trip in Santa Cruz. Today it seems significant to see both of these events occurring at the same time in history, because they represented two different views of the meaning of America, two contrasting attempts to shape its destiny.

Without completing their intended journey, the participants in Amereida returned to Valparaíso with a new understanding of the American condition. A collection of poetry called Amereida was soon published, and became an important basis for later work done at the Valparaíso School. An inverted map of South America, with the south pointing up (an image taken from an ancient map), became a public sign of Amereida, signifying a change in the South American cultural condition.

Amereida can only be understood as a complex phenomenon: a voyage of discovery, a gesture inscribed in the tradition of manifestoes, and above all, the genesis of an original form of historical and cultural research. If on the one hand, *Amereida* can be considered an effort to generate a new basis for the school's architectural research, on the other, it can be seen as a positive investigation of the American geographical condition and the origin of a later series of poetic research journeys known as the Travesías.

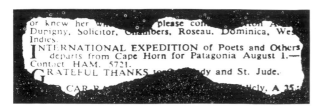

Newspaper notice published in the *Times*, announcing the journey.

The thesis of the interior sea—
a new map of South America emerges, showing the uninhabited regions of
the continent.

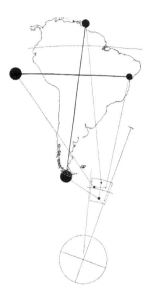

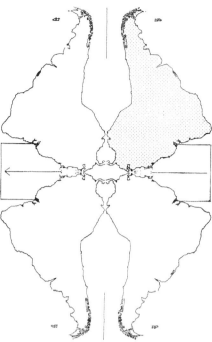

The thesis of the proper north.

.. in their cross they expand
                    all the cardinal points
        the north names them south
                    but they are not south
        for in this American sky
                    their light also misleads expectation—
                    gift or constellation
        to illuminate the map again

and more than south
                is it not our north?[21]

15. The ideas of Edmundo O'Gorman, one of Mexico's most famous historians, were transmitted to the Valparaíso School by Mario Góngora.

16. Edmundo O'Gorman, *La invención de América* (1958; Mexico: Fondo de Cultura Económica, 1986). Also in English translation: *The Invention of America* (Bloomington: Indiana University Press, 1961; Westport, Conn.: Greenwood Press, 1972).

17. "Colón/ nunca vino a América/ buscaba las Indias/ en medio de su afán/ esta tierra irrumpe en regalo."*Amereida: Volumen Primero* (Santiago de Chile: Editorial Cooperativa Lambda, 1967).

18. Mario Góngora, "Una cultura Americana," *Revista hombre y universo* 2 (1983): Góngora asserts that the lack of a foundational sign in the cultural history of America inhibits the development of an autonomous cultural identity. This sign would be the equivalent of Europe's classical culture and mythology.

19. Fabio Cruz and Claudio Girola, from the journey's chronicle in *Amereida: Volumen Segundo* (Valparaíso: Talleres de Investigaciones Gráficas de la Escuela de Arquitectura de la Universidad Católica de Valparaíso, 1986), 198.

20. Cruz and Girola, *Amereida: Volumen Segundo*, 170.

21. "Ellas abren en su cruz/ todos los puntos cardinales/ El norte designa sur/ pero ella no es el sur/ porque en este cielo americano/ también sus luces equivocan la esperanza/ regalo o constelación/ para encender el nuevo mapa/ y más que sur/ ¿no es ella nuestro norte?" *Amereida: Volumen Primero*.

Lunch meeting in the Music Room.
Members of the Open City.

THE OPEN CITY

In the late sixties, a group of architects linked to the school bought a piece of land almost thirty kilometers to the north of Valparaíso, in a place called Ritoque. The site was a poor, sandy field, divided in two by a road running north-south and having no special value other than the impressive presence of the Pacific Ocean and the sand dunes. One could speak of the almost ordinary condition of the place—the same ordinary condition of so many places and landscapes in America, hiding some deeper meaning. This was the place where the Open City was founded.

The Open City is a direct answer to the question raised by Amereida, a gesture intended as a foundational sign of new possibilities for modern American culture; here, standing before the sea, open and inviting to any passer-by, is a city ruled by poetry.

Since its foundation, the Open City has been the main focus of the school's efforts in construction.[22] Almost all of the twenty-some buildings in the Open City are the result of collaboration between several architects, occasionally assisted by students or recent graduates of the school. There is no client in a conventional sense; commissions are formulated through the intervention of poets, who are given freedom to interpret the activities that will transpire on a certain site. The architectural response to the poet's words develops from a shared vision about human life and inhabitation rather than from a set of external requirements.

The experimental character of architectural projects in the Open City arises from several exceptional circumstances, not the least of which is the site itself; its geographic condition imposes great difficulties on construction projects. Soil conditions are relatively poor, and the Pacific coastline is known for its severe winds. In the face of a range of logistical problems, the group has adopted a flexible, experimental attitude toward each act of construction.

Because the Open City has been built entirely with funds contributed by individual members of the cooperative, the projects are built almost exclusively of standard, inexpensive, or discarded materials, such as wooden posts and planks, corrugated metal, and handmade bricks. The astonishing variety of ways that these simple materials are combined in the Open City is a reflection of numerous experiments in collaborative design and construction processes.

From the beginning, the city was conceived as decentralized and sparsely built. It has developed incrementally over two decades, with few formal guidelines and no overall preconceived order. Each addition reflects a new facet in the city's pronounced destiny. The idea of a city center is conspicuously absent from the Open City—even the agoras are not conceived as central places in any conventional sense. Here, the classical word *agora* is used to designate not only a place of public discourse, a place to hear and to speak about the rules and projects of the city, but also the act itself in which these discussions take place.

In the Open City we can speak about two basic types of constructions. Public spaces constitute the first type: buildings and places developed primarily for collective use and based on a unitary spatial concept. Each of the communal spaces—the agoras and gardens, the Music Room and the Palace—is a formal celebration of a public act, living out the meaning of the poetic words that designate it. The Pajaritos Chapel could be considered a prototype for some of these spaces—a form of absence to house and give form to a variety of human acts.

22. The Cooperativa Amereida was formed to administer the Open City's funding, building, and infrastructure. Thus, while a great number of faculty members participate in the Open City, it is essentially a private institution, independent from the university; only recently has an agreement between the university and the Open City been established, allowing university facilities such as classrooms and workshops to be located on the site.

Water Tower, 1973.

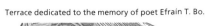

Terrace dedicated to the memory of poet Efraín T. Bo.

Agoras are conceived as meeting spaces in the Open City. They are usually defined only by a few elements—primarily the paving, some retaining walls, and sculptures or other symbolic (frequently vertical) elements. They are not plazas in the traditional sense of being confined by walls or buildings; rather, they are conceived as marks in the continuum of the landscape. This is partly due to the low-density occupation of the site, but is also consistent with the open condition attributed to the city.

Garden of Bo, 1980. Pavement detail.

Cemetery of the Open City.

The Music Room (1972) was founded on the relationship between music and space, seen through the medium of light. Dedicated to performances of both classical and modern music, the room is a simple, introverted volume built of wood. Its location was decided in order that the sound of the ocean would still be perceptible. The room is isolated from the exterior by opaque walls; a single pillar of light illuminates the center.

Throughout the spaces of the Open City, similar inversions (of interior and exterior, center and periphery, public and private, and so on) point to an essential key to the Valparaíso School's understanding of Modernity. In their search for new knowledge, one frequent technique for escaping an accustomed order has been to look in one thing for its very opposite. Hence the "thesis of proper north" of Amereida overturns the map of South America, and the interior of the continent becomes the "interior sea."

The second type of construction in the Open City is family houses, known as *hospederías* (guest houses). Based on the principle of hospitality, families in the Open City do not own their dwellings and do not assume traditional boundaries regarding private property; all inhabitants regard themselves as guests in the Open City. Each *hospedería* combines a private dwelling with some specific public function that gives the *hospedería* its name. These public functions range from studios and workshops to banquet spaces. As a hybrid building type that combines public and private realms in a complex architectural form, the *hospedería* is intended to connect every individual dweller to the city as a whole.

While the composition of communal spaces in the Open City can be described as unitary, the *hospederías* tend to be additive, even fragmentary, in composition. And if programmatically the *hospederías* are intended to address simultaneous individual and communal needs, in architectural terms they are also an expression of the individual-group dynamic. One of the most notable experiments in the construction of the Open City has been the concept of working *en ronda* (in the round). Cruz and Iommi have described this collaborative process:

In it are shared observations, acts, what is on the tip of the lips, the return to ignorance, the generation of form and its construction. The ronda can elaborate the work at the building site. Working mentally, talking to one another and listening to technicians at the same time, without being forced to rely on the use of previous plans . . .[23]

Thus the resulting composition might be regarded as an architectural conversation of many voices. The complex building including two *hospederías* and an extension used as a studio (el Banquete, las Máquinas & el Confín) is perhaps the clearest illustration of this process. Its aggregation of separate volumes of wood, brick, and metal also illustrates one of the earliest ideas of the group: architecture as the "skin of human acts."

Hospedería de la Entrada, 1984.

The Hospedería de la Entrada houses three separate functions. First, it is a family house with sleeping, eating, and working spaces. Second, as its name suggests, the hospedería stands at the entrance to the Open City, overseeing this entry point much like an ancient guard house. At ground level are terraces and platforms that serve as a reception area for people arriving and departing. Third, an outdoor cinema, not yet built, will be located on one of these open terraces.

Formally, the project is based on a repetition of skewed modular cubes, each a separate room of the dwelling. Inside, an open corridor connects the cubes, producing an ambiguity between individual rooms and a single interior space. The upper dwelling is a skeletal structure of light timber, and the expansive terraces at its base are formed by standard bricks. The dwelling is raised above the ground on slender stilts, both to give inhabitants some privacy and to allow a view through to the city and ocean beyond. As an entrance piece for the Open City, the Hospedería de la Entrada achieves through its broad frontality and crown of overscaled skylights an almost monumental character that belies its modest size and inexpensive materials.

23. Godofredo Iommi and Alberto Cruz, "La Ciudad Abierta: de la utopía al espejismo" ("The Open City: from Utopia to Mirage"), *Revista Universitaria* (Pontifícia Universidad Católica de Chile), 9 (April 1983).

Hospedería del Confín, 1983.

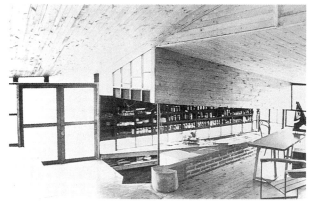

Hospedería de los Diseños.

Hospedería de la Alcoba, 1976.

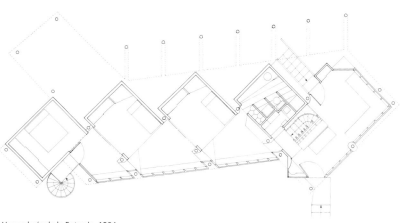

Hospedería de la Entrada, 1984.

Critics have associated the formal experimentation of the Open City with contemporary trends in late Modernism and Brutalism. More recently, stylistic similarities with the work of Deconstructivist architects have been pointed out—although it must be noted that the morphological experiments of the Open City precede the dissemination of Deconstructivist ideas by several years. While it may be useless to maintain that forms used by the Valparaíso School are free from external influence, it is clear that they have always emerged in connection to a specific, autonomous discourse.

Both in architectural and urbanistic terms, the Open City may be regarded as a highly evolved version of the Achupallas project. As in the earlier proposal, preconceived formal constraints are largely dispensed with; the overall conception of the city is left open, adaptable to new ideas from its inhabitants. The authors of the Open City place great emphasis on maintaining discussion and consensus as the basis of a truly urban architecture.[24]

Without a doubt, utopian aspirations are implicit in this vision of the Open City. The idea of creating an environment where everyday activity and poetic acts are integrated as one is perhaps the most fundamental utopia of all. Yet unlike most utopian experiments, the Open City was never intended to be a self-sufficient model in economic or societal terms; rather its basis is metaphysical. Iommi describes the concept of this utopia paradoxically as *el no-lugar que ha lugar* (literally, "the no-place that has a place")[25] to describe the real presence, even in its fragility, of what is supposed to be physically absent or situated far in the future. It is in this context that the Open City can be considered utopian. The city must not, therefore, be seen merely as a collection of interesting buildings, but rather as the presence, however incomplete or fragile, of a profound vision of the world from a modern American point of view.

Palace of Dawn and Dusk (1984 to present).

24. Ironically, Enrique Browne comments on the similarity between the fragmented buildings of the Open City and the chaotic forms of contemporary Latin American cities. See Enrique Browne, "La Ciudad Abierta en Valparaíso," *SUMMA* 214 (July 1985).

25. Here, the phrase *ha lugar* is used in its double sense to mean both "takes place" and "has a place (is accepted as true or valid)." Based on the original meaning of the Greek *ou-topos* ("not place"), Iommi's words also convey a sense of wonderment: something is taking place in the Open City that, by definition, is not supposed to happen in any place. See Iommi and Cruz, "La Ciudad Abierta: de la utopía al espejismo."

Palace of Dawn and Dusk. Interior patio.

The Palace of Dawn and Dusk, as its poetic name suggests, is intended to capture two transitional moments in the continuum of the day, moments when, under the transforming light of the sun, things acquire an unusually clear, distinctive shape. In the Open City, dawn and dusk assume not only temporal but also geographical associations: the sun rises in the east (over the interior sea) and sets over the Pacific Ocean (the exterior sea). Charged with addressing both the day and the cardinal directions—absolutes of time and space—the palace began with an ambitious program of dwellings (two hospederias), associated patios, a common dining hall, and a public bath. The Palace represents a search for an ever more complex union of public and private spaces.

Disappointingly, the work remains unfinished, interrupted in the initial stages of construction. Instead of the monumental forms intended, foundation walls and terraces alone mark the site. Yet the Palace has a certain beauty in its incompleteness, and its poetic intentions are legible in the spacious, walled patios that suggest what may be yet to come. The symmetrical ordering of the plan, unusual for projects in the Open City, is a response to the site's ambivalent situation between twin seas, between sunrise and sunset. The uniformly precise and repetitive apsoidal walls of the palace capture and amplify the effects of strong, angled light.

Awaiting the palace's completion, residents of the Open City have adapted its walled patios for outdoor ceremonies.

Lateral addition.

. . . les vrais voyageurs sont ceux-là seuls qui partent
Pour partir . . .

Baudelaire[26]

The Travesías (Crossings) are one of the latest proposals of the Valparaíso School. The Travesías emerged during the early eighties as a way of linking teaching and research experiences. At the end of a semester, professors and students make a trip together with the idea of revealing the poetic meaning of a place through the building of a work or installation.

The trip itself is not considered an instrumental means to arrive at another place, but rather an experience that changes the meanings of things and makes one more acutely aware of the world's reality. The original text of *Amereida* proposed that a journey suspends an accustomed mode of thought and opens the senses: "Travels teach us (among other things) that words are foreign to the things they designate."[27] Conceived in this spirit of discovery, each of the Travesías acts as a prolongation and partial development of Amereida's fundamental journey.

The poetic origin of the Travesías, like that of the Phalène, lies in the idea of improvisation, in the condition of a gift or a work without commission. The final result is frequently a lone sign or gesture, left in the most remote places, only to be found by unknown people in an unknown time. Each of the Travesías is an attempt to reveal something new about a specific place. Taken together, they form a body of research about architectural possibilities in the most remote and varied places in America, from the cold southern regions to the tropical rain forest, from metropolis to desert.[28]

The school considers the Travesías a fundamental pedagogical experience, a way of learning about management and organization in the hard conditions of an underdeveloped country and continent. In their conception of architecture as positive action, as enterprise, the Travesías have been recognized by many students as a useful experience for their later professional work.

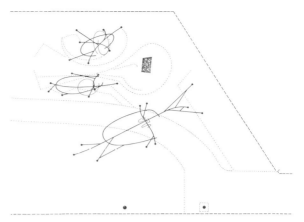

Athenea. Plan.

The Travesías are not restricted to timeless unpopulated landscapes; cities and historical sites are also open to new interpretation, as a recent Travesía to Santiago by the students of Alberto Cruz and Miguel Eyquem has shown. Studying the development of the city, they selected a significant site beside the Mapocho River, at the edge of the colonial grid's expansion, in view of the Cordillera mountains. The constructions erected by professors and students in the course of a few days were inspired by a poem by Godofredo Iommi, which speaks of the relationship between this city and land. The poem is engraved on a sculpture by Claudio Girola, set among shifting ground planes and virtual curvilinear volumes suggested by fragile metallic arcs.

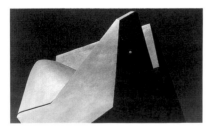

Athenea. Detail of sculpture by Claudio Girola.

26. "The real travellers are only those / Who leave for leaving's sake . . ." Charles Baudelaire, "Le Voyage," in *Selected Poems*, trans. Joanna Richardson (London: Penguin Books, 1975), 206. Also *Obra poética completa, edición bilingüe*, Ediciones 29 (Barcelona: Libros Rio Nuevo, 1977), 362.

27. "Los viajes nos enseñan (entre otras cosas) que las palabras son extrañas a las cosas que nombran." *Amereida, Volumen Primero*.

28. A book documenting the experiences of more than thirty Travesías to varied and remote places on the continent will soon be published by the school.

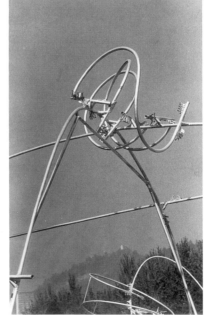

Athenea. Detail.

Construction of the Santiago Travesía, entitled Athenea. Night view.

ATHENEA	ATHENEA
1 As promising	*Cual promisorio*
2 or behind	*o detrás*
3 enclosed light	*cercada luz*
—the secret does not register—	*—el secreto no registra—*
4 Even another	*Aún otra*
5 intimate	*íntima*
6 tells herself	*se dice a si*
stirring her appearance	*conmoviendo la aparencia*
7 As of yore	*Tal antaño*
by black snow	*por nieves negras*
8 in threads	*al hilo*
she girds	*ciñe*
blind	*ciegas*
recurrent	*libertades*
liberties	*recurrentes*
9 This land keeps	*Esta tierra guarda*
the inviolable silence of her echo	*el silencio inviolable de su eco*
10 and forbidden	*y vedada*
she falls in love with her people	*se enamora de sus gentes*
11 Lamp	*Lámpara*
that every oblivion returns.	*que todo olvido vuelve.*

Godofredo Iommi

Notes to the poem "Athenea"

1 Even a catastrophe contains hope; an expectation.
2 The Cordillera, the background or rear of the city, builds, encircling the magnificent light of the city like an open glass.
3 But at first sight, the reason, the cause of this effect—the secret—is not registered.
4 The earth makes herself into another.
5 when she trembles.
6 She tells herself when trembling, stirring her appearance.
7 As ever the Cordillera's snows
8 untie themselves in threads (Mapocho, Maipo) and channel as through a girdle the violent, liberated, recurrent waters. Through those beds telluric currents descend.
9 But this place nurses the silence of the echo that is produced between its tremors and its secure and enduring presence.
10 As if in trembling she would indicate that no one may possess her (she is only an echo of herself), thus keeping her distance, she falls in love with her people.
11 Cordillera, rivers, the meeting of both in the San Carlos that joins Mapocho and Maipo— they are the lamp that reminds of the destiny of the city. That is why all oblivion, all will to obliterate, brings destiny back.

RESEARCH AND PROFESSION: A PERSPECTIVE VIEW

The fundamental aim of this essay has been to expose, even in an incomplete and fragmentary way, some of the issues and circumstances that have shaped the history and present reality of the Valparaíso School. The group's perseverance through almost forty years stands as testimony to the school's significance; this is particularly true within the limits of the Latin American context, where one is always dealing with the changing and the ephemeral. The school has not only resisted public misunderstanding and the lack of economic resources, but has explored the possibility of transforming these deficiencies into positive elements, working precisely with the provisional, the unfinished, the unrooted.[29]

Since the beginning, professionals have criticized the group for its complex language, radical views, and lack of professional orientation. Nevertheless, some significant commissions developed in the early years of the school seemed to express its confidence in the possibility of building a fluid relation between research, teaching, and practice. Group participation in the competition for the new Naval School in Valparaíso (1956)[30], in the reconstruction of a set of churches destroyed in an earthquake in southern Chile (1960), and in the alternative proposals for a new highway linking Valparaíso and Viña del Mar (1969)[31] demonstrates that this goal of joining research and professional activity remained active for many years. Individual members of the school have also entered into several more conventional commissions, many of which have enjoyed wide publication.[32]

Since the late sixties, however, the school's main efforts have been concentrated on the Open City, leaving aside group participation in conventional commissions. We can understand this move as a practical necessity; the long-term project of developing an experimental way of practicing architecture demands the full energy of the group. Yet a more critical interpretation might introduce doubts as to whether the requirements of conventional commissions could ever be met starting from the group's radical point of view.

In a broader sense, the relations between the Valparaíso School and the profession can be understood in two separate aspects: the activity of the architects educated at the school and the intellectual influence of the school itself. A survey of several generations of architects educated by the Valparaíso School might constitute an independent study; there is little doubt as to the imaginative renewal that many of them have brought to the fields of architecture and urbanism. Simultaneously, the intellectual influence of the Valparaíso School has grown significantly over the years, so that today it represents one of the clearest poles of architectural thought in Latin America. Presently, with growing acceptance among professionals and academics for its work, the School is faced with broadening its theories to interact with a more complex reality.

The Valparaíso School has devoted over forty years to the investigation of the idea of architectural research. Starting from a conviction about the value of research itself and about the necessary connections with different arts and sciences, they have attempted to penetrate the most difficult and underdeveloped area of research: research connected with the project, the very core of the architectural discipline. Although it may be tempting to think of the formal, spatial, and tectonic experiments of the Open City and the Travesías as the main body of this architectural research, these experiments were never intended to be generalizable; they were conceived as specific solutions to specific sites and to a decidedly atypical mode of dwelling. The most significant research contribution of the Valparaíso School seems to lie elsewhere—in the school's philosophical foundations, in its conception of what architecture is and of how architecture relates to our daily lives.

By promoting an alternative model of architecture as a collaborative enterprise, the Valparaíso School has demonstrated that architecture can thrive under adverse conditions. Architects of the Valparaíso School have created buildings inextricably linked with the words and acts that generated them, crystallizations of a way of living and thinking. The beauty and vigor of these projects are only manifestations of a deeper current of thought, akin somehow to Jacob's concept of nocturnal science.

The necessity of generating specific conditions for this special way of working, different from what conventional commissions usually allow, emerges as one of the critical issues of the school. It points to a reexamination of the different levels of activity included in what we consider globally as architectural practice.

The development of experiences like those of the Valparaíso School may allow architecture not only to achieve the sort of prestige exhibited by the intellectual paradigms of science, but also to contribute to the enrichment of human knowledge with its own resources and methods.

29. I am indebted to Rafael Moneo for this observation, which he made while visiting the Open City in 1983.

30. *Revista Oficial del Colegio de Arquitectos de Chile*, 3d ser., 43 (May 1983): 29-34.

31. "Avenida del Mar," in *Fundamentos de la Escuela de Arquitectura*.

32. Among these private commissions, most notable are the partially built Benedictine monastery in Santiago by Jaime Bellata and others (see Patricio Gross and José Vial, *El monasterio Benedictino de las Condes, una obra de arquitectura patrimonial* [Ediciones Universidad Católica de Chile, 1988]; and private houses by Fabio Cruz, Miguel Eyquem, and Juan Baixas (see respectively "Casa Cruz," ARQ [Escuela de Arquitectura de la Pontificia Universidad Católica de Chile] 16 [March 1991]: 31-39; "Casa Luis Peña," *Revista Oficial del Colegio de Arquitectos* 31: 24-28; and "Casa José Mingo," *Revista Oficial del Colegio de Arquitectos* 57 [1989]: 72).

Casa Cruz in Santiago, 1961. Fabio Cruz and others. Courtyard facade.

Casa Cruz. Interior view.

Casa Peña near Santiago, 1980.
Miguel Eyquem.

Plaza José Vial in Valparaíso.
This public plaza is dedicated to the memory of one of the school's founding members.

Plaza José Vial. Aerial view.

Collaboration offers an alternative context in which to consider the subject of research in architecture. Projects, ideas, and authorship overlap and an unexpected cross fertilization occurs. When the relationships of author, subject, product, and method of production become more complex, the process of research becomes tactical, and the way in which the problem is formulated, the construction of the research, becomes as important as the product.

Our research begins with direct observation. We look at what is known, what is visible in the city, but we also consider forces which act upon the city that are not immediately visible or known. Research is the process of looking again in different ways at the set of issues within a field of interest. There is no fixed beginning point to research. At the start of a project, we are already in the middle of the problem because we bring to the work our personal history, our interests and biases, and ideas from past work. There is a subjective condition in research: we as individuals are a part of the problem.

A tension emerges between the subjective condition of research as personal inquiry and the legal, economic, social and physical forces inherent in the "objective" mechanisms of architectural production. This tension is unavoidable for architects who choose to work in the public territory. While the work occupies the space of the battle, it is also resistant. The deadening institutionality of conventional architectural production can't be resisted by ignoring issues of use, scale, and cost, for the work becomes subject to commodification in other markets, and to the privileges and problems of the gallery.

The Computer Laboratory at RISD is an architecture which enables the perception of connections between the products of technology (power, information, light) and the networks of electrical infrastructure through which technology is transmitted, accessed, and located within the School. In this project, the space of the wood stud wall is excavated as a site of research. Materials are studied at their source to understand the intersection of their visible and invisible properties. Fiberglass resin sheets used in the trucking industry provide privacy between work stations, resist transmission of electromagnetic waves, and record the presence of power within the walls as shadows projected onto its translucent surface. The color of L.E.D., incandescent and fluorescent light, and the translucency

COMMENTS FROM THE MARGIN

Sheila Kennedy and Frano Violich

Kennedy and Violich Architecture, CAD Laboratory, Rhode Island School of Design, 1991.

or opacity of materials in space suggest possible relationships between what is present or visible and what is hidden or not perceived.

Elements of electrical infrastructure which are usually not considered to be in the "domain" of architecture–electrical conduits, outlets, and surge suppressors–are used as material. The excessiveness of what is necessary in the Computer

Laboratory produces a surplus of meaning that is always ambiguous and that raises questions about the resolvability of the technological and the spatial. The architecture supports a continual re-reading of structure and infrastructure by exposing the points of contact and connection–the cords, wall cavities, plugs, and network systems–which enable technology and make it vulnerable.

At the scale of the city, in Reclamation Park #1, the planning and representation of urban artifacts became the subject of a collaborative project of research, "Drawing on Site." A group of artists asked us to construct a system of pathways to provide public access for a temporary, site specific installation on an abandoned piece of waterfront land. Using old maps of the site and engineering plans for its proposed development, we marked with lime chalk on the surface of the site the former, existing and future lines of its infrastructure. The distant aerial view depicts the oversite/sight of the Master Plan; it edits and reduces the visibility of local conditions that characterize urban public territory. The projection of planning maps upon the site reveals the instrumentality of the Master Plan, enhancing perception of the complexity of local environmental and topographical conditions.

Through this process of mapping, a representation of the site is drawn out as the infrastructure above and below ground is superimposed and inscribed onto the surface of ground. Horizontal networks of movement which were stratified at different moments in the site's history are collapsed together on the surface of the site. The intersections of this collapsed network of infrastructure are marked by localized excavations which allow visitors to construct relationships and "map" this urban landscape for themselves.

There is a political dimension in any examination of research in architecture. If research in architecture is to be critical and speculative, then the inevitability of the "givens" of a site or situation must be temporarily suspended to address the more significant issue of making visible the nature of the problem itself. As scientific models have been challenged as paradigms for research in architecture, traditional modes of architectural practice must be criticized. The thinking that comes from alternative forms of practice raises questions about the scope of the architectural intervention, its duration

Kennedy and Violich Architecture with Linda Pollak and Matthew VanderBorgh, *Drawing on Site*, installation overview, Charlestown, 1990.

Kennedy and Violich Architecture with Linda Pollak and Matthew VanderBorgh, *Drawing on Site*, installation excavation, Charlestown, 1990.

and the location of its audiences and territories. Yet the consequences of this thinking remain marginalized as they are irreconcilable with many aspects of the existing organization of the profession. Who benefits from research? Who needs help? What are the products of architectural research? Whom do they serve? How are projects funded and how are they made public? These questions must be addressed if we are to confront the subject of research in architecture and of architecture in public territory: an elusive construction which we remake every day in the work of research.

INTERIM BRIDGES PROJECT

Introduction

In 1955 the construction of Boston's elevated Central Artery and the advent of large-scale urban renewal projects compounded the city's problem of the separation of its historic waterfront from the downtown core. The elevated artery structure cuts through Boston at its most vulnerable point, and acts as a visual and physical barrier that isolates the historic peninsula from the city's "mainland." The decision to demolish the existing elevated artery and replace it with two miles of new underground roadway was to be the first step toward the reunification of Boston. Ironically, the "depression" of Boston's elevated Central Artery will make the city even more vulnerable to division, because of the disruptions this large-scale public works project will cause.

The Interim Bridges Project is an architectural design project for three pedestrian bridges located on three sites along the construction zone of the new underground roadway. The Interim Bridges will provide the only means of dedicated pedestrian access from the Boston waterfront to the rest of the city during the estimated ten to fifteen years that the roadway project will be under construction.

The design of the Interim Bridges explores how ordinary, functional urban amenities can be activated to challenge the anonymous character of temporary public structures and combat the atrophy of the public realm in American cities. The connections between people, program, and public space is essential for a sense of security, diversity, and vitality in the environment of the Interim Bridges. The architecture of each bridge is different, and recognizes a different group of users in the planning of its public programs. All three bridges share the same set of technical requirements and respond to design issues such as the best use of natural and artificial light, pedestrian access, life safety, shelter from the construction environment, and pedestrian security.

The architectural form and language of the Interim Bridges is derived from technical and design criteria established through research sponsored by a grant from the National Endow-ment of the Arts. Standard conditions that permeate building construction are accepted and everyday construction materials, such as

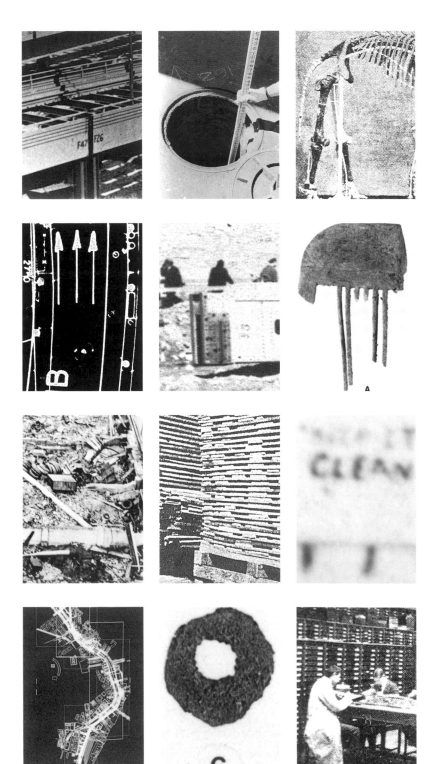

Bent no. 62, construction of the Central Artery, 1952. [Bostonian Society/Old State House]	Survey of underground utilities.	Vertebrate reconstruction. [Archives d'Architecture Moderne, Belgium]
Temporary on-ramp, engineering proposal. [Bechtel, Parsons, Brinkerhof, Engineers, Inc.]	Pedestrian crossing at Bent no. 43, 1953. [Bostonian Society/Old State House]	Comb fragment, iron, ca. 1820, NE 02 Trench C. [Office of Public Archaeology, Boston University]
Debris field, Demolition Block no. 23, 1952.	Construction lumber stacked on pallets.	"Keep It Clean," wrecker's slogan on the party wall of 47-49 Haverhill Street, 1952.
Terminal display, master plan for the reconstruction of the Central Artery, 1992. [Bechtel, Parsons, Brinkerhof, Engineers, Inc.]	Shoe eyelet, tin, ca. 1850, NE 02 Trench C. [Office of Public Archaeology, Boston University]	Entomological Collections Research Hall, Musée d'Histoire Naturelle, Brussels, 1913. [Archives d'Architecture Moderne, Belgium]

two-by-fours, plywood, and sheet products, are particularized and transformed through the ways in which they are assembled. The Interim Bridges resist a singular, fixed architectural configuration, as they must respond to changing technical requirements of construction phasing, surface traffic circulation, and different structural conditions associated with the underground construction. The bridges' lightweight wood frames and standard construction materials can be easily adapted on site, and each bridge is designed to change over time according to the fluid conditions of the construction field.

The interior environment of the bridges encourages a sense of spatial openness through the disposition of volume and the use of translucent materials. Openings in the skin allow natural light in and provide views out to the changing landscape of the construction site. Natural light is filtered to avoid excessive heat gain, but limited direct sunlight always permeates the interior space to create a changing interior environment that marks time, orientation, and season.

The Interim Bridges Project supports both changing and fixed programs of public use. Each bridge provides unassigned areas of open space along its passage, which are intended to receive a variety of small program elements such as vendors, newsstands, and public amenities as well as more spontaneous performances and events.

The Interim Bridges are designed to be horizontal and vertical connectors that serve to make the public more aware of the relationships between different levels of the city. Changing programs of cultural and historical information about the city, temporary artworks, information about the construction process, and archaeological exhibits will allow the pedestrian to see, hear, and understand the changes that are being made to the city. In this way, the environment of the bridges allows the pedestrian to become a participant in the process of construction, which would otherwise remain hidden underground.

The Interim Bridges make clear that temporary structures as urban interventions can influence the future use and perception of reclaimed public land in the city. The project offers a unique precedent for rethinking the role of such temporary structures, and sheds new light on those urban structures that are perceived to be permanent.

The material history of the city is made up of its fragments. The city can be understood as a living artifact; decipherable, open to interpretation. The city's former, present, and intended conditions are re-assembled, re-configured in the archaeological fragment on an urban scale: subway and utility lines, foundations. Infrastructure is the city ledger, to be read through excavation, which suggests and questions relationships among elements in the city.

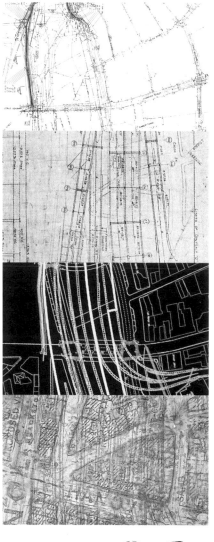

Demolition Block no. 23, 1952.
[Bostonian Society/Old State House]

Top to bottom:

Plan of underground utility lines at Haymarket Bridge crossing, 1992. [Massachusetts Department of Public Works]

Steel infrastructure, Central Artery FHC Engineering plan, 1950. [Massachusetts Department of Public Works]

Terminal display, slurry wall infrastructure, Central Artery, 1992. [Bechtel, Parsons, Brinkerhof, Engineers, Inc.]

Composite site plan, Haymarket Bridge crossing, 1992.

Bottle fragments, glass, ca. 1850-1900, NE 03 Trench C. [Office of Public Archaeology, Boston University]

Aerial view of Boston, 1992.

A DRIFTING ARCHITECTURE

The provisional needs of the construction site and the potential for the public use of its urban edges produce conditions for a drifting architecture, a temporary architecture that changes and moves over time.

A description of this architecture is elusive. The figuration of the whole is relinquished in favor of the configuration of relationships between the parts. The design is determined by a series of decisions: an amount of time, a choice of materials, a set of directions for the assembly of parts, the discovery of points in the city to be connected.

Material is placed and replaced, cut to fit, butted together, and joined again in new configurations. The ongoing process of construction records each former location of the Bridge in the patches and seams in the surfaces of the boardwalk and barrier wall. The length and position of sheathing boards within the order of the elevation forms a changing and unpredictable pattern–a mosaic of waste and reuse.

Different moments of time within the history of the city—past, present and future—may be brought together to reveal how urban artifacts are constructed, used, discarded, and replaced. The repetition of cycles of production, and the accelerated placement and replacement of neighborhoods, highways, and domestic objects, contribute to the new sense of inevitability between the "not yet" and the "no longer": the Temporary City.

Construction site materials waste and surplus stock.

Haymarket Bridge, day and night views

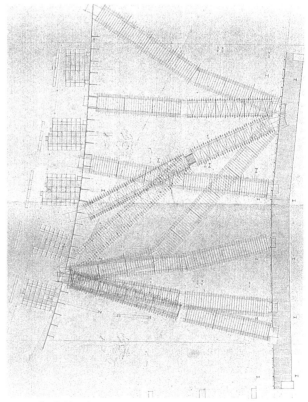

Haymarket Bridge plan.

Right: Positions of Haymarket Bridge head and market stalls over time.

The Hollow Space Between Structure and Skin

The separation of volume from mass, and of sheathing skin from structural skeleton produces a layer of hollow space between inside and outside. At the scale of the city, this layer of space is found between the thin skin of the urban ground plane and the steel frame structure of the existing elevated Artery.

Blighted and discarded at the urban scale, hidden and ignored at the scale of the building, the geography of gaps produced by frame construction can be rethought as another kind of space, one to be excavated and explored as a site for programs of public use.

The space between structure and skin offers an ear to the ground poised to listen to what is beyond itself; an aural presence of an "other," of footsteps amplified, chance encounters overheard.

It is a space that resonates in the public memory with echoes of the anonymous architecture of wood frame construction: stage sets, scaffolding structures, and backyard storage places. Continuity is found in the repetition of the wood stud as an inexhaustible and irreducible artifact of frame construction. The visibility and universal prevalence of the 2x4 make its commonness its most significant characteristic. The 2x4 is inherently public because it is common to the culture of contemporary construction. Through its commonness, the 2x4 inadvertently acquires a new value as a medium for an architecture that is of the public.

Listening Bridge, view of skin at intersection with Bent no. 43.

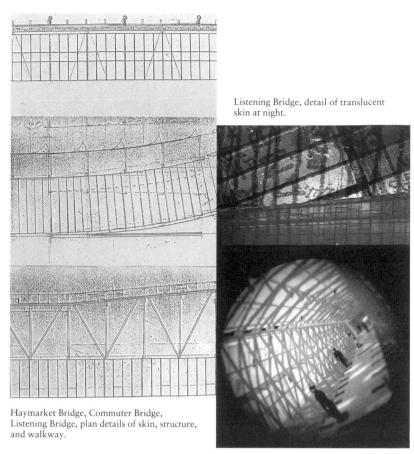

Listening Bridge, detail of translucent skin at night.

Haymarket Bridge, Commuter Bridge, Listening Bridge, plan details of skin, structure, and walkway.

Listening Bridge, interior view.

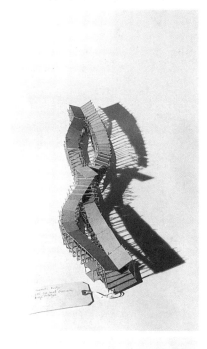

A Space of Crossing

A space of crossing is understood through movement, and different conditions of time and use. To and from, coming and going, the crossing of people, light, and cars is doubled in the daily exchanges of the Commuter. The space of crossing is doubled again by the intersection of the bridge with the highway structure which bisects the pedestrian passage, dividing its space in a fluid crossing from one side to the other. The merger and divergence of people moving at different speeds and directions produces the possibility of unexpected crossings, adjacencies and encounters.

The symmetry of the doubled passage is broken by the bias of morning and evening light. The standard plywood sheet is transformed in its assembly as a skin. The surface is bent back, crossed

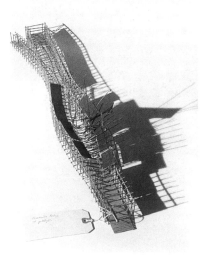

Commuter Bridge working sketch and models.

Commuter Bridge, interior view at junction with Bent no. 62.

over the perimeter and warped to provide oblique views out in different directions of travel.

The necessary redundancy of the doubled passage offers a strategy for making public space in the city. The act of crossing produces a doubling which enables choice and allows the space of passage to be made and remade by the public each day with each new crossing.

Crossing in space supports a crossing of use, where the program of passage and public space flip-flop back and forth. Public space is produced by the act of passing through; it occurs on the way to something else. The necessity of crossing allows the space of transit to activate the transition from public passage to public space.

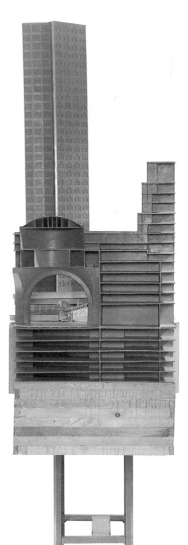

Commuter Bridge, diagram of program and volume over time (above) and site model at waterfront edge.

Special thanks to Matthew VanderBorgh and Pam Davies.

Bruce T. Martin, photographer

Panel 2   # RESEARCH IN ACADEMICS AND PRACTICE

October 6, 1990
Harvard University Graduate School of Design
Cambridge, Massachusetts

Panelists
Henry Cobb, Pei Cobb Freed & Partners, New York City
Linda Groat, University of Michigan, Ann Arbor
Kyong Park, Storefront for Art and Architecture, New York City
William Porter, Massachusetts Institute of Technology
Mack Scogin, Harvard University; Scogin, Elam, and Bray Architects, Atlanta
Denise Scott Brown, Venturi Scott Brown and Associates, Philadelphia
Jorge Silvetti, Harvard University; Machado and Silvetti Associates, Boston

Moderator
Peter Rowe, Harvard University

Peter Rowe The title of the second panel is "Architectural Research in Academics and Practice." In essence we're going to be dealing with the culture of research, as opposed to the epistemological basis of research. Hopefully, we can get into the politics of architectural research—how its various agendas become shaped.

There are various models for research in practice. From the arts and sciences of academia, we have various historical and theoretical forms of scholarship. Here perhaps the fine arts relate most closely to architecture. Various forms of logical-empirical orthodoxies, as well as ethno-methodological and hermeneutic forms of interpretation, are operative in technical areas and the social sciences—both of which are fairly close to architecture in certain ways. These are usually criss-crossed, as we saw rather well in the first panel, by various philosophical colorations.

Introduction

In professional practice, knowledge about projects accumulates in firms or groups of firms, as does research into building products and building systems. These are necessary for the technical, as well as, to some extent, the theoretical advancement of the field. And if I were to speak to Italian or Spanish colleagues, they would see design itself as a form of speculation and would not be at all troubled if I called it a form of research.

In addition to this, we have various ways in which these models of knowing are employed. Here I'm talking about the agents involved, the way research agendas become set, and the way support is given to research. Research is often an expensive undertaking; it may involve a large amount of resources and people requiring financial support. It essentially involves a political debate. The established disciplines of knowledge in academia form lobbying groups for what they do and perpetuate themselves. We are well aware of the machinations of the government agencies that guide and coerce funds in support of research. Interest groups exist within, across, and beyond disciplinary lines, as well as between schools of similar kinds of thought; journals get started; we have professional societies; and we have alternative venues that deliberately offer some kind of, if you like, "other place" for investigations into architecture that lie outside of the mainstream. The panel today represents people from all walks of this life. We have a mix of academics, practitioners, people who have worked in research organizations as well as in alternative venues of research. I have asked each of the panelists to comment briefly on the general topic, mentioning how they understand architectural research.

Denise Scott Brown[1] There have been a lot of tall men at this conference, and their words are going over my head.

As an architect, I was very lucky to enter the University of Pennsylvania planning school in the late 1950s and be taught by social scientists in planning who were skeptical about the role of architects in the city and churlish about architecture. They rocked my convictions and made me think hard, but I found their views "some sort of killing lifeline."[2]

As I came onto Penn's faculty in 1960 a set of debates was held on curriculum that helped me define where I stood in architecture, planning, and urban design. I learned that a field such as architecture is defined academically as a discipline by having a research-based body of knowledge, theory, and principles. Yet architects know that, in their work, design does not automatically evolve out of a research process—that the relation between design and research in architecture is complex indeed.

During the 1960s, as planning tended even further toward social studies, everyone fought the architects, who were considered to have little knowledge and to make decisions by intuition. During the Civil Rights movement, as the social activists took over in planning, they criticized the social scientists for being prepared only to study trends, not to act or to set out values and goals, and they called the architects elitists.

Much of my career, I've been a circus horse rider trying to relate architecture and planning as they've gone their diverging ways. "Can't there be design in economics?" I

asked, "I certainly know there can be analysis in architecture; and there are ways—there have to be ways—of doing architectural research as well." But where are we today with architecture as a field of research?

Another part of the curriculum debate was a discussion of the difference between academic and professional education. Should professional school educators teach differently from academic educators? Can professional educators in different professions learn from each other? The model of medical school may not be a good one for artistic education, but the two fields do share the fact that their practitioners act or prescribe actions and must learn how to do it. In school they practice this acting, one way or another, they don't just study theories of action.

Research in architecture after Modernism: a personal history (1)

My model for that kind of education was our five-year-old learning to ride a bicycle. He went away from the family, found himself a grassy bank, and rode down it over and over; he frequently landed at the bottom in a mud puddle. Finally, from the distance, approached this wobbling child bicycling toward us. "I did it!" That, I think, is a metaphor for how you learn to design. You try it over and over, introducing, in succession, more and more complex arguments. Although the presence of sympathetic guides who can suggest informative sources and useful philosophies is helpful, you must really learn to do it on your own, by trying again and again. You have to do it.

Where does research come into this process? If it's not carefully organized, research can inundate the designer and hinder the sequence of trial and error. With this in mind, I have tried to devise ways of relating research and design in studio. I based my early urban design studios on planning studios. These were defined as workshops or case studies where subject matter learned analytically in courses could be synthesized, through the solving of realistic problems that involved creativity and design. Yet, too often it seemed as if the students did a ritual dance called research and then another unrelated one called design. We tried to help them find ways to connect these two. I began teaching urban design studios called FFF (Form, Function, and Forces), to stress that the design of the city required an understanding not only of form and function, but also of social and economic forces within the society.

Later, at Yale, we tried a similar (although more loosely structured) studio, for architects. Its focus was research in architectural form and symbols. Formal analysis was treated as our design research. An unusual panoply of subject matters was introduced to the students and we proposed that loving beautiful buildings, in an analytic way, would help us to become good designers.

I must admit that many of the people who took my studios became good administrators and few became designers. But how many people have the chance to be designers in our profession? Was the training suitable for administrators rather than designers? If studio is a wonderful method for teaching design, how come designers tend to be inflexible and you find the work of the last guru at their last school on their drawing boards twenty years later? How come we're not training all that many good designers?

JORGE SILVETTI One must be concerned today about the status of architectural research in academia, about the models of inquiry in academia, and, of course, about issues of power and the manipulation of knowledge through the means of validation that are prevalent in the university and that bear upon the status of architectural research in the university. When I talk about this subject, I tend to get gradually angry, because I don't like to be at the periphery in the setting of academia, but I think that is where we are relegated as architects. I have a certain degree of animosity toward the current conditions that one must abide by in order to get any kind of research going or validated in an academic setting.

Research in architecture after Modernism: a personal history (2)

I would like to go back to the morning session and take from John Whiteman something I liked very much, which is the way I try to define the object of inquiry for architecture. That is—and we use the same word—"excess," that little bit that is beyond building, beyond all the technical aspects; that little bit extra that has kept research, theory, and history going now for centuries; that little bit that every theoretician and every historian has tried to define. It is that excess that we should be concerned with, not because the other sciences or disciplines that converge in architecture—like technology, physics, chemistry, or history—are not important to us, but because they are not indispensable to define the object of architecture. My point is that research in architecture should be conducted about the excess that is architecture in the construction of the physical world, and that this research should be done through the *project*.

The issue of the project has not been touched today, and I think we must. This is my position now, a position that has evolved through practicing and involving myself

with different modes of research. Why do I think that the project is the preferred mode we should use in research? Not because I privilege drawings over words. Both are obviously removed from the given world; they are both prior to the fact, they both deal with something that does not exist, and they work a different medium than that of architecture itself; they are both representations and simulations. I privilege drawings because I would like to give them a chance, since words have not helped in these last attempts of research in architecture.

I think it will be not too simplistic to say that research, as we talk of it today, is a result of some ideas that have been elaborated in the last twenty years or so; it is that history that I would like to briefly recount from personal experience. The lines that were explored in this period left, in my view, two dead ends of architectural research: the transformation of theory into technique, and the transformation of theory into illustration. Neither of these is the true essence of architectural research, although both may help to build buildings.

When this history starts in the late 1960s, we are dealing with the last gasp of the bastion of Modernism that dealt with scientific approaches to problems. Architecture became a case study for behavioral sciences, for social sciences in general, for operations research. We were all very fascinated with that, but it resulted in trivial, simple platitudes: after long periods of collecting data, one would, for instance, find that people really would rather sit in the sun than in the shade on a cool day, and vice versa.

At that moment, the notion of culture became a tool for criticism. It opened all kinds of paths that established the field of theory as firmly grounded in academia. One turned to anthropology (I would say this started with the concentration of anthropology on linguistics), because it was the most scientific kind of discipline that could help explain some issues about meaning, which was then the thing we thought needed to be explained. That opened many doors, but it basically led to two approaches: one, an iconographic line of thinking; and the other, a philosophical line of producing architecture. Both were rooted in the notion that architecture is a part of culture and operates somehow as language. Those interested in iconography were very concerned with explaining the structure of meaning, how things are signified. They exerted a very important critique on the language of architecture, but iconography inevitably became a technique, a formula: "If you want to produce X rhetorical fact or Y particular effect of meaning, you do Z." The technique might be good, but it stops the idea of research right there.

The philosophical line—obviously, because it's philosophy—got entangled in a lot of words. It produced an important critique of some aspects of architecture, ideology, and metaphysics, but because it was so dependent on words, architecture became an illustration; words were invariably needed to explain what one was supposed to see in these projects. The philosophical line did produce important ideology, but it was not conducive to architecture.

Both of these lines of thinking depended on the model of scholarship usually associated with the humanities, instead of using the scientific model of validation. The university required the scholarly model, and I think that is  something that still needs to be criticized, because I don't think architectural research will always be subservient to these models of thinking and validating. Both were also very introspective, trying to explain the internal workings of architecture. What I see now is the need to reverse these views—locate ourselves inside architecture as we know it, without asking too many metaphysical or epistemological questions about its nature, and look out at those other things, the ones we used to use to validate our own discipline, look at them from inside architecture and through the project.

Defining a locus for architectural research

A few years ago I proposed that some of the subjects we could analyze this way are the fundamental relationships of architecture and power, and of architecture and art, largely because there is incredible confusion that's probably disturbed all the relationships of architecture today, including its relationship with scholarship. Harry Cobb demonstrated so clearly why the university needs architecture in a speech he gave a few years ago called *Architecture and the University*, and I recommend that you read it.[3]

Now, what I am trying to do in this institution is to do projects. My idea is that I would like to saturate not just this school (because it is saturated almost), but this university with projects, to demonstrate that what architects do—projects—is also the means and the product in the field of architectural research.

HENRY COBB I have lived almost all my life in practice and hence am very familiar with the inadequacies of practice as a vehicle for research. I have had also a brief engagement in academia, in which I discovered the inadequacies of the academic world as a vehicle for research. I would like to define research in architecture as any activity undertaken with the objective of advancing knowledge in the discipline of architecture. If one accepts that definition, I think it immediately becomes apparent that we are continuously producing knowledge both in practice and in the activities of the academic world, be it through individual study in research or teaching.

What then is wrong or missing, and why did I begin with a negative assessment of both practice and the academic world in terms of their support for research? For me it has to do not with the absence of research: as I said, I think it is continuous and ongoing in both realms. It has to do more with what I would describe as a poverty of epistemological and heuristic strategies that exist in both those realms with respect to the advancement of knowledge in the discipline. Our poverty of strategies, it seems to me, does deprive us of the ability to come to grips with a most important obstacle to architectural research: the inescapable relationship between architecture and power in culture. That relationship makes me want to refine

Jorge Silvetti's definition of the object of inquiry. He said the object of inquiry is that little bit of excess beyond building. It seems to me it's important to be more precise. For me that little bit of excess beyond building has to do with pushing architecture beyond a prescriptive status, beyond the status of being normative, into a speculative status where the work of architecture is more concerned with raising questions than with answering them.

It has seemed to me for some time that this is the most significant object of inquiry for architectural research, and it's for that reason that I am pessimistic about both the realm of practice and the academic world as vehicles. It's hard to push inquiry beyond assumptions that are so fundamental to the activity in question that they seem to confine it; and yet it is precisely that confinement that one wants to get beyond. For that reason, while I applaud every effort within the realm of practice and within the academic world to pursue the advancement of knowledge in architecture, I think that we may be at a point in the discipline of architecture where we do need some institutional framework outside of both those worlds in order to pursue the question that most concerns me, the question of architecture as a mode of speculative inquiry.

This kind of investigation—which obviously has to be sponsored by society, the same source that supports both practice and the academic world—nonetheless may need at this moment an alternative institutional framework. I think Jorge might agree that some of the efforts that he refers to as projects are, in fact, efforts which are not particularly comfortable in the framework of the university. That may be one of the best things about them, as a matter of fact. Another way to look at the issue is that by introducing a kind of virus into both practice and the academic world, one may modify those structures to be more hospitable to this kind of inquiry.

BILL PORTER I would like to pick up where Jorge left his history and suggest that there are a couple of directions to move from there. It seems to me one of the reasons to have an active program of architectural research—which I will attempt to define—is to provide a stage for as much creative architecture as we possibly can. Although I have a great faith in the sort of work which borders on the introspective, which I'll call research on practice, I believe we cannot turn our backs on the work of people who truly are part of the discipline and who may cause shifts in thinking to which the ingenious members of the profession may

Institutional Frameworks (1): MIT

respond, resulting in extraordinary and revolutionary change. If one tries to imagine what the sources of creative change in architecture are, I think one finds that they do not come primarily from within the profession, but from outside it, and the profession ingeniously responds to those changed conditions. One can't help but think of the extraordinary moments in the history of architecture as moments in which something about the world was being exhibited and explored through architecture.

I want to stress the need for exploration and research within the framework of "cultures of research" that overlap with the boundaries of architecture. I think, for example, of history, an area in which wonderful creativity has been exhibited, not only within the proper domain of architectural history itself, if you like, but in the border regions. Building technology is another area in which major shifts in available materials, in technologies, of even construction and assembly change the way in which buildings are built, and change what architecture can become.

Our strategy in the department of architecture at MIT is to reinforce at least three of these slightly foreign cultures and contain them within our own department: architectural history, building technology, and art. These cultures are populated by people who come from different backgrounds and have different goals. They are substantially different from us, if you like, and have reputations to make in their own fields. They are not warmed-over architects doing these sorts of things; they are people who are valid within their own professional frame of reference. Their work may not bear directly on the profession of architecture, but it may bear spectacularly on it. The standard of legitimacy for research related to architecture within these groups are promulgated within their own cultures of research, and these fields are well defended by professional journals and/or other forms of recognition. We are the beneficiaries when their work overlaps with architectural research.

But I am more interested in this business of research in practice; let me rapidly outline a multi-layered approach to research in the realm of practice. Designers move back and forth between two activities, which I term *conjecture* and *appreciation*. By appreciation I mean the full capacity of the creative individual, the architect, to understand, to read, to imbue with images and ideas that which he/she sees as the situation for design. Conjecture is the activity of mind which projects possibilities, which inflects and transforms it. The appreciative and conjectural processes happen over and over again. As there is a new conjecture for a particular circumstance, it's reread or reappreciated by the individual and so on. The situation is not objective; it is imbued with the person's feelings, understandings and prior images, and becomes further transformed. It's not a question of a personal transformation of something objective—a simplistic model of what design is about—rather design is the further transformation of an already heavily interpreted scene, where a need for change has been partly formulated. In other words, the individual responds to both personal and historical overlays on an objective situation. There is also a normative overlay because the individual as architect makes changes to the situation.

The test is different for this kind of research than for the first kind, which takes care of itself by virtue of the mature formation of the cultures in which the activities of building technology, history, and art occur. Here the test is the plausibility of action in the world within some sort of value framework. Were it not for this, that which is being researched would either be of antiquarian interest or of no interest at all. This value framework is a choice that an institution has to make in order to ensure that it has some consistency of view.

LINDA GROAT I want to talk about institutional constraints at two levels: at the level of the academic program in architecture, and at the intersection of architecture with the university as a whole.

I will start with the academic program and our experiences at the University of Michigan. Architectural research may be significantly advanced when the apparently discrete domains of social science, engineering, and historiographic research are examined at their points of intersection. If we are trying to describe a domain of architectural research, it may be important to look at where these different related disciplines intersect; that's what we tried to do when we revised our doctoral program at Michigan. In particular, we tried to develop a curriculum that would both facilitate the development of expertise in one of the four

Institutional frameworks (2): The University of Michigan

specialty areas that we offer and simultaneously foster an understanding of the complementary and integrative potential of these four areas. Our purpose was quite directly to address the issues that the *Harvard Architecture Review* set out in its introduction to this symposium. In our program proposal, we developed a four-part conceptual framework describing domains of architectural research. The four components were research orientation, temporal focus, thematic focus and the four specialty areas. We hoped to identify potential areas that haven't been explored, the points of intersection between, for instance, architectural history and building technology, and so forth.

We're still committed to that objective, but it's a lot easier to state it than to actually work it out. First, the faculty must live up to the standards of such an integrative model. Since we each had training in these conventional specialty areas, we needed retraining in order to provide such a program. Second, there is a tension between the integrative ideal and the need to train future faculty who are going out into a job market that is defined in terms of these preestablished specialty areas. Third, there is the challenge of marketing this comprehensive model to potential students who are already very focused in their interests. Fourth, there is the desirability of maintaining curricular cohesion within specialty areas while simultaneously encouraging interaction and solidity. So far, I think we've navigated this reasonably well, but it remains an ongoing challenge, and a continuous and lively source of debate.

The second institutional context is architecture in relation to the university as a whole. As many people have observed, the scientific paradigm and the expectations of external funding sources dominate how research is conceived in the larger university context. Given the situation, it's not surprising that so-called scientifically grounded aspects of architecture (say computer-aided design or technology) seem to constitute the body of what is termed "research in architecture." In this scheme, architectural history, with its traditional links to scholarship and the humanities, sometimes falls into uncertain territory. As a consequence, those who care about issues central to architectural discourse are often reticent, intimidated or ill-prepared to define alternative approaches and standards which make sense for architecture as a discipline. Now on the one hand, I argue that it's important and necessary to proffer such alternatives. My own experience is that university administrators and scholars from other disciplines are more than willing to entertain such alternatives. But the alternatives should not simply be to claim that all design inquiry is research. The better alternative is to pose a different view of what real research is. If we are going to get on with being able to do research in architecture or other disciplines that involve the production of cultural artifacts, we really need a different kind of epistemology.

KYONG PARK We've been talking about research within the academic and professional realms, and I'm very happy that Mr. Cobb brought up this idea of an alternative institution. For almost nine years now, I've been running what I believe is an alternative institution, called Storefront for Art and Architecture, in New York. I think it's my own example of research, because I am still not certain what its goals and future are to be.

It is not a definition of research that I am interested in, but in finding conditions or frameworks that make it possible for a greater amount of research to take place. Architecture as a field has to renovate itself with the changing world today. It needs

Institutional frameworks (3): Storefront for Art and Architecture

something comparable to science—a research laboratory—and that needs to be funded, as Mr. Cobb pointed out, by the industry itself.

Storefront is a cultural institution, in relation to educational and professional institutions, and it provides a forum for research and advancement for postgraduate architects and nonprofessionals. The definition of who those people are could be expanded, if the impoverishment of research capacity within the academic and professional realms, is accepted. At times I feel it is a majority of the architectural community when I hear their frustrations on a personal level. Storefront mounts exhibitions of architects who are doing research, conducting work "on the edge," expanding the perimeter of architecture. Our open projects are a collaborative form of research in which everybody may participate. The issues that we raise are sometimes very obscure. This allows for exploration of a wide range of ideas that are not found in conventional situations.

AUDIENCE (Jeffrey Sugarman, New York City Department of City Planning) I'd like the panel to consider what the implications of substituting the word *criticism* for *research* might be and whether architectural criticism today actually serves or hinders architecture as a speculative endeavor.

COBB You are asking the question, "Isn't the fundamental aspect of research a critical habit of mind or the ability to be self-critical?" That is perhaps a necessary habit of mind for research, but it is not necessarily sufficient. I think, therefore, that I would not be prepared to substitute the word *criticism* for *research*, because I think research has a broader implication involving operations which clearly go beyond criticism.

ALBERTO PÉREZ-GÓMEZ In the first panel I drew a distinction between practice, which has to do with ethical action and real possibilities, and research, which has to do with appropriate rhetoric, theory, and possible realities. I found it a very moving and provocative way of stating the case. I believe that research in architecture is not a disinterested activity. It is a profound ethical obligation of the discipline to conduct research to advance knowledge in the discipline. The incapacity of architecture to get itself out of what John Whiteman referred to as the constant condition of overstating,

Research as an ethical obligation

overfixing, overprescribing; that is a condition of architecture that I think we have been trying to get beyond. We'll never get beyond it, except through research. We won't get beyond it through practice or the conventions of practice or the conventions of professional training.

SILVETTI I think there is a crisis of words and that maybe helps the project acquire a bit more validity. I would agree that *research*, the English word, probably should be left to other kinds of activities or to the most traditional activities. It's interesting that the same words—same root—in Italian, *recerche proggetale*, would be used for just about any project, which is one of the most revered activities. An architect might actually never build a building and still be considered an architect because of the projects.

MACK SCOGIN Oddly enough, when I was in school, I can't ever recall the word *research* being uttered. We, in fact, had no theory courses ever in my school. It was basically a Beaux-Arts education. We did *analytiques* and drew the alphabet in very precise ways; we were taught the rules of the traditions of architecture as they were being applied in that day. Our study of history barely touched on Corb and a few modern architects. Frankly, I think I had a good education in architecture despite all of that, and it all seems to relate to the word *discipline*, which has a lot to do with our attitude toward architecture today.

The word *possibility* was brought up by Alberto. I like that word, because I think that has the essence of architectural research. Architectural research to me does two things: it defines the world of possibility for an architect, and it expands the world of possibilities. It does those things simultaneously, which is a real trick frankly, because we are involved in a world of infinite possibilities. But we are also involved in a world of excruciating preciseness. In the end we have to make decisions to make architecture,

many very precise decisions. We cannot experiment in architecture. In practice, we do not experiment.

Well, what does that mean for our attitude toward architecture? When we start projects, our mind-set is like that of an artist staring at a blank canvas. It's not difficult for us to assume a position of ignorance, believe me. We like to look at a project as a very intensive exercise, where we take into consideration all of the things surrounding a situation that influence or may influence the architecture: from social, economic, contextual, and behavioral influences down to very precise textual influences, adjacencies, contingencies, etc. The point of the analysis is not to aim towards a particular solution, but in our minds, ironically almost, to suspend judgment. It seems to me that it is in that suspension of judgment is the realm in which research in architecture has its greatest contribution: how you can get enough information, do enough research, pique enough interest, advance your particular knowledge of architecture and suspend judgment, until you have to make a decision and move forward.

AUDIENCE (Sheila Kennedy, Harvard GSD) I'm responding to Mack Scogin's comment on the difficulty of experimentation in practice. It is difficult, and yet this discussion has pointed out that research is not a luxury, but an ethical responsibility. So somehow, within this notion of research, I'd like you to address what this kind of project is. New strategies are needed. My concern is that the strategies being offered actually result in the marginalization of research out of architecture, at a time when we have so much need for it.

SCOGIN Perhaps I can clarify my definition of experimentation, because it is something that we don't use in our practice, or at least I hope we don't use. Experimental to me implies an element of the unknown that may be an undue risk. That's a risk that you as a practitioner simply can't impose upon a client or upon society. That's an ethical position that we take. That doesn't mean that we don't push the limits of our knowledge of architecture. We push ourselves as far as we can go in terms of research and investigation, but we don't push ourselves past the point where we take risk. Within the institution, however, experimentation could be a possibility. You don't have the same risk. That is the difference from the situation of practice, this excruciating precision that we as practitioners have to deal with. In academia you really do not have to have that same degree of precision.

William Adams

SILVETTI So far the issue of boundaries had not been brought into the discussion today and I was glad, but I'm going to touch on—shall we call them—architectures, or different realms—almost subpractices within architecture. We all like to be critical in school. I think that is our responsibility, even before research, to be critics of culture and of the institution of architecture itself. Two distinct ways of approaching architecture emerge: one includes those projects that are interested in knowing the limits of the risk one can actually take in real life when you build a building, and the other includes those projects which are, in a positive way, illustrations of a critique. Those are some of the narratives that I imagine Alberto was talking about. These may never pass the stage of being a pictorial representation whose subject matter is architecture, but they may have the power to alter the culture of architecture. And of course, the risks you can take in that realm of investigation are very different from the one in which you operate professionally. I know there are a lot of dangers in this division, but it sorts out two lines that I think are very clear in the schools today, even within our own school. To put experimentation in terms of risks might seem a bit conservative, but it's absolutely important that we understand exactly what it is we are talking about: criticism of ideology and criticism of institutions and culture.

STANFORD ANDERSON There is a distinction between the discipline of architecture and the profession of architecture. The practice of architecture and the profession of architecture understood in its current conventional sense, form one extraordinarily important part of what we in a larger sense call architecture. They are also an important part of our schools of architecture, since we are legally accredited to aid in the development of people who will take positions in a licensed profession.

But for all the importance of professionalism it is far from being the extent of what we understand as architecture. The discipline of architecture reaches outside the profession into the population at large, incorporating amateurs (in the best sense of the word), historians, preservationists, and others. The discipline incorporates knowledge developed in other times or cultures and which seemingly may be of little interest within the profession or the activities of the moment, but which nevertheless is a resource. The discipline also offers the opportunity to speculate and push beyond what is likely to be available within the constraints of practice.

Research should reach across the entire range of the discipline of architecture, including those things that are not currently important to practice, and those things that are not yet available. But at the same time it should also be concerned in the most professional way with those things that practice does require. Both the material and the style of Lars Lerup's presentation pointed to this potential for simultaneity of practice and discipline, and that is something which the architect himself can intensify, and those of us looking on from the side can attend to more carefully.

PÉREZ-GÓMEZ I think that the kind of research we are talking about here—design as research—takes its questions very seriously. The formulation of the question is the problem. When we do a project with a set program for a client, those kinds of questions aren't asked. We see the activity as problem solving, and that frightens me.

COBB I don't think that there is any professional worth his or her salt who only responds to the problem as defined by the client. I think we may be weak in many ways but we are all inventing our own problems, and to me that's terribly important. The practice of architecture is always hermeneutic with respect to the client's program, to society's program.

But Sheila Kennedy phrased her question in a way that carries an implication that I want to disagree with. She asked, "Aren't we marginalizing research in the profession and in the schools?" Well, I think we are to a degree marginalizing it, but I don't think that we should look at that as pejorative. It's precisely those marginal interventions that can be enormously effective. If there is a resolution to this paradox of how architecture can be an autonomous discipline and at the same time integrate other bodies of knowledge and other aspects of life into it, it is in this notion that there is something about architecture that is hospitable at its margins to these other issues. I think that it's quite dangerous to say that because these issues are marginal they should be made central; if they are made central, they will, in fact, overwhelm architecture. They have to be left marginal, but architecture has to find a way to absorb them, somehow. That's true in practice, and it's true in the university.

Some of the most exciting moments that I recall from my time in this school were those moments when people from other disciplines came into this school to speak with the faculty and students. They certainly brought their own disciplines and bodies of knowledge with them, but they came to talk about architecture, to be part of our discipline. Somehow they entered always on the margins of our discipline. In fact, it's very hard for them to connect to us. Somehow we have to make the effort.

ROWE One thing I've noticed about the discussion is that two large points have emerged. One is a fair amount of agreement on the idea of project, either in the form of speculation or as suspended judgment (using Harry's or Mack's terms) as being the locus of architectural research. There was also this idea that came from Linda and Bill—and it certainly squares with my own experience—that a vital domain of research is precisely in the intersections between the curious areas that gravitate around architectural problems. There is a bit of a paradox involved; getting the various members of Noah's Ark to work together is difficult in itself and with the idea of a project one is premiating the role of the designer in architecture, while the other disciplines play subordinate roles. I am interested in how you square the two to engage in projects which reach out beyond the architectural profession into the other areas.

PORTER In the universities it's been possible to discount the value of some of the metaphors which have been lately drawn from other fields and used as a basis for generating architectural knowl-edge that has proved not to be terribly useful. I refer specifically to work in the behavioral area, which is supposed to yield information about user behavior that is translatable into guidelines for design. Many of us believe this has come up short. And indeed, there are metaphors from other fields—procedural paradigms if you like—for how to do research which have been criticized over the course of the day as "linear," "reductive," etc. I think to visualize research as that which precedes design, not as an integral part of a process of inquiry, is bound to decrease the value of the research.

Reconciling traditions of research

I think there are two distinct directions that research ought to go in architecture. One of them has to do with maintaining work in the allied disciplines. The other direction is into what I earlier called "practice-oriented" research. I see these as distinct. Instead of relying heavily upon metaphors or borrowed patterns of work from other fields, I feel we must start as much as possible from within the discipline of design itself. So it is a dual strategy.

COBB Peter asked a question about a reconciliation that is probably unanswerable in theory. If I've drawn one conclusion from my life as an architect, it is that we live with certain paradoxes that are unresolvable. I don't think that should be allowed to deflect us for one instant from the determination that architecture as a discipline is the center of our focus. We can and must adhere to that. I think that's our posture in the university, and in the world. It has to be a completely uncompromising posture,

and therefore the reconciliation of that posture with the issue of how you absorb different bodies of knowledge into the discipline comes down, in the end, to the mind of the individual. These bodies of knowledge become integrated into the discipline of architecture not through frontal attacks, but through what I would call "glancing blows," tangential blows which illuminate in some way the discipline of architecture. I would argue—since the discipline of architecture is the threatened species here—that we need to be fairly polemical in our defense of it. At the same time, because we are in a university we need to find ways of connecting that don't threaten the basic premise that architecture is an autonomous discipline.

A political agenda for architecture in academia

To be optimistic for a moment, part of the positive aspect of this moment in our culture is that many disciplines are finding ways of absorbing other bodies of knowledge at their margins, and this is enriching all aspects of the culture, including architecture.

SILVETTI I think that until the status of architectural work—the project—is changed and put on equal standing with other academic endeavors, we should, in fact, be very careful of integration. Any attempts at integration will again bring the languages of the other disciplines which we will have to use in order to justify what we do. We always lose that way because that is not what we do, not how we think and produce. So I would say this is, in a way, the political agenda for academic architecture today.

ROWE I think we are reaching a state of semi-exhaustion. Thank you to the panel and to the organization.

1. Denise Scott Brown's remarks are © 1992, Denise Scott Brown.

2. For further description of this period, see Denise Scott Brown, *Urban Concepts* (New York: St. Martins Press, 1990).

3. Henry Cobb, *Architecture and the University* (Cambridge: Harvard University Graduate School of Design, 1986).

ON PROJECTION

Stan Allen

1. Phillippe Sollers, "Program," in *Writing and the Experience of Limits* (New York: Columbia University Press, 1983), 4.

0.0 PRETEXT: "ITS EXERCISE, UNDER CERTAIN CONDITIONS"

What is at stake in the definition of architecture as fundamentally a "projective" discipline? To answer this question involves asking about the relationship between drawing technique and architecture's understanding of itself as a discipline. It might be noted, for example, that in certain European languages, to "project" is synonymous with to "design." The linguistic affinity signals a delimiting condition for the discipline: architects are displaced from the material object of their work and of necessity effect construction only indirectly, at a distance. This distance is encoded in operations of projection. The present project begins to describe and enact some of the consequences of these transactions across the gap.

In a fragmentary essay entitled "Program" (1967), the French novelist and critic Phillipe Sollers writes:

1. A COMPREHENSIVE THEORY DERIVED FROM THE PRACTICE OF WRITING DEMANDS TO BE ELABORATED.[1]

From this decisive beginning, Sollers continues:

1.2 *From the practice* signifies that it has become impossible, beginning with a rupture that can be precisely situated in history, to make of writing an object that can be studied by any means other than writing itself (*its exercise, under certain conditions*).

Any research project begins of necessity with the definition of the object of research and the specification of its geometrical locus. In an operation which is already architectural, the first object is to define the site of the research. Fully aware of the illegitimacy of the transposition, (but also perhaps its inevitability) I would like to extend Sollers' formulation to the architectural field:

It has become impossible to make of architecture an object that can be studied by any means other than architecture itself (its exercise, under certain conditions).

What follows is a theoretical research into certain questions of representation and projection. The site of this research is double: a project and a text. The exact question of what constitutes theory and what constitutes practice is left unanswered. The project precedes the text; the text illustrates the project.

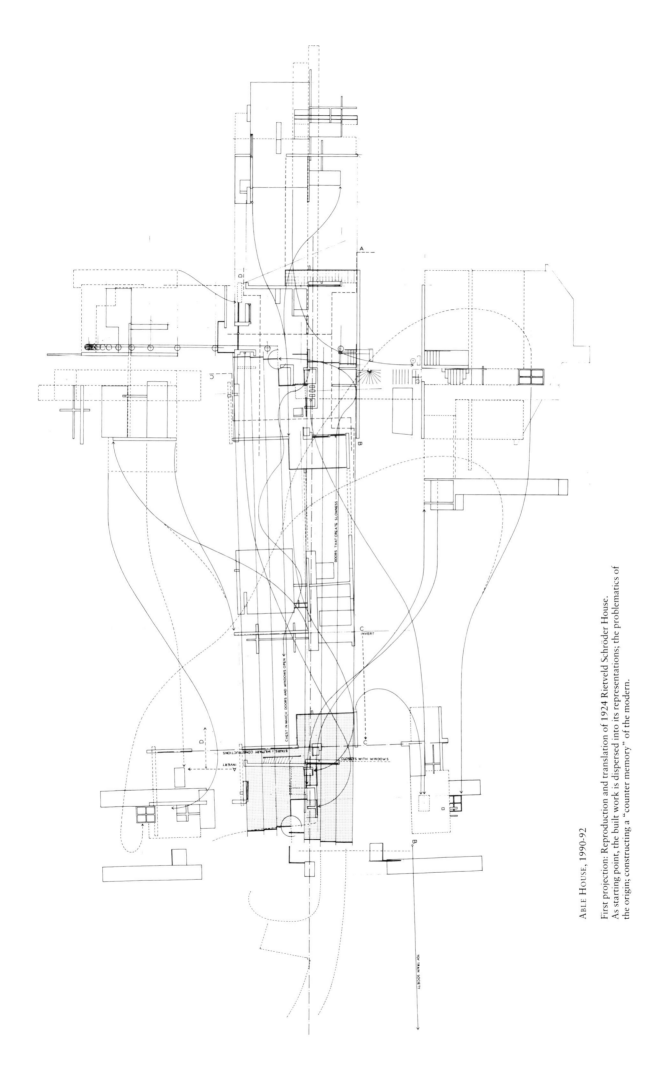

ABLE HOUSE, 1990-92

First projection: Reproduction and translation of 1924 Rietveld Schröder House.
As starting point, the built work is dispersed into its representations; the problematics of
the origin; constructing a "counter memory" of the modern.

2. Leon Battista Alberti, *On the Art of Building in Ten Books*, trans. Rykwert et al. (Cambridge, Massachusetts: MIT Press, 1988), I.4-4v.

3. Werner Oechslin, "Geometry and Line. The Vitruvian 'Science of Architectural Drawing'," *Daidalos* 1 (1981).

4. Edmund Husserl, *Origin of Geometry*, trans. John P. Leavey and with an introduction by Jacques Derrida (Lincoln: University of Nebraska Press, 1978), 160.

5. See Derrida's "Introduction," in Husserl, ibid., 66. "In other words, ideal formations are rooted only in language in general, not in the factuality of languages and their particular linguistic incarnations." Husserl, Derrida argues, constructs this ideal objectivity against the grain of the actual practice of language and the movement of history.

6. "And what is thematic here is precisely ideal objects, and quite different ones from those coming under the concept of language." Husserl, ibid, 161.

7. See for example Hans-Georg Gadamer's formulation: "The word [theory] does not mean, as it does from a standpoint of a theoretic construction based upon self-consciousness, the distance from beings that allows what is to be known in an unbiased fashion and thereby subjects it to anonymous domination. Instead, the distance proper to *theoria* is that of proximity and affinity. The primitive meaning of *theoria* is participation in the delegation sent to a festival for the sake of honoring the gods." Hans Georg Gadamer, "On the Philosophic Element in the Sciences and the Scientific Character of Philosophy," in *Reason in the Age of Science* (Cambridge, Massachusetts: MIT Press, 1981), 17. (This is not to overlook

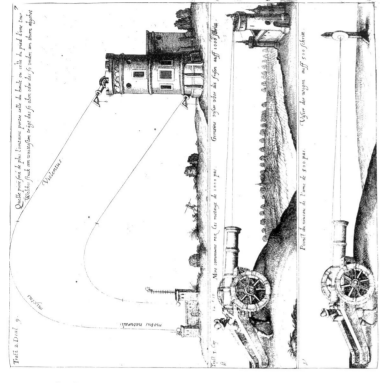

R. Norton: *The Gunner*, 1628 [*The Art of the Engineer*, Lund Humphries].

It is quite possible to project whole forms in the mind without recourse to the material, by designating and determining a fixed orientation and conjunction for the various lines and angles.   L.B. Alberti[2]

0.1 Axonometric Projections: Geometry and Origins

In order for classical architecture to identify itself with the exact sciences, architecture had to establish its foundations in mathematical reasoning. Architecture could be scientific only to the extent that it was mathematical.[3] In his 1936 essay "The Origin of Geometry," Edmund Husserl examines geometry's unique capability of construing an "ideal objectivity" distinct from both scientific instrumentality and the vagaries of the subject. In a key passage, Husserl situates geometry beyond, or better, *over* history and local circumstance:

Works of this class do not, like tools (hammers, pliers) or like architectural and other such products, have a repeatability in many exemplars. The Pythagorean Theorem, indeed all of geometry, exists only once, no matter how often or even in what language it may be expressed. It is identically the same in the "original language" of Euclid and in all "translations," and within each language it is again the same, no matter how many times it has been sensibly uttered, from the original expression and writing down to the innumerable oral utterances, or written or other documentation.[4]

For Husserl, geometry is a kind of sacred speech: untranslatable, precisely because its origin is always present. (There is no lack for translation to supplement.) This perfect transparency is not uncontested; Husserl is fully aware that it necessitates a bracketing of the contingencies of language and practice.[5] But geometry, as distinct from language, proceeds from "primary intrapersonal origins."[6] Husserl wants to ground the sign in geometry. He would use geometry as a model for language, not language as a model to describe the geometric.

Husserl's essay and the broader project outlined in *The Crisis of European Sciences and Transcendental Phenomenology* (1936) can be seen as a reaction to the instrumentality of 19th-century positivism and an attempt to recuperate for "scientific" thought its original meaning: the synthesis of humanist inquiry and mathematical reason.[7] It is in this sense parallel to certain aspects of the theoretical project of the early

modernists who also sought new paradigms of representation in order to renew contact with origins.

Significant among these new paradigms is the integration of axonometric projection into architectural practice. Despite its long history, in modern (i.e. post-Renaissance) practice, axonometric is first identified with technical concerns. The earliest systematic description of axonometric projection occurs in the context of military use.[8] Axonometric drawing was taught in engineering schools, and its development and dissemination is closely related to mechanization and industrialization. The use of axonometric projection in architecture extended the scientific/mathematical basis for architectural representation already initiated with the widespread teaching and use of descriptive geometry. In the 18th and 19th centuries, the re-definition of the profession of architecture in relation to new political structures, social institutions, and new typological demands contributed to the emergence of functionalist ideology. The

Piero della Francesca: *De prospectiva pingendi*, c.1480 [Bibliothèque de l'institut d'Art et d'Archéologie (fondation J. Doucet)].

William Farish: "On isometrical perspective," 1822 [*Transactions of the Cambridge Philosophical Society*, I].

significant differences between Husserl's and Gadamer's versions of phenomenology.)

8. Christian Regier, 1756, *Perspectiva Militaris*; This citation in Yve-Alain Bois, "Metamorphoses of Axonometry," *Daidalos* [1] (1981). The discussion of axonometric here elaborates and extends a schema suggested by Bois' text.

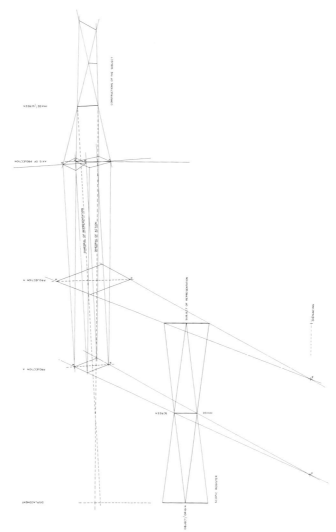

ABLE HOUSE, 1990-92

Left: Site plan: The site is one-and-one-half acres, subdivided from the lot of a larger house, located one hour north of Philadelphia.

Right: Diagram, constructions of the subject: Based on Lacan's mapping of subjectivity and image formation, this version introduces a swerve to disturb the symmetry of Lacan's diagram.

9. El Lissitsky, "K und Pangeometry" (1925), trans. Eric Dluhosch (Cambridge, Massachusetts: MIT Press, 1970), 142, 145. Note also Malevich's earlier formulation: "Analyzing the canvas, we see, primarily, a window through which we discover life. The Suprematist canvas reproduces white, not blue space. The reason is obvious: blue does not give a true impression of the infinite. The rays of vision are caught in a cupola and cannot penetrate the infinite." "Suprematism" (1920), in *K.S. Malevich, Essays on Art 1915-1928*, ed. Troels Andersen (Copenhagen: 1971). The preoccupation with rendering visible the infinite coincides (paradoxically) with an assertion of painting's essentially realist character.

etry and mathematics. These artists were looking for a notion of geometric practice comparable to the position held by perspective in the Renaissance world view—but now in the face of the evident exhaustion of the visual and conceptual paradigms offered by perspectival geometry. Early modern practice sought to put back together what the instrumentality of the 19th century had taken apart.

The operations of technical disciplines, mechanical drawing, optics and ballistics, and in architecture, axonometric projection, were taken over by visual artists and given a new meaning. In 1925, El Lissitsky writes as follows: "In the period between 1918 and 1921 a lot of old rubbish was destroyed. In Russia too we have torn A. [art] from its holy pedestal 'while spitting on its altar'." Old forms of representation could no longer hold together under sustained innovation. "Perspective," he writes, "limits space; it has made it finite, closed." The world is put into a cubic box, which creates a static "facade view" of the world. El Lissitsky constructs an analogy between visual practice and the most advanced scientific developments of the day:

Suprematism has extended the apex of the finite visual cone of perspective into infinity.

It has broken through the "blue lampshade of the heavens".

Suprematist space can be formed in front of the surface as well as in depth. . . . Suprematism has swept away the illusion of three-dimensional space on a plane, replacing it with the ultimate illusion of *irrational space* with attributes of infinite extensibility in depth and foreground.[9]

In a dialectical effort to elide abstract mathematical precision and an incipient spirituality, Lissitsky collages contradictory logics. In a positivistic manner, he attempts to inscribe visual practice into the compass of mathematical and scientific progress. At the same time, he follows the logic of avant-garde practice which turns to the irrational and the spiritual in the face of the horror of technological rationalism. In Lissitsky's "irrational" space, viewpoint, and vanishing point are located at infinity. The infinite extension in depth coincides with the suspension of the subject's privileges of self-location. The viewing subject and the object of representation both inhabit the same field of extensibility. Projection collapses distance.

architect was no longer able to mediate conception and execution through actual contact with the fabric of construction. The developments of drawing practice reinforced this separation of design and construction. The ideology of functionalism demanded that the operations of projection and representation be accountable, subject to the control and oversight of the emerging managerial classes. Technique no longer sought to model a poetic act.

El Lissitsky:
Schema from
K und pangeometry, 1925.

Kazimir Malevich:
Spatial Suprematism, 1919,
Lithograph [*Malevitch*,
Thames and Hudson].

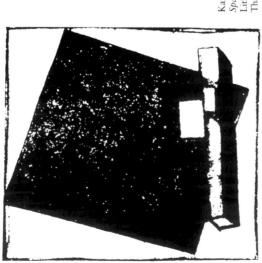

Able House.
Study model—projections.

Indeed, the most basic terms of technique itself were being called into question. By the early 20th century, the ability of a representational system based on classical notions of the object and consequent conventions of perspective to offer privileged contact with symbolic origins seemed increasingly suspect. On the one hand, drawing practice had become more instrumental (emptied of its metaphysical resonance). On the other hand, notions of space, time, and subjectivity had become more complex. Avant-garde practice radicalized this incipient crisis. It worked out of a mismatch between the desires and ambitions of artistic practices and the available visual paradigms. Among abstract artists of diverse tendencies and distinct means (Mondrian, Kandinsky, Malevich, or Klee), there existed a common necessity to re-inscribe drawing practice within a symbolic and spiritual understanding of geom-

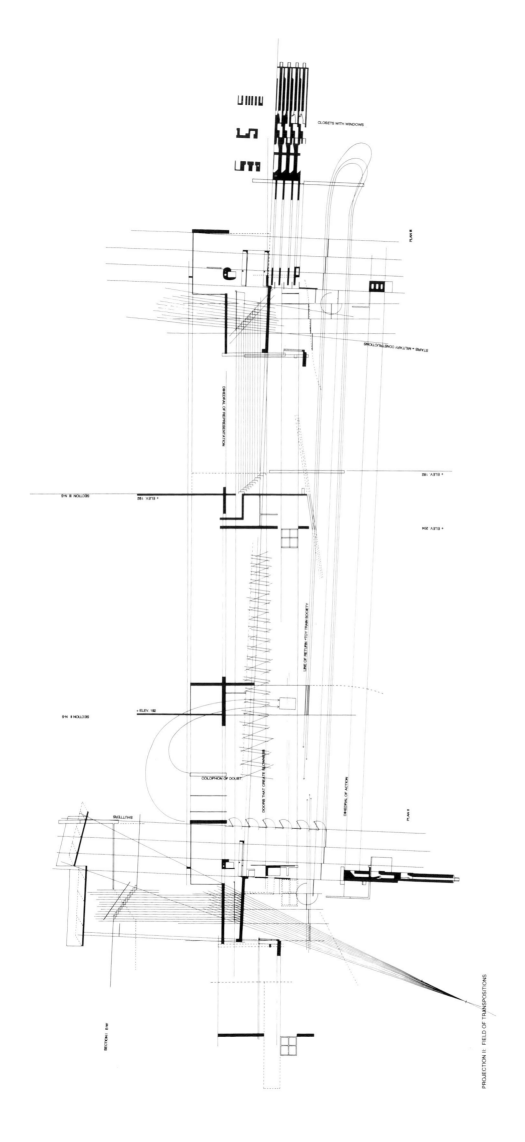

ABLE HOUSE, 1990-92

Second projection: To erase the traces of the starting point through the exercise of process; at precisely the point at which the self-sustaining logics of the project acquire their own identity, the origin will disappear.

In practice, though, the smooth space of projection mapped out in El Lissitzky's diagram must work against multiple resistances. The implied metaphysics of infinity is only incompletely realized. As the three dimensional *Proun* construction reveals, the infinite extension of the visual field is possible only as "ultimate illusion." Modifications have been introduced, but the basic framework of Euclidean geometry is untouched. The stable body of perspectival space persists, now in an idealized form.

Rather than an overturning of metaphysics—"spitting on the altar"—there is here a substitution. The classical metaphysics of measurable, figurative space is exchanged for a metaphysics of infinite abstract space. The appeal to mathematics as transcendental and foundational is not diminished. The humanist subject and the privilege of the body are maintained.

The question of translation, which this essentialist argument would like to defer, turns out to be central. If geometry, as Husserl understands it, offers an ideal objectivity (an unmediated and univocal means of being in contact at all times with its origins), then the distance between the object and its representation is nullified. If this were the case, the history of representation would have to be understood as the gradual and constant unfolding of meaning and the distillation of the origin through invariant operations of historical process. But if we argue otherwise, that any geometric construction only incompletely maps perception and that vision of necessity operates through the social, then the history of representation becomes a history of the forms of its mediation.[10] History must map both the resistances of geometry itself as material and the subject's always mediated and partial access to geometrical thinking. The recent appearance of concepts such as "index" and "trace" in the architectural field represents one attempt to map this partiality.[11] The operations of translation, the mediations across this gap, are not the reflections—weak or strong—of a distant, but still present origin, but rather, a series of constructions which only as construct make possible the idea of the original.

Architectural practice maintains this contradictory collage. Drawing's original identification with abstraction is re-established. Axonometric space is essentially atopical; the fixed point of the spectator is abolished. From Theo van Doesburg to Peter Eisenman, architects have exploited the implied reversibility of depth and foreground which characterizes the axonometric projection and links it to early modernist spatial investigations. Infinity, if not represented, is at least rendered thinkable. Yet axonometric, originating in the technical disciplines, also maintains the linearity and objectivity—the measurability—of the architect's plans, and is therefore attractive to architects such as Hannes Meyer or Walter Gropius not for its "irrational" qualities but for its objectivity. Transparency here implies not privileged contact with origins (Husserl), but a guarantee of technical performance.

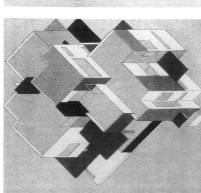

Left: Theo van Doesburg and Cornelis van Eesteren: *Maison Particulière*, 1923, Axonometric Drawing [The Walker Art Center and Abbeville Press].

Right: El Lissitsky, *Proun Space*, 1965, Reconstruction of 1923 original [Harvard Art Museums].

Peter Eisenman, *House X*, 1981, Axonometric Model [Peter Eisenman].

10. This notion of history proceeds from Michel Foucault, specifically the position outlined in "Nietzsche, Genealogy, History," from *Language, Counter-Memory, Practice* (Ithaca: Cornell University Press, 1977). "If interpretation were the slow exposure of the meaning hidden in an origin, then only metaphysics could interpret the development of humanity. But if interpretation is the violent or surreptitious appropriation of a system of rules, which in itself has no essential meaning, . . . then the development of humanity is a series of interpretations." From *The Foucault Reader*, ed.Paul Rabinow (New York: Pantheon, 1984), 87.

11. A full discussion is impossible here; see Rosalind Krauss, "Notes on the Index: Seventies Art in America," *October 3* (1976-77): 68-81. For Krauss, the indexical signals a "tremendous arbitrariness with regard to meaning, a breakdown of . . . the linguistic sign."(77) The concept of the trace is fundamental to Jacques Derrida's work and cannot be isolated to one particular instance. It is of necessity *unspecifiable*: "The mode of inscription of such a trace in the text of metaphysics is so unthinkable that it must be described as an erasure of the trace itself. The trace is produced as its own erasure." Jacques Derrida, *Margins of Philosophy*, trans. A. Bass (Chicago: University of Chicago Press, 1982), 76. Derrida writes elsewhere: "This principle compels us not only not to privilege one substance—here the phonic, so called temporal, substance—while excluding another—for example, the graphic, so-called spatial, substance—but even to consider the very process of signification as a formal play of differences. That is, of traces." Jacques Derrida,

Positions, trans. A. Bass
(Chicago: University of Chicago
Press, 1981), 26.

ABLE HOUSE, 1990-92

Elevations and Sections (Orthographic Projections) — A, B, E, F.

12. Sigmund Freud, "Metapsychological Supplement to the Theory of Dreams," in *Freud: Dictionary of Psychoanalysis*, ed. Fodor and Gaynor (New York: Philosophical Library), 36.

13. Norman Bryson, "The Gaze in the Expanded Field," in *Vision and Visuality*, ed Hal Foster (Seattle: Bay Press, 1988), 88.

14. Ibid; Note that this "decentering" occurs not in the context of modern fragmentation of vision or post-modern "dislocation," but in absolutely normative, canonical perspectival representation. Bryson cites the 1504 Raphael *Sposalizio della Madonna* as example in his text.

15. Jacques Lacan, *Four Fundamental Concepts of Psychoanalysis*, ed Miller, trans. Sheridan (New York: Norton, 1978), 86. I would like to thank John Whiteman for first pointing out these chapters in Lacan on optics and the gaze.

A dream is, among other things, a projection: an externalization of an internal process.
Sigmund Freud[12]

0.2 VISION AND PERSPECTIVE:
THE CONSTRUCTIONS OF THE SUBJECT

In classical thought, perspective offered an ideal means to order the constructed world in accord with an idea of nature. Culture presented itself as nature accurately re-produced as artificial nature. But perspective also functioned as a concept of time: ordering, surveying and re-creating the past from the privileged viewpoint of the present. Just as the distant Roman past was rediscovered/reinvented on the basis of ruins and fragments, so the viewing subject could reconstruct the narrative space of painting by means of the scaffold of perspectival projection. Space is read in depth—locating the spectator in front and in the present, from which distance and the past are entered and traversed. Perspective establishes a temporal field which supports narrative history.

The mathematization and calibration of the visual world would allow other correspondences. The analogies between musical and visual harmonics were established on the basis of their common foundation in geometry. Cosmological, religious and philosophical consonances were played out on the basis of the geometry of space and its relation to an idealized body. Emerging sciences of ballistics and fortifications could be given a metaphysical overtone by contact with geometry. Seeing was understood as a natural function of the eye; the paradigms of Renaissance painting naturalized an idealized concept of vision.

The constructions of perspectival geometry then, appear to enforce the privilege of the observer. But Norman Bryson, elaborating on the speculations of Jacques Lacan concerning optics, has pointed out that the presence of the viewing subject implies a corresponding absence:

The moment the viewer appears and takes up position at the viewpoint, he or she comes face to face with another term that is the negative counterpart to the viewing position: the vanishing point . . . The viewpoint and the vanishing point are inseparable . . .[13]

If, as Renaissance theory wants to suggest, the proper perspectival con

struction contains within it an ideal viewing distance which fixes the position of the spectator, then the spectator is at this moment also effaced. The viewer, in facing the vanishing point, is confronted with a "... black hole of otherness placed at the horizon in a decentering that destroys the subject's unitary self possession."[14] The very possibility of the subject's being in the picture—in as much as the architecture of the perspectival construction includes the viewer—is inextricably linked to its displacement from the picture.

Albrecht Dürer, "Drawing of a Woman," 1525 [Bibliothèque de l'institut d'Art et d'Archéologie (fondation J. Doucet)].

This displacement is already visible in Dürer's 1525 codification of perspective practice. This device, a conceptual structure made manifest in material form in the diagram, contains all the essential elements organizing the conceptual underpinning of perspectival projection. The fixed (monocular) location of the viewing point (male) is marked by the tip of the obelisk (with obvious phallic connotations) and the picture plane is defined by the gridded screen, a kind of trellis against which the projection is measured and registered. The rays of light, like threads, are drawn from the contours of the object to the eye of the observer, tracing out, in the intersection with the picture plane the foreshortened (distorted) outline of the (female) body.

The physicality of this framework has led Jacques Lacan to remark: "The geometral space of vision—even if we include those imaginary parts in the virtual space of the mirror . . . is perfectly reconstructible, imaginable, by a blind man."[15] It must be noted as well, that the system of projection here is a one-way system. The interpretive desire of the viewing subject is short-circuited in the capture of the represented object. The act of representation is depicted as an objective, scientific activity—the recording of already established relations and facts. And

Masaccio: Holy Trinity, 1426-27, Santa Maria Novella, Florence.

Jacques Lacan, Diagrams from *Four Fundamental Concepts of Psychoanalysis*, Norton.

Object   image   Geometral point

Point of light   screen   Picture

The gaze   image screen   The subject of representation

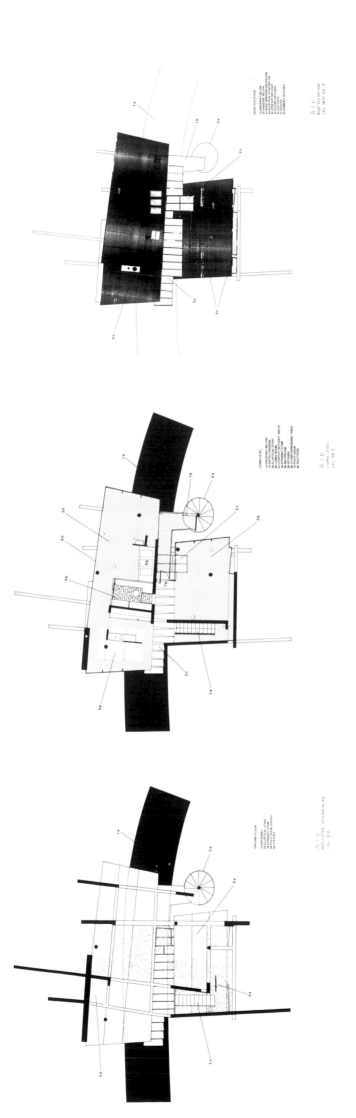

ABLE HOUSE, 1990-92

A,B,C: Plans, as indicated. The client is a single person and the house is organized in an open loft-like fashion around the services. The house straddles the drive and is entered from below.

16. Ibid., 86.

Athanasius Kircher: "Application of the Magic Lantern"; from *Physiolgia kircheriana experimentalis* c. 1660 [Ediciones Siruela, S.A.]

following from that, what is represented is of necessity falsely objectified. The scene of representation enacted here is itself represented utilizing exactly the same conceptual framework which it describes. And even in this idealized scene, the eyes of the observer are slightly displaced from the geometrical viewing point. The fluidity of his gaze is frozen and relocated to the abstract pin-point at the tip of the obelisk. The artist hovers over and observes the scene of representation while he remains trapped within it. The representation of architecture (which is the representation of empty space and not the representation of an object), confirms Lacan's assertion: "perspectival construction allows that which concerns vision to escape totally."[16]

Operations of projection make thematic what is left out, lost or hidden in the exercise of perspective. It is an evacuation. The representation of architecture necessitates an effort of geometrical imagination, a mental and intellectual projection, like the reading of musical notation, which might synthesize the always multiple and always incomplete representations. The active intervention of the interpreting subject is required to supply what is "lost in the translation."

The codification of the practices of perspective carry another consequence: within the logic of the system of perspectival projection, there exists the possibility of its reversal, turning the one-way system (Dürer) into a two-way system. Athanasius Kircher, in his engraving "Application of the Magic Lantern" (c.1660) turns projection into an active construct, in this case, magical and secret: the conscious production of illusion through projection. (Note that the mechanics of this illusion directly anticipate cinematic projection.) From "proper" perspectival construction to anamorphosis only an instrumental inversion is required. Simply tilting or warping the screen of projection in Dürer's diagram has the effect of making the construction visible. The artifice is no longer hidden, and perspective no longer conceals itself as the natural outcome of vision. The evidence of disorder (distortion, dissonance) is contained within the rational limits of the system itself. Anamorphosis functions to make visible the limits of the perspectival system and its arbitrariness. A legitimate exercise of the established rules of the system has the capacity to produce monsters and aberrations. Like conventional perspectival construction, anamorphosis locates the viewer, but now in an oblique and de-centered position. The

image coalesces only in the moment of turning away from the painting. The geometral dimension of vision is used in order to capture the subject—a "trap for the gaze." (Lacan)

For Lacan, the discussion of anamorphosis confirms that Euclidean geometry is inadequate to map the complexities of perception and the fluidity of the gaze. The constructions of subjectivity always exceed their geometrical description. Unlike Husserl, Lacan asserts that geometry's meanings cannot be given in perception. The subject is always in the picture; at the very moment that the gaze sees itself seeing, all of the pathologies repressed in the rational construction of vision return. In turning away, the viewer sees that which is hidden in the "normal" construction of the picture: the contingency of the act of viewing and the collaboration of the subject's desire.

If projection is understood here not as natural, scientific and objective, but as the product of active subjectivity, as the construction of illusion through "irrational" means, what are the consequences within architectural practice? If geometry cannot map perception, if the constructions of

Mario Bettini: "Reproduction of an eye by means of catoptric anamorphosis upon a cylindrical surface," *Apiaria Universe Philosophiae* 1642 [Van Pelt Library, University of Pennsylvania].

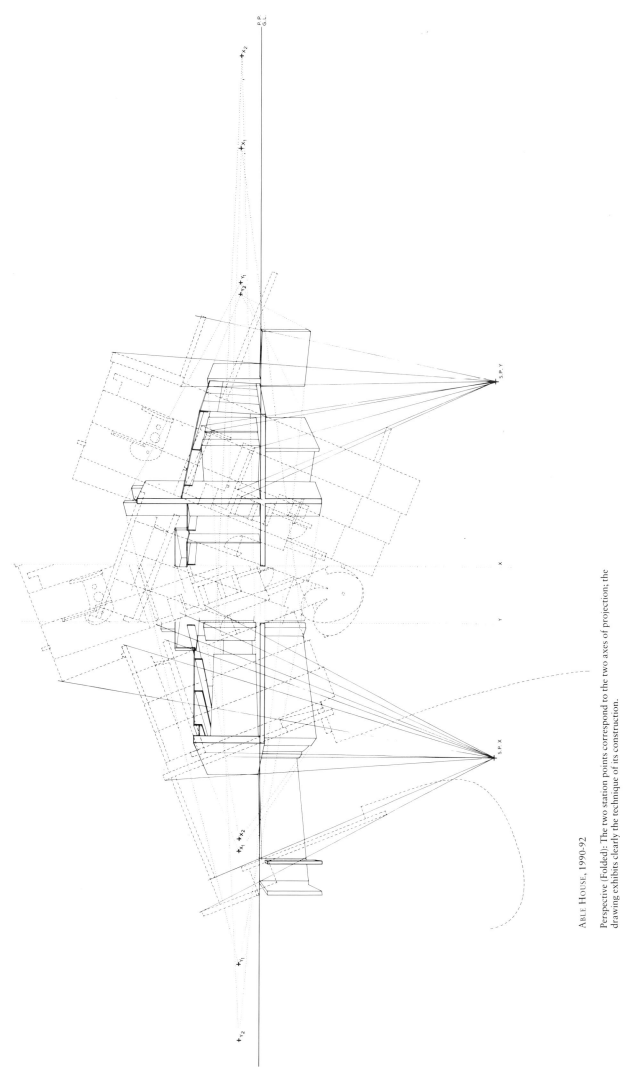

ABLE HOUSE, 1990-92

Perspective (Folded): The two station points correspond to the two axes of projection; the drawing exhibits clearly the technique of its construction.

17. Norman Bryson, "The Gaze in the Expanded Field," 91-92. "Between subject and the world is inserted the entire sum of discourses which make up visuality, that cultural construct, and make visuality different from vision, the notion of unmediated visual experience. Between retina and the world is inserted a screen of signs, a screen consisting of all the multiple discourses on vision built into the social arena."

18. Martin Jay, "Scopic Regimes of Modernity" in *Vision and Visuality*, ed. Hal Foster (Seattle: Bay Press, 1988), 3-28

19. Svetlana Alpers, *The Art of Describing: Dutch Art in the Seventeenth Century* (Chicago: University of Chicago Press, 1983) cited in Bryson, "The Gaze in the Expanded Field."

20. Christine Buci-Glucksman, *La folie du voir*, 1986, cited in Bryson, "The Gaze in the Expanded Field." 17. "For Buci-Glucksman, the baroque self-consciously revels in the contradictions between surface and depth, disparaging as a result any attempt to reduce the multiplicity of visual spaces into any coherent essence."

21. For a detailed and precise account of the transformations of scientific and visual paradigms over the course of the nineteenth century, see Jonathan Crary, *Techniques of the Observer. On Vision and Modernity in the Nineteenth Century* (Cambridge, Massachusetts: MIT Press, 1991). I mention Crary here because he explicitly criticizes the historical model of the twentieth century avant-garde as a decisive break from a hegemonic perspectival tradition dating back to the Renaissance.

22. Victor Burgin, "Geometry and Abjection," *AA Files* 15 (1987): 35.

subjectivity exceed geometrical description, how can geometry maintain its foundational privilege with regard to architecture? If contact with reason's origins through geometry is foreclosed, how can the frontier between rational and irrational be secured? And finally, if drawing practice maps vision only through the mediated conventions of the social, how can this "screen of signs"[17] be made visible?

At this point it is important to note that there already exist practices which have been developed outside of the frame of Cartesian perspectivalism. Martin Jay, in "Scopic Regimes of Modernity,"[18] questions the actual hegemony of Albertian perspective and "ocularcentrism" in post-Renaissance Western art. Among other practices, Dutch art of the sixteenth and seventeenth centuries, as outlined by Svetlana Alpers in *The Art of Describing*, provides a counter example.[19] Alpers describes a painting practice which was not mediated through the codified systems of Albertian perspective (with its emphasis on narrative time compressed into the visual space of a painting), but which related to other practices: cartography, surveying, the experimental and optical sciences. The multiple and overlapping viewpoints and vanishing points, the encyclopedic, descriptive quality of Dutch painting, the suspension of real time, the importance of landscape, topography, still life and the object all work against the explanatory models enforced by the dominance of Italian Renaissance models.

These two episodes—Anamorphosis and "optical" painting as described by Alpers (other examples could be advanced as well: certain episodes of Baroque Art which in the "excess" of the visual show representation itself as a self-referential system[20])—signify a challenge from within the historical framework: internal tensions within the traditions of Cartesian perspectivalism. The relationship between perception and representation is called into question, and the multiplicity of practices underlines the arbitrary nature of the foundational role of mathematics as understood in classical theories of representation. These cracks within the edifice of perspectivalism must be seen in light of a parallel process of instrumentalization.[21] As the operations of drawing become emptied of metaphysical content, drawing practice itself becomes more complex and sophisticated. Artistic innovation advances from crisis. The heterogeneity of early modernist practice reprograms this incipient instrumentalization. Cubism's "misreadings" of scientific theories of perception revise the positivistic notion of instrumentality. Dziga Vertov's dissection of the technical oper-

ations of movie-making in order to "lay bare the device" begins to rewrite the received notions of linear technological progress and its political value. The realities of practice outstrip their own theoretical description.

Analogies to cubism and the cinema open out to the present. The experiments of early modernism did not overturn Euclidean geometry or, finally, abandon the foundational appeal to geometry. In recent practice, Victor Burgin has noted the persistence of spatial (geometral) metaphors in representation:

In so far as this metaphor is drawn from physiological optics, it is inappropriate to the description of psychological functions. In so far as it is drawn from Euclidean geometry, it is inadequate to describe the changed apprehension of space which is the attribute of so called post-modern culture.[22]

The question, often raised, of what the geometrical description of post-modern electronic space would look like is misleading. In post-modern practice, geometry's authority to establish limits and closure has not so much been negated as bypassed. The visual paradigms of post-modern practice recapitulate obsolete, "exhausted" visual practices. It is only by this movement, this "bypass," that geometry's foundational-theoretical authority (its privileged capacity to organize and structure representation) might be overturned, and its autonomy from subjective inflection reasserted.

Mark Tansey: *Short History of Modern Painting*, 1982 [Curt Marcus Gallery, New York].

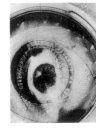

Dziga Vertov: Still from *The Man with a Movie Camera*, 1929 [Museum of Modern Art Film Stills Archive].

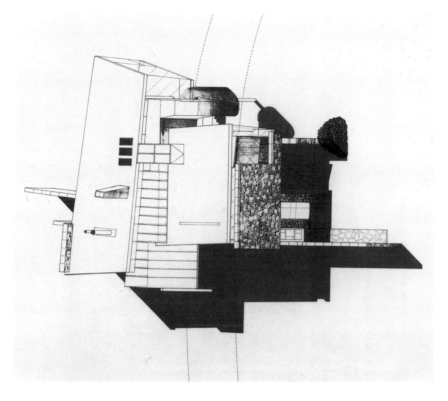

23. José Quetglas, "Fear of Glass: The German Pavilion of Mies van der Rohe," trans. Allen, Colomina, Marratt, in *Architecture/Reproduction*, ed. Beatriz Colomina, Revisions:

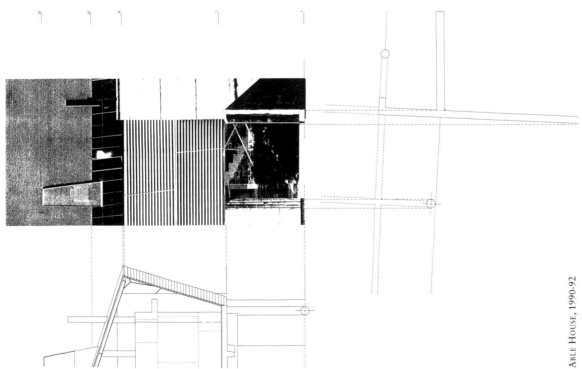

ABLE HOUSE, 1990-92

Left: Elevation study.

Right: Axonometric projection.

Papers on Architectural Theory and Criticism volume 2, (New York: Princeton Architectural Press, 1988), 122-151.

24. Michel de Certeau, "The Laughter of Michel Foucault," in *Heterologies*, (Minneapolis: University of Minnesota Press, 1986).

25. Roberto Mangabeira Unger, *Knowledge and Politics* (New York: The Free Press, 1984), 36.

26. Ludwig Wittgenstein *Lectures and Conversations* (Berkeley: University of California Press, 1983), 21.

27. Contrary to expectations, this does not result in a fragmented object. The fragmented object maintains the authority of the subject as the only stable position from which to apprehend the shattering of the object. Moreover, the fragmented object always presumes the theoretical possibility of the reconstruction of the whole from which the fragments derive. To mirror the displacement of the subject in a de-centered object is to leave intact all of the classical teleologies of representation.

In fact no one can imagine or project anything modern. By definition there exists an essential contradiction between the terms "project" and "modern." To project literally means to throw forward. But in order to throw something forward both thrower and projectile must be behind. Every project is an emissary from the past.   José Quetglas[23]

0.3 POSTSCRIPT

The operations of projection, as they unfold in time (as an articulation of the idea of the project and the position of the architect), can only escape with difficulty from a linear idea of history. If space itself has a history, we are necessarily located within it; but the movement of history within this space is not self-sustaining. It is produced by active subjects and sustained by the social body. The "forward" and "behind" of Quetglas' comment are concepts imposed over a heterogeneous field of activity. In face of the evident exhaustion of visual paradigms rooted in foundational thinking (both the geometry of perspective and the idealized metaphysics of infinity), it is necessary to ask what it might mean now to work within the web of representation itself and not in its reflected content. If the grounded authority of the "theoretical" is no longer credible, we must begin to work within the "field of operations within which theory is itself produced."[24]

The present project, in a provisional way, begins to explore the consequences of this position. On the one hand, operations of projection are made thematic to the project; on the other hand, these operations are not assumed to carry any intrinsic meaning.

As Roberto Unger has stated:

Thinking and language depend on categories. We must classify in order to think and speak. But we have no assurance that anything in the world corresponds to the categories we use. Our ideas about science and nature seem to imply that we believe both that our classifications can be true or false and that the question of their truth or falsehood is unanswerable or illusory.[25]

Stan Allen:
Buell Hall Installation, 1991.

Architecture is a discipline of limits and boundaries. These limits operate in time as well as spatially. Architecture maintains categories and is in turn supported by these definitions. The authority of architectural representation to extend a local picture of reality over the space of the world depends directly upon this question of categories. The practice of architecture entails a fundamental paradox today. In order to work critically (i.e. in a fashion which does not simply rehearse and reiterate currently available paradigms) we must *appear* to endorse the very categories and limits we set out to overturn. To call this a paradox is to suggest that the validity of those limits is essentially undecidable and always provisional.

If, therefore, as Unger suggests, these questions are illusory, then the operations of process cannot by themselves constrain meaning and subjectivity. The self-sustaining logics of practice must be allowed to play themselves out. "As long as I can play, I know the rules are in place."[26] Nor can the internal coherence of the process legitimize the object, as process is always already outside of the field of the object. The specificity of the operations of projection, design and construction cannot be subsumed to the overarching authority of the "concept." Practice always disrupts theory; the exercise of theory solicits practice.

In the present project, two effects resulting from the operations of projection are given particular attention. First, by disturbing the symmetry of subject and object in perspectival representation, the displacement and de-centering of the subject is made apparent.[27] The consequence of these operations is a collapsing inward and a disturbing of the axes of perception—a spatial warp, the formal counterpart of which is compression and folding over. Second is a form of "geometrical drift" where the stability of the rules of projection—the perpendicular rails which control orthographic projection—are allowed to bend, warp and drift, creating new juxtapositions and unpredictable eruptions in both the formal and the programmatic fields. The provisionality of these investigations should be taken as thematic. This is not to suggest that they do not intend construction or aspire to realization. What is intended is rather to extend doubt to construction itself.

Research and text 1990-91; Design 1991-1992;
Design Assisted by Catarina Tsang

Model Builders: Harry Gaveras, Saif Sumaida, Eric Wong

Photography: Peter Tolkin

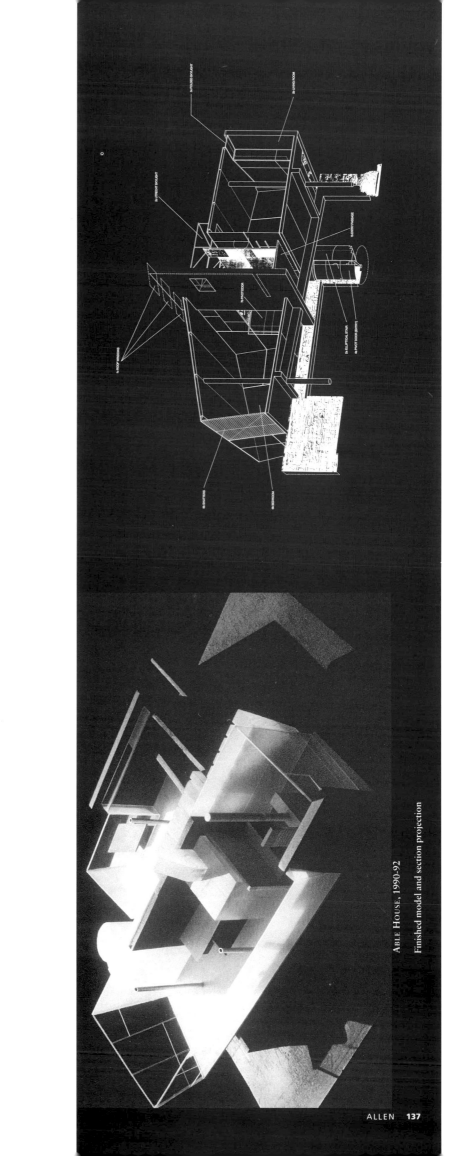

ABLE HOUSE, 1990-92

Finished model and section projection

CORNERED HOUSE

In the ideology of contemporary architectural practice, the discourse of architecture is not located and developed within its form, but rather within the society that validates and produces it. Formal research has been criticized as reductive, as aspiring only to embody compositional or geometrical principles, and as disinterested in cultural phenomena. Form, however, is not unambiguous. If architectural form is the material actualization of ideas, it can also be understood as the ossification of conflicts between conceptual, spatial, and material forces, or as a repository of historical residues. In this way, formal analysis becomes crucial to realizing the potentials of architectural meaning. Formal analysis situates form in culture not by attending to constituents of form that are externally predetermined or culturally autonomous; instead we must look to those constituents that are determined immanently.

Preston Scott Cohen

View from living room looking toward kitchen.

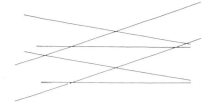

A-E Development of abstract schema.

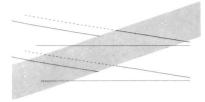

B

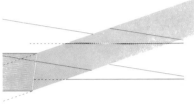

C

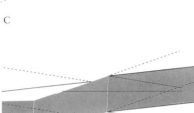

D

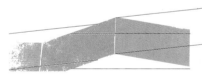

E

Cornered House is the result of a search for architectural forms that appear as an after-image of discourse. The house invites the viewer to engage in possible reconstructions of its formation. It encourages a multiplicity of readings, many of which are not unmistakably symbolic. Interpretations develop within the discrepancies among several preiconographic structures, and between those structures and their visual and material presence. The structures refer to the real or ideal objects, organizations, processes and histories that the house both resembles and opposes. Interpretation is simultaneously motivated and frustrated by conflicts between the structure's underlying formal schema and the concrete form in which it is inscribed.

Two morphological schemas, one iconographic, the other an abstract formal structure, were used to map the decipherment of the house's possible referents and to supplant the usual status of program and site as originators. The iconographic schema includes and elongated and folded frontal pediment, and lateral hip and gable roofs superimposed and situated so as to suggest axonometric and perspective projections of altogether different objects. The abstract structural schema is developed by way of three sets of parallel lines that have been bent and broken, such that they are in the process of severing, displacing, and bending one another. In order to merge, the lines are demarcated simultaneously as folds, intersections, edges, or planes. This process replaces a logic of structural lines in perceivable and discrete parallel sets with and anti-logic of systemic indeterminacy.

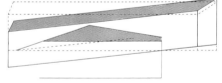

F Iconographic schema, already transformed.

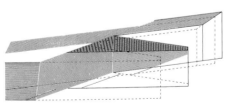

G-H Convergence of abstract and iconographic schemas

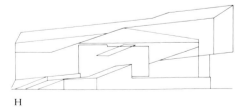

H

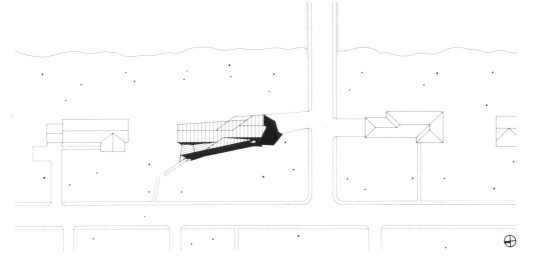

Site plan.

Dimensions of the house partially identify with the roof edges and ridges of nearby houses. As the forward-most wall inflects away from the street corner, the elongated and skewed volume embedded in the house becomes orthogonal to the site.

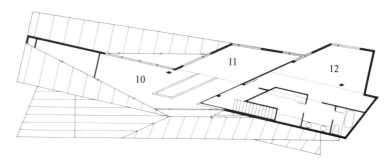

Upper floor plan.

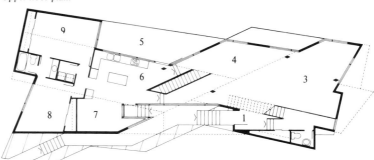

Main floor plan.

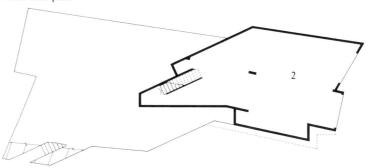

Ground Floor plan.

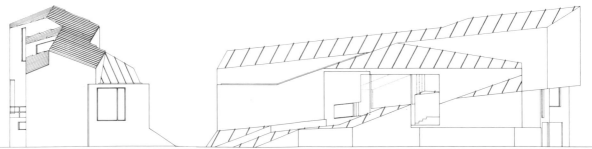

North elevation.

West elevation.

Key segments of selected edges and folds disappear where the three implied horizontal volumes intersect and are cut, shifted and spliced. The spacing and orientation of the standing seams on the roof and ramp align to further confound the third dimension.

Key to plans:

1. Entrance.
2. Garage.
3. Living room.
4. Dining room.
5. Terrace.
6. Kitchen.
7. Den/breakfast room.
8. Bedroom.
9. Bedroom.
10. Open to below.
11. Open to below.
12. Bedroom.

The final schema, a combination of the iconographic and structural referents, does not give rise to the configuration of the house by means of a simple plan or section extrusion. Derived from several angles and distances of projection of the elements in the schema, the resultant form seems to betray its initial referents. Together, as realized, the lines turn, forming now a pediment, now a fold–moving from form to meaning to form again. By continually inverting the conventional relationship of abstract form to iconography, the underlying schema and its referents both resist and accommodate the program and environmental context, influences that are generally thought to delimit the use, context, and meaning of architecture. The house establishes a distance between its outward appearance and latent structure, denying the schema's standing as origin. In the interpretation of the final configuration of the object, as with the schema, possible explanatory scenarios compete, each providing a plausible history, a possible before and after. The house may be thought to be three elongated volumes compressed into one space, or it could be a single hollow vessel that is folding in response to pressures from within. Another possibility is that an additive process is occurring, that the central volume has been skewed and sheared in order to accommodate several appended faceted masses. The facets also hint at a number of motifs from their America suburban domestic site: a split level-style skirt, a giant picture window, a meandering sidewalk, and front and back porches. These associations make concrete the various non-exclusive abstractions that the house points toward.

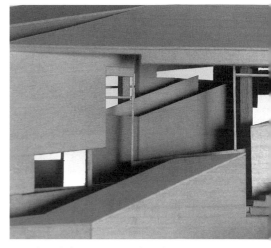

View through front picture window plane. The top of the forward-most ramped plane and the stair enclosure are aligned. The staircase suggests that the interior is bisected not only in plan, but also at an oblique angle in section.

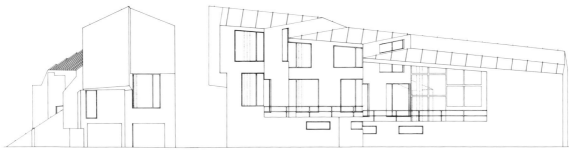

South elevation.   East elevation.

Indeterminacy of reference and meaning results from the multiplication of possible referents, and from the interdependence of their formal components. These components are very precisely drawn into relationships in which elements they share overlap and interfere with one another. The shared areas are unable to coalesce into a coherent system nor do they identify completely with any of the individual constituent parts or systems. Transformation of the house would be necessary to recover the logical and formal integrity of each of its components. However, in order for the formal components to remain tightly bound to one another, they also must remain unchanged. Theoretical richness derives from the manipulated overdetermination of these formal components. They appear both clearly shaped, but tremendously distorted. This distortion undermines the conventional logic by which meanings and historical origins are attributed to forms; meaning suffers systemic indeterminacy. In this way, a resistance to peremptory coherence is built into the house at the formal level. The house distills this resistance while remaining very close to realizing a coherence that is impossible to extract.

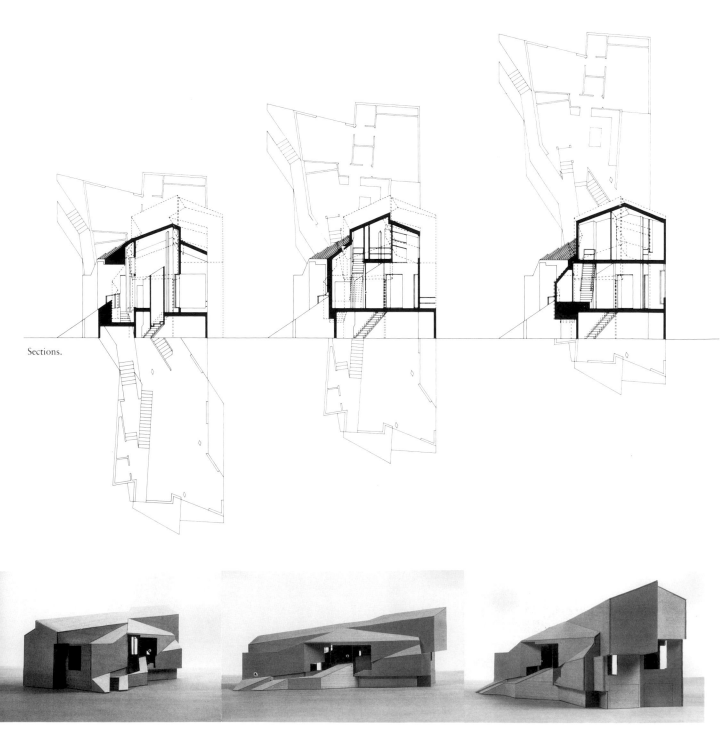

Sections.

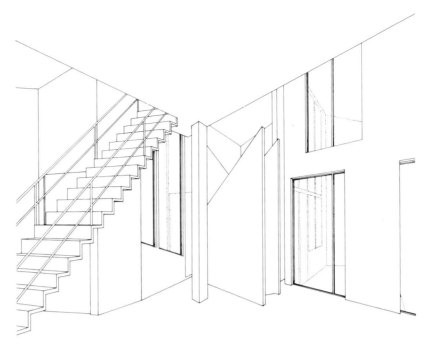

View from breakfast room looking toward main entry, living room, and upper bedroom.

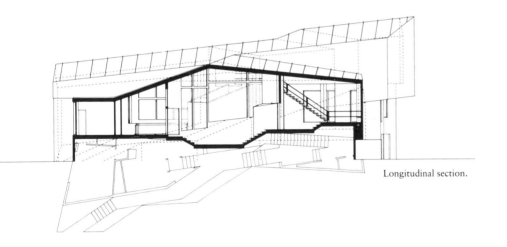

Longitudinal section.

Christopher Macdonald and Peter Salter

Both as teachers and practitioners it is our inclination to trust our senses. We allow the direct experience of the material world to serve as inspiration and measure of our architectural speculations. Our understanding of the essential frame of architectural research seems at direct odds with much contemporary debate, in which architecture is too often asked to illustrate current critical positions of a hermetic and essentially literary nature. Such work is often baffling. It denies the direct understanding of architecture as a palpable artifact and diminishes society's sense of architecture as a valued public art. The unwieldy trajectory of this situation seems both extraordinary and deeply troubling.

One way beyond this impasse might be a continuing inquiry into the act of building, the most immediate way in which architecture continues to reveal itself to the world. Throughout our work we have cultivated a sensi-

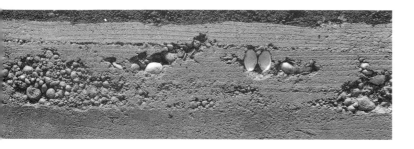

bility that restores value to our sense of materials and their manners of construction; we have discovered a need to **ground** our works. The juxtaposition of organic and Cartesian orders is for us a motif of enduring interest.

The recently completed Osaka Folly reflects these concerns, for it makes evident our own sense of the work as deliberate research. The condition of being at once temporary and devoid of function encouraged serious consideration of motive alongside technique; it provided a kind of laboratory in which preoccupations could be entertained with unusual intensity. Certainly in the context of the techno-pop landscape of a World's Fair in Japan, the need for **grounding** appeared pressing, even paramount. The short duration of the fair also provoked us to speculate on the means for expressing appropriately the **mortal** quality of architecture: to make evident the passage of time so often resisted in building. This was explored in literal constructional terms, and also in the interplay between the formal elements termed **gourd** and **cage**.

As our first constructed work after many years of drawing, the folly proved to be at once exhilarating and provocative: challenging certain orthodoxies that had developed in our practice.

PREFACE   The commission for a small folly, to be built as part of the Osaka Garden Festival of 1990, presented a very particular architectural program: a building bereft of any explicit function. Past studies of ours had explored the inherent capacities of the materials that shape buildings. It seemed that here one could discover fundamental qualities of architecture, qualities capable of providing a sensual frame in which contemporary meaning could be located. As the proposal developed, three essential components of the folly were refined and clarified: **ground, cage,** and **gourd.**

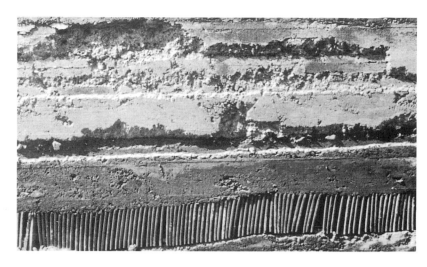

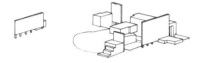

GROUND   In an effort to **ground** this small building–to establish a sense of locale within its shrill surroundings–the earth was excavated and scoured. The excavated earth was reconstituted as a small mound planted with bamboo and a series of walls and plugs constructed of rammed-earth or *pise*. Associated with each of the plugs is a screen–wall of earthen render on bamboo lathe–a traditional construction introduced by our collaborators Team Zoo: Atelier Mobile. In general, the excavation and mounded garden offer a first degree of containment and withdrawal from the surrounding asphalt. The rammed-earth structures and their screens create a series of navigational features–a series of differing elevations turned towards the different points of entry to the folly and its plaza. These pivotal structures reconcile the vortex of moving visitors with the relative calm of the folly's interior.

GROUND CONSTRUCTED

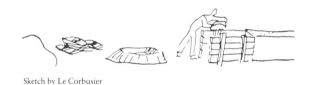

Sketch by Le Corbusier

The construction of ground elements was to some extent a consequence of the temporary nature of the construction. For example, it was impossible to use in situ concrete. The possibility of using *pise* construction was raised and discussed at length with our Atelier Mobile colleagues. While the precise construction was endlessly modified as the balance between material and labor was refined, we agreed upon an essential technique. Each daily batch of compaction would be revealed as a horizontal stratum in the final elevation, varying as the work progressed and marked by occasional exceptions: a string course of tiles at original ground level, a dusting of charcoal after the first week's work, and so on.

The fascination of this technique was that an "accurate" elevation could never be drawn. An analogous process could be diagrammed and drawings made to evoke the quality of the walls, yet finally the density and depth of the strata and the exact composition of the earthen material were unpredictable. For us, as architects, this tolerance of and reliance upon the vagaries of the building site provided the thrill and wonder of unassisted flight. An improvisational quality arose that would normally be firmly relegated to the techniques of the design studio.

If I must ascribe a meaning to the word craftsmanship, I shall say as a first approximation that it means simply workmanship using any kind of technique or apparatus, in which the quality of the result is not predetermined, but depends on the judgement, dexterity and care which the maker exercises as he works. The essential idea is that the quality of the result is *continually at risk* during the process of making.
—David Pye[2]

CAGE   The dominant figure of the folly is a three-dimensional cage of timber construction. It consists of a heavy timber frame set on large cylindrical columns filled in by a grid of much more finely dimensioned timber elements. In its essentially cubic form a deliberately static frame is established, against which the sensuous nature of the **gourd** trapped within can be measured. Initially it was proposed that the external layer of grid be filled—with flowers, for instance—on occasion through the course of the fair.

The large cage, built by putting together plain timbers and solid earthen walls, plastered with an ancient technique, makes you feel the warmth of Nature. A high, tough Folly with serenity, as if you are relaxing in the grove surrounding a village shrine.
—Kinyu Maruyama[1]

CAGE CONSTRUCTED   The construction of the cage was positively orthodox in contrast to ground and gourd. Its orthogonal form and role as frame—it is the most reticent piece of the composition—allowed conventional timber construction to be used throughout. Carpenters from Nara trained in traditional tea-house construction were employed for the main structural portion of the cage. The cage as constructed omitted a third layer of even finer timber members, leaving the structure rather more open than was intended. Our desire for truly stout columns—they were built 900 mm in diameter—immediately prompted debate with Atelier Mobile on the ecological wisdom of using such large trees for an essentially frivolous use. Ultimately we settled upon a farmed tropical softwood that reaches this girth in only fifteen years of growth.

GOURD   The third essential element, the gourd, operates in two quite different roles. From some distance its elevation, partly masked by the cage, completes the dynamic composition of the various free-standing screens. Seen from nearby and within the folly, isolated from the surroundings entirely, the gourd appears to hold light and offers a meticulously framed view of sky.

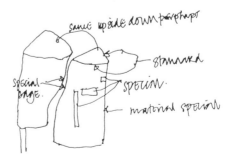

GOURD CONSTRUCTED The gourd appears in the first sketches for the project as a pair of bottle-like volumes: one of galvanized sheet steel and one of *cor-ten*. As pressures of budget and a sense of the building's intense use affected the scheme, the gourds in turn were withdrawn from direct contact with the public and caught within the cage. Here we intended them to be constructed of laminated plywood, a technology common in boat building that proved to require a lead-time inconsistent with our very tight schedule. Finally we agreed upon a fabric structure stretched back to the timber cage, to be built by sailmakers in southern England. The pressures of the completion date required that the inner cage construction take place while the gourd was still a drawing; again the design was forced to acknowledge the large tolerances of our improvised constructive means.

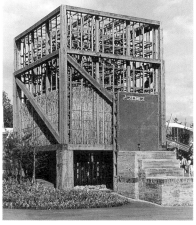

A certain sensibility concerning building, architecture, and landscape is evident in this extremely modest structure. In order to establish sufficient composure to resist the arbitrariness of contemporary architecture, we look to a direct—even primitive— manipulation of material for both inspiration and form. The threshold between the architect and craftsman is made explicit, foreshadowing a more gracious collaboration between architecture and its subsequent occupation.

1. Inscription at the building site.

2. David Pye, *The Nature and Art of Workmanship* (Cambridge: Cambridge University Press, 1978).

3. Daniele Sallenave, introduction to *André Kertesz* (London: Thames and Hudson, 1989), 4.

Credits:
Folly Number One
Osaka Garden Festival
1 April–15 October 1990
Macdonald and Salter
Architects

Sponsor:
Promise Col. Ltd.

Collaborator:
Team Zoo, Atelier Mobile, Kinya Maruyama and Mark Winford

Photographs:
Macdonald, Salter, Winford, and Héléne Binet

An idea in vogue has it that the artist must necessarily work in opposition to his language, that he has to force it, constrain it, and twist its syntax in order to mold it to his own design. However, another definition of art is perhaps not only possible but more accurate: that the real artist is someone who has been able, through patient work, to discover the profound nature of the art he has chosen and its laws . . . . These two types of artist will always be in opposition. The first lives in a state of continual conflict between his ego and his language, while the second is constantly learning about the increasing *concordance* of his works and his world.
—Daniele Sallenave[3]

FROM
THE
CORNER
OF
YOUR
EYE

**Tod Williams
and
Billie Tsien**

"Domestic Arrangements: A Lab Report" is one result of a series of projects entitled "Architecture Tomorrow" developed by Mildred Friedman of the Walker Art Center. Friedman asked six American architects and teams of architects to create installations addressing the subject "Architecture Tomorrow."* Thirty thousand dollars was provided for each project. While no prescribed format was established, Friedman suggested that the architects not approach this as a retrospective, but more as an exploration, one capable of being reassembled in other venues. The accompanying notes and images were compiled as a kind of diary of thoughts as we worked with our office on the project, "Domestic Arrangements."

*Architects selected:
Frank Israel (1989),
Morphosis (1989),
Tod Williams/ Billie
Tsien (1990), Stanley
Saitowits (1990),
Elizabeth Diller and
Ricardo Scofidio (1991),
Steven Holl (1991).

As our subject we selected the home—a home that would be low in cost, that would be experimental in its materials and construction, and that would speculate on a way of life in which we, ourselves, might choose to live. The home has traditionally been a subject of scrutiny by architects, and is a problem that we believe lies at the heart of architectural thought.

Moreover, "Domestic Arrangements" allowed us to consider a question with which we continue to struggle: How can our evolving philosophy, the way we choose to live, become a more integral part of our work for others? This research, indeed all of our work, is driven not by theory or history, but by experience. It represents a personal, and perhaps quixotic, acceptance of and grappling with the dailiness of our lives, as individuals, within a collective, and as architects. We look in many directions: to our own child's bookshelf, to the natural history museum, to Africa and Asia, and to architectural history, our own and that of others. We do not look only straight ahead in pursuit of one correct answer, for this is to operate in and as part of an exclusive world. It is peripheral vision that brings the happenstance that connects us to an inclusive world. So we peer out the corners of our eyes for those side steps and digressions that bring us new directions and lead us to new questions. For in the end, it is the questions, not the answers, that are most vital to us.

Of course, this image diary is incomplete. We subtitled this project "A Lab Report" because we believe it is ongoing research, not only for us, but for any others who are interested, inspired, or made thoughtful by our results. We believe the value of research lies in sharing its results, so that we can all continue to grow from the questions, successes and failures.

We thought about cutting the 6'H x 4'W x 12'L stack of donated homasote like a puzzle. As a cabinet shop does, we created diagrams for the most efficient and effective use of the material (we call this "mining the stack"): minimum waste with maximum use of material.

"Art on the Beach" was a collaboration with Jackie Ferrara where we used concrete landfill blocks 6' x 3' x 3' as building elements. Purchased for ten dollars each, they produced a great volume with little expenditure. These overscaled modular elements led us to consider the walls and the roof as large elements, each with its own structural integrity. Both concrete and foam use casting as a form of making.

Scott Burton's witty and thoughtful furniture has always been an inspiration to us, especially his ability to expand the materials and the expectations that apply to furniture. The clarity of his understanding of materials is evident, as is his subsequent decision to work either with or against this understanding. We attempt to achieve the same level of clarity in our research with materials.

This photograph of Brancusi's studio shows him using a piece of sculpture as a workbench. The art was not precious to him. He made the bases for his sculpture with the same intensity as his sculpture. Where is the dividing line?

Architecture is an art of use. We try to cross the dividing line.

The magical red carpet rolls on and on.

Japanese garden; islands in the stream; stepping stones of moss. The floor is a plane of imagination.

Rauschenberg's prints present a layered and transparent sense of time. We would like to make rugs that are transparent, that can have additional layers added to them.

This fossil contains 40-million-year-old fish. We are interested in making a rug that marks or holds time.

The incised lines of Nazca. The rug seen as an aerial view allows the sudden ascent of the viewers. We think of rugs in their relationship to markings on the earth—the making of places.

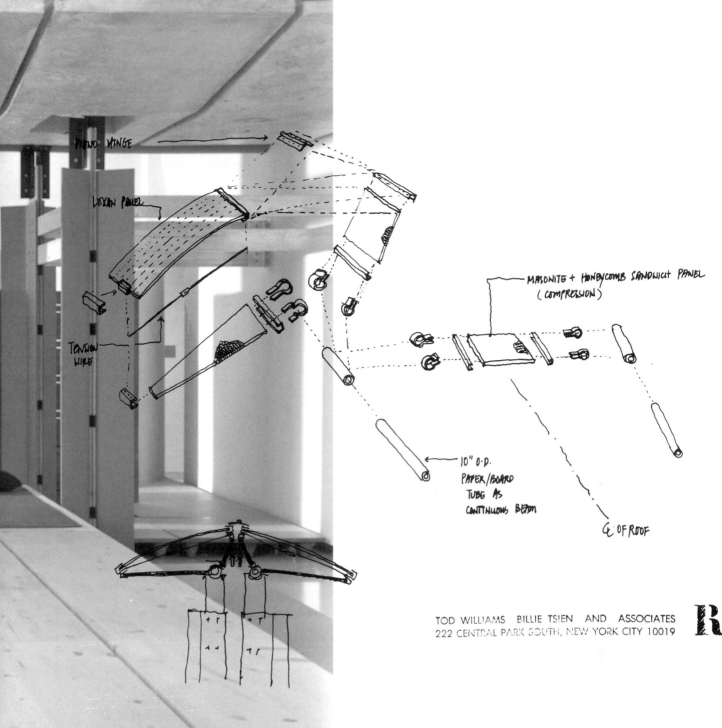

PIANO HINGE

LEXAN PANEL

TENSION WIRE

MASONITE + HONEYCOMB SANDWICH PANEL
(COMPRESSION)

10" O.D.
PAPER/BOARD
TUBE AS
CONTINUOUS BEAM

C OF ROOF

TOD WILLIAMS BILLIE TSIEN AND ASSOCIATES
222 CENTRAL PARK SOUTH, NEW YORK CITY 10019

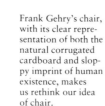

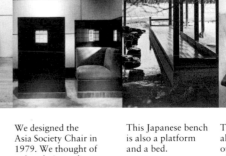

We have always been interested in the back of the rug—the canvas and latex. It is both quiet and rich in texture. It can be played with like sand and can, like embroidery, become a map of personal notations.

Frank Gehry's chair, with its clear representation of both the natural corrugated cardboard and sloppy imprint of human existence, makes us rethink our idea of chair.

We own both of these chairs but we sit more often in the smaller one, a kindergarten chair, that we bought for our son, Kai. It is the size of the many small chairs we "mined."

We designed the Asia Society Chair in 1979. We thought of sedan chairs and we wanted to make the furniture become a room.

This Japanese bench is also a platform and a bed.

This Senufo bed is also used for laying out the dead. Made of a solid piece of very heavy dark wood, it is very long and flat. We often use its surface as a kind of chair and table.

An earlier chaise designed by Tod thinking about the flatness possible in a chaise and specifically about the Senufo bed and Le Corbusier and Perriand's chaise. We think about several uses for each object.

New York is a city of small spaces so there is a luxury in a long empty flat surface. A table can easily be used as a bed.

The Dutch combined a bed with a closet and made a small room.

When Tod was at Cambridge, the dining tables were so long the students stepped on them to get to the seats on the other side. Try walking on your dining table sometimes. We do.

Prouvé's roof structure—each piece has its own structural integrity.

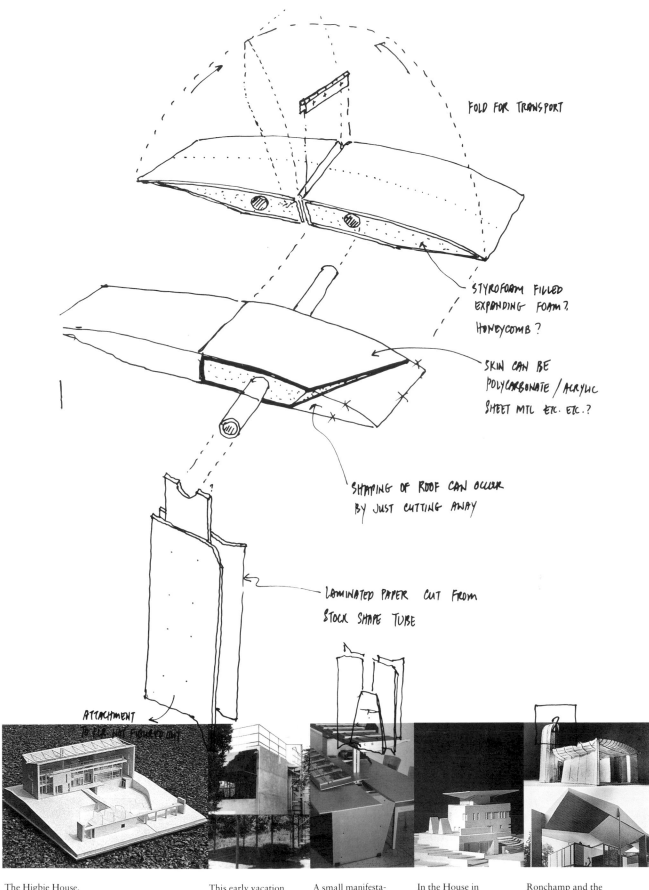

FOLD FOR TRANSPORT

STYROFOAM FILLED
EXPANDING FOAM?
HONEYCOMB?

SKIN CAN BE
POLYCARBONATE / ACRYLIC
SHEET MTL ETC. ETC.?

SHAPING OF ROOF CAN OCCUR
BY JUST CUTTING AWAY

LAMINATED PAPER CUT FROM
STOCK SHAPE TUBE

ATTACHMENT
TO PLA NOT FIGURED OUT

The Higbie House, designed by Tod in 1979, was an early look at the idea of the floating roof. It was also related to the roof research of Le Corbusier.

This early vacation house by Kocher and Frey is a child's tree house cum tent. A floating house waiting to fold up and steal away. The sense of freedom is exilarating.

A small manifestation of an early roof idea for the Higbie House.

In the House in Rowayton, designed in 1986, we continued to think about the release of the roof from its support.

Ronchamp and the Heidi Weber Pavilion give inspiration and suggest avenues of research for our own roof structure. Can it be stretched on a light framework, or be made of folded planes?

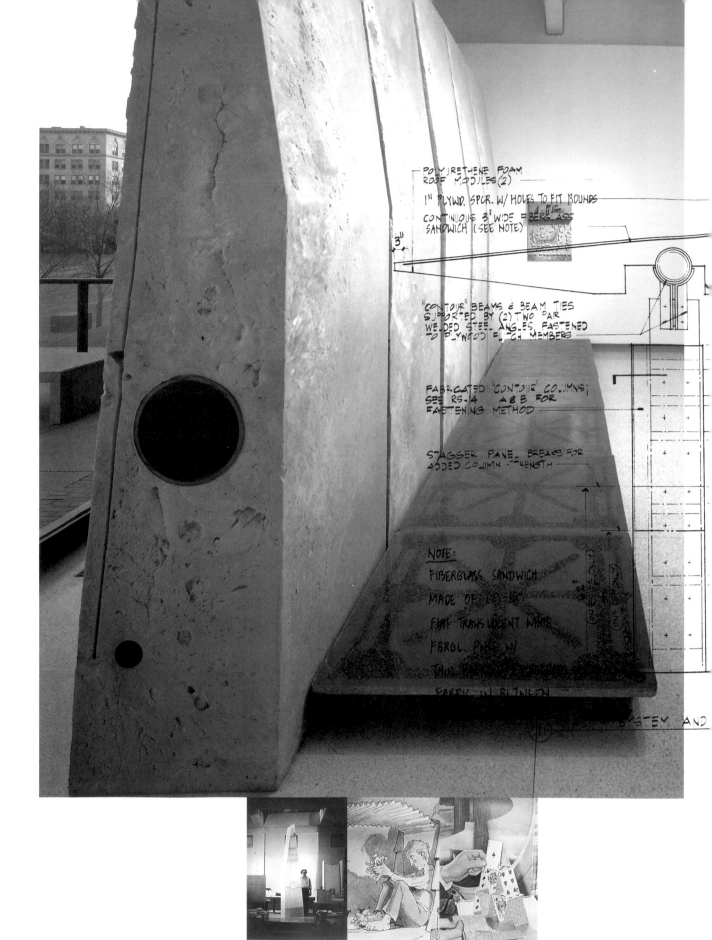

POLYURETHENE FOAM
ROOF MODULES (2)

1" PLYWD. SPCR. W/ HOLES TO FIT ROUNDS

CONTINUOUS 3' WIDE FIBERGLASS
SANDWICH (SEE NOTE)

3"

"CONTOUR" BEAMS & BEAM TIES
SUPPORTED BY (2) TWO PAIR
WELDED STEEL ANGLES FASTENED
TO PLYWOOD FLANGE MEMBERS

FABRICATED "CONTOUR" COLUMNS;
SEE RS-4 A & B FOR
FASTENING METHOD

STAGGER PANEL BREAKS FOR
ADDED COLUMN STRENGTH

NOTE:
FIBERGLASS SANDWICH
MADE OF (2) 1/8"
FLAT TRANSLUCENT WHITE
FBRGL. PN W/
THIN FIBERGLASS
FABRIC IN BETWEEN

SYSTEM AND

Our first roof experiment in our studio. Folded corrugated plastic—a failure.

Paper John, a character in a children's book, folds his whole world. We continue to try to fold a roof. This technique proves unwieldy, but we discover that bent and tubular cardboard works well for the structural support of our roof.

We think of the house of cards. We try to use tilted planes to make the roof—the connections are too complicated and fussy.

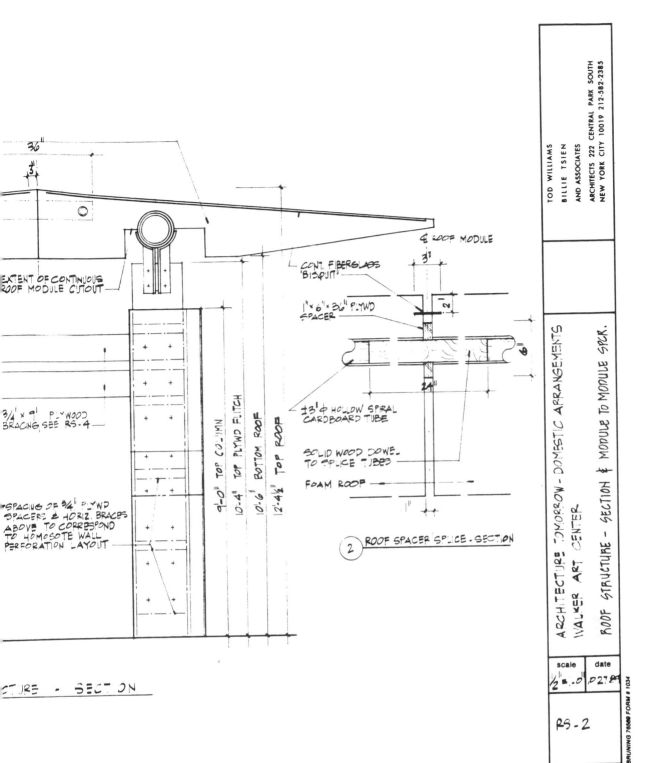

36"
3"

EXTENT OF CONTINUOUS
ROOF MODULE CUTOUT

¢ ROOF MODULE

CONT. FIBERGLASS
'BISQUIT'

3"

2"

1" × 6" × 36" PLYWD
SPACER

3/4' × 9' PLYWOOD
BRACING SEE RS-4

9'-0" TOP COLUMN
10'-4" TOP PLYWD FLITCH
10'-6" BOTTOM ROOF
12'-4½" TOP ROOF

6"

24"

±3' ø HOLLOW SPIRAL
CARDBOARD TUBE

SPACING OF 3/4" PLYWD
SPACERS & HORIZ. BRACES
ABOVE TO CORRESPOND
TO HOMOSOTE WALL
PERFORATION LAYOUT

SOLID WOOD DOWEL
TO SPLICE TUBES

FOAM ROOF

1"

(2) ROOF SPACER SPLICE-SECTION

CTURE - SECTION

TOD WILLIAMS
BILLIE TSIEN
AND ASSOCIATES

ARCHITECTS 222 CENTRAL PARK SOUTH
NEW YORK CITY 10019 212-582-2385

ARCHITECTURE TOMORROW - DOMESTIC ARRANGEMENTS
WALKER ART CENTER

ROOF STRUCTURE - SECTION ¢ MODULE TO MODULE SPCR.

scale	date
½"=1'-0"	02.27.89

RS-2

BRUNING 76500 FORM # 1034

Teaching at Southern California Institute of Architecture in Santa Monica, we drove past a surfboard manufacturing shop. We saw the foam slips curing in the sun. They are stiff, have their own built-in structure, and are light; not to mention that they float. We eventually made our roof elements from expanded polyurethane foam, the same material as surfboards. The process is trial and error on the part of the fabricators. Many technical problems remain to be considered in future research.

Now that the roof elements have their own built-in structure, we realize we can slice and carve them like slicing pieces of bread. Bread, like foam and concrete, is a cast material. This provides great freedom in the development of form.

Lebbeus Woods

Architecture
that
arises
from
and
sinks
back
into
fluidity,

into the turbulence of a continually changing matrix of conditions, into an eternal, ceaseless flux—architecture drawing its sinews from webbings of shifting force, from patterns of unpredictable movement, from changes of mind, alterations of position, spontaneous disintegrations and syntheses—architecture resisting change, even as it flows from it, struggling to crystallize and be eternal, even as it is broken and scattered—architecture seeking nobility of presence, yet possessed of the knowledge that only the incomplete can claim nobility in a world of the gratuitous, the packaged, the promoted, and the already sold—architecture seeking nobility of persistence in a world of the eternally perishing, itself giving way to the necessity of its moment—architecture writhing, twisting, rising, and pinioned to the unpredictable moment, but not martyred, or sentimental, or pathetic, the coldness of its surfaces resisting all comfort and warmth—transforming architecture, that changes both those who effect it and those who are affected by it—transcendent architecture, rising above the turbulence even as it sinks deeper within it—A group of fluid-dynamic structures originates in the ocean, far from Long Beach. Ideas are forming "offshore," where constraints of meaning are at a minimum. Only the physical constraints of the ocean itself prevail: its tides and currents, its turbulent movements, densities, temperatures. Between the fluid realms of air and water is a shifting surface, the wasteland of the ocean, a distorting, frictional plane caught between two differentially moving masses. Across these, the slow-moving icebergs will come. Their movement is the movement of the surface, and of the churning currents in the fluid masses just above, just below. They are formed separately, crystallized from a matrix of indeterminate forces. Each is an island, isolate and lone. Seabirds, the harbingers of continents, bearing the seeds and spores of primordial life seeking soil in which to take root, simply land and leave. Nothing can grow here, except the cold, crystalline life within: cold, fractured, intellectual. **The drifting icebergs come together** in occasional groups, more by chance than design. The complexity of the fluid currents above and below dictates the uncertainty of conjunctions, the impossibility of unions and totalities. Yet the surrounding kinetic domains are the media of a more universal communion. Waves travel freely in fluid domains, curiously unimpeded by mechanical currents, by the precedents of ideology and the contingencies of the expedient, the useful, the merely intentional. What travels on the waves is a matter of origins and destinations, which need not be connected by intention, but nonetheless are equally given and received. **Inevitably, the icebergs are driven onto the land.** The force behind them is the same force driving the evolution of things, a

probability inherent in the particular and the transient. By chance they cleave the urban soil of Long Beach, plows tilling fields of an inevitable, perhaps inevitably violent social change. To catalyze it, to crystallize it, to give it an "other" form. **Today the meaning of change comes from outside cities**, and it comes in forms that are alien to the cultures within, propelled by "outside agitators." They are the root of all local evil, to be sure, but are necessary, if change is to be understood finally *from* within. Edmund Burke has something to say about this phenomenon in his comments about "the Sublime." So does Kazantzakis, when, in his "Odyssey: A Modern Sequel," he describes with mordant glee the overrunning of Knossos by barbarians from the North–the Greeks. But why cannot the meaning of change come from within? Are the cities of the advanced nations incapable of understanding the changes spawned by their own evolutions, their own histories? Are they corrupted by too much self-satisfaction, manifest as a desire to maintain at all costs a status quo? Or are they paralyzed by too much self-loathing, arising from deep flaws, manifested as social and political problems? One need only look at the 1992 riots in Los Angeles, at the strikes in Germany's major cities, at the war that has devastated cities in Croatia and Bosnia-Herzegovina, and at the unrest in a hundred other cities on every continent to know that the answer to these questions comes too often in the form of rebellion, violence, destruction, and death. To the extent that a need for restructuring of cities, their politics, and their social conditions, is straining everywhere against the self-satisfaction of a

(handwritten annotation below image) 94700 - EN

few and the self-loathing of many, against the lethargy or incapability of established institutions to give coherent form to change, violence seems inevitable. The only question is, what form will it take? Is it conceivable that there is a form of constructive violence? Might there be an architecture that is a form of tectonic attack, healing the wounds it causes by the same architectural and technological means it uses to assault meaning that has become regressive, even pernicious; an architecture of indeterminate form and space combined with uncensored, open communications and community? *Anarchitecture* is the term I have coined to describe an architecture of unpredictable transformation. **Heterarchical history, or the history of heterarchies.** In my Underground Berlin project of 1988, a continuous civic space is constructed beneath the Wall, subverting its political purpose, which is not division, but the concentration of power that is centered elsewhere. Within the underground space, the fragile structures called "living-laboratories" are constructed as subtly kinetic structures, vibrating harmoniously or dissonantly with one another on wavelengths of geomechanical and geomagnetic forces animate within the earth's planetary mass. In the Aerial Paris project of the following year, the aeroliving-laboratories, mobile sites of experimental living, move freely in the fluid environment of the atmosphere, forming a turbulent, heterarchical community that is a gentle invasion of the Parisian skies. The Berlin-Free-Zone and Zagreb-Free-Zone projects of 1990 and 1991 describe heterarchical communities formed by a different kind of turbulence and fluidi-

Aerial Paris (1989)
Magnetic vortex at the
Eiffel Tower

Berlin-Free-Zone (1990)
Composite section-perspective
Französischestrasse

Berlin-Free-Zone (1990)
Communications heterarchy

ty, produced by rapid political and social changes already underway. The free-space structures move in invisible fields of electronic energy and matrices of continuous communication. The Long Beach Heterarchy, a project also made in 1991, extends these concepts into fluidities of a different order of physicality and politicality than those found today in Eastern Europe: the throes of an American city on the edge of the continent, where the ocean abrades the land with all the uncertainty of a coming *el Niño*, and of the rising urban violence flowing from deep structural flaws in American society. Los Angeles and Long Beach are simply names dividing a continuous urban fabric turbulent with changes, both present and promised. Next to this, in the ocean itself, where the floating architecture of a new type of community is constructed, the forces of nature seem benign. **In each of these projects, the architecture is conceived as an instrument of change that has many dimensions—spatial, temporal, aesthetic, epistemological, political.** Each freespace structure is itself fluid in the particulars of its presence, changing in form and space, in relative position above, on or beneath the existing urban fabric. Each living-laboratory, each freespace structure is an element initiating change or actively participating in changes inherent in present conditions. As urban ensembles, they do not seek to de-stabilize urban conditions which, after all, are already highly unstable. Rather, they seek to provide forms for change, tectonic armatures about which many kinds of change can occur. Because they are undefined in their purpose, they provide an occasion for change to take form without pre-determining the results of change, without, in other words, attempting to control change. This

is an architecture that means to support the idea of change and its unpredictable outcomes, and knows that this can be accomplished only by giving up
the idea of design as future control, by embracing indeterminacy as a first principle of thinking, making, living. **How** could such a principle exist in architecture, a noble profession that has always aimed at "firmness, commodity, and
delight"? Isn't architecture supposed to provide a sense of place, a point of origin, a touchstone in the vicissitudes of existence? Home and hearth, a sanctu-
ary, a "sacred and primordial site"? So long as the aim of the people for whom
architecture is intended is to find themselves, ground themselves, locate themselves securely in a known and intelligible world, then the role of architecture
must be one of confirming the already known. But what about those people
who are not part of a status quo, who–by choice or chance–are uprooted, geo-
graphically, intellectually, and spiritually, and who embrace (however reluc-
tantly) this state of uprootedness as the primary condition of modern, or post-
modern, or postindustrial existence? This latter group might include artists,
restive intellectuals, or people who are disillusioned with the status quo; dispossessed, or disenfranchised, laborers, farmers, or white-collar workers. It
might include citizens of countries torn apart by war, by the failure–or the tri-
umph–of ideologies. It might include those who find they have no home, polit-
ically. This is a growing group of people who have experienced the effects of
rapid changes in society and who now acknowledge them as a strength.
Architecture for them must be more than an artifact confirming the already

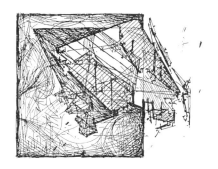

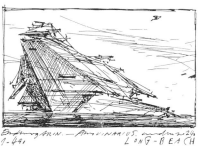

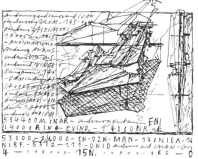

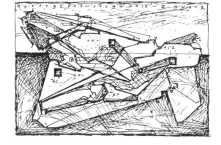

known. Architecture must be an instrument of mobility, fluidity and dynamic capacity, an instrument by which those who are affected by change effect changes, by engaging in dialogue and establishing networks for exchange and action. Architecture for this disparate and heterarchical community must be a means for engaging the unknown—architecture that moves, slowly or quickly, delicately or violently, resisting the false assurance of stability and its death—architecture that comforts, but only those who ask for no comfort—architecture of gypsies, who are hounded from place to place, because they have no home—architecture of circuses, transient and unknown, but for the day and the night of their departure—architecture of migrants, fleeing the advent of night's bitter hunger—architecture of dissidents, of dispossessed farmers, automotive workers, accountants, and philosophers, of those who have felt the sting of rapid and uncontrollable changes, but who see their pain as strength—architecture of abandoned citizens, whose countries are no more, and perhaps never were—architecture of war, aiming at thoughts wedged too comfortably in the vanity of certitudes—red and yellow and violet architecture, carrying the heat of anger and too much compassion—silver architecture, tarnished by the interminable grayness of rains, glinting in the first instant of sun—architecture of steel crushed by forces directed by more powerful, less material instruments—architecture of disillusioned idealists, who understand at last that ideals and ideologies are opposite and conflicting—critical architecture that brings into question every assumption, especially that of its own presence—undeniable architecture, insistently present, even though its reasons are yet to be known—architecture of emptiness, waiting to be filled, then emptied again—architecture of icebergs, formed of metal's crystals, in the waves of invisible seas, driven onto land by storms of chance—architecture that reaches at once above, on, and below, devouring space as though its emptiness might then be filled—architecture of a philosophy of interference, the forms of which are infinitely varied, a vocabulary of words spoken only once, then forgotten—architecture bending and twisting, in continual struggle against gravity, against time, against, against, against—barbaric architecture, rough and insolent in its vitality and pride—sinuous

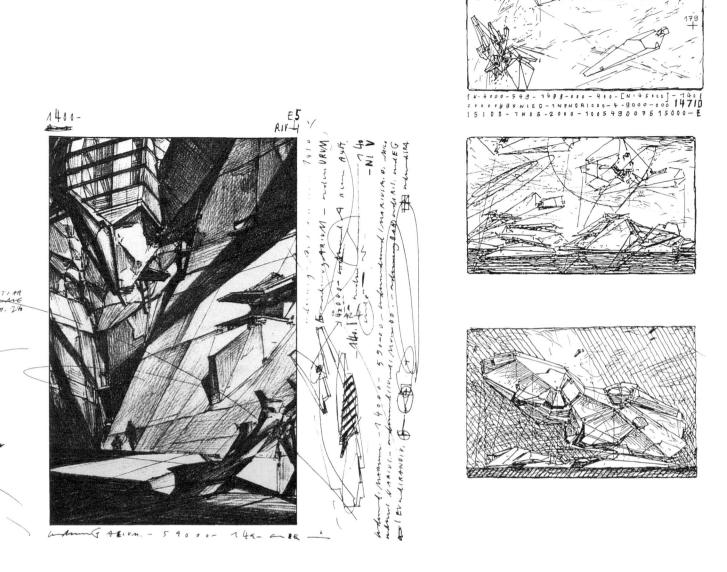

architecture, winding endlessly on and through a scaffolding of reasons—architecture caught in sudden light, then broken in the continuum of darknesses—heroic architecture, which always reaches for more than it can grasp, possessed of the wisdom that there are no more heroes—architecture, the forms of which are modest, never showing too much of the hidden sources of its strength—architecture embracing the sudden shifts of its too-fragile forms, therefore indifferent to its own destruction—architecture of complexity in the way that any moment is complex: being what it is and what it is becoming—architecture of relentless materiality, never symbolic, never metaphysical, never appealing to authority other than its own—architecture that destroys, but only with the coldness of profound respect—neglected architecture, insisting that its own beauty is deeper yet—abandoned architecture, not waiting to be filled, but serene in its transcendence—architecture that transmits the feel of movements and shifts, resonating with every force applied to it, because it both resists and gives way—architecture that moves, the better to gain its poise—architecture that insults politicians, because they cannot claim it as their own—architecture that refuses to monumentalize mediocrity, or institutionalize one more time the already confirmed—unsponsored architecture, drawing itself from the nothingness of autonomy, the meaninglessness of existing, the anger of having to exist in a world demanding as a first cause the reasons of its own decay—architecture for architects, or at least those who have no choice—experimental architecture, which proceeds with the fury of the obsessed, from uncertain beginnings to unknowable goals—architecture whose forms and spaces are the causes of rebellion against them, against the world that brought them into being—architecture drawn as though it were already built—architecture built as though it had never been drawn—

New York City 1992

Storefront for Art and Architecture. James Keyden Cathcart, Frank Fantauzzi, Terrence Van Elslander, "Portable Toilets Inserted Through Gallery Wall," outside view.

October 20, 1990
Parsons School of Design
New York, New York

Moderator
Kyong Park, Storefront for Art and Architecture

City of Lines

Wellington Reiter teaches at the Department of Architecture at MIT. His projects have been exhibited at galleries in New York and Boston, and published in several American publications.

Offshore Structures

Donna Goodman is an architect practicing in New York City. She is the author of "Visions and Inventions" (forthcoming), on large-scale infrastructural projects. Her research into offshore structures was supported in part by a grant from the Graham Foundation.

The Universal City

Michael Kalil practiced architecture in New York City and worked extensively with NASA on designs for long-term space habitations. Since his death in 1991, his interests and work have been carried on by the Kalil Trust and Foundation.

Fabric-formed Concrete

Mark West was raised in New York City, where he survived the public school system, worked as a carpenter and builder, and studied architecture at the Cooper Union. He is presently teaching at the College of the Atlantic.

Arch/Truss Wall

James Carpenter is a sculptor, film-maker, and industrial designer working out of New York City. With his firm, James Carpenter Design Associates, a collaborative team of architects, he has worked on a variety of projects with, among others, Barton Myers, Edward Larrabee Barnes, and Norman Foster.

Metroplex: The Expenditure of Dreams

Dan Hoffman is head of the Department of Architecture at the Cranbrook Academy of Art.

September 18, 1990 – September 28, 1990

Allan Wexler teaches at the Parsons School of Design. His work has been widely exhibited, and is currently represented by the Ronald Feldman Gallery in New York City.

CITY OF LINES

Wellington Reiter

Every city should be followed by a shadowy half-brother that exists only on paper. Drawing and redrawing the city is a necessary act, one that can powerfully alter our perception of the physical city. For example, it is no longer possible to view Rome free of the influence of Piranesi's reconstruction of that city. In fact, so potent are his works that the ruins and scattered fragments seem adjusted to conform to a Piranesian vision—the shadow casts its image in reverse. The contemporary model for such activity should consist of a perpetually updated collection of drawings that speculate upon the city's past, present, and future. They can reformat the city we thought we knew, making it more available to criticism.

For drawing to become the critical tool that is proposed, drawing itself must be defined. Pen and ink media have here been purposefully chosen in order to reinforce the issue of line. The inability to erase requires that alterations or changes occur only by an increase in density—one must overwhelm the undesirable. Each line carries the potential to become the germ or site of future speculation. This method of drawing finds inspiration in the successive layers of foundations to be found in Rome and elsewhere; the buildings we saee today have origins in circumstances no longer visible.

Research proceeds in a rigorous manner without a preconceived conclusion. This drawing is certainly not intended to be conclusive. Its primary function is to create a truly raw material, a resource that will later be exploited and purified in response to other circumstances. Drawings like this one suggest the autonomy of drawing while simultaneously denying it, and make the case for improvisation in architecture.

Drawings of the city had, in the past, the advantage of being able to locate the subject, if not in the landscape, at least in the mind. The long history of aerial views of Venice, and the idealized diagrams of Vauban offer examples of the advantages of compactness when imagining the city. The frequent need for walls of fortification necessarily circumscribed the city, thus framing it for inspection. The city could be considered as a discrete still life, rather than as an undifferentiated expanding field—an object more available to being represented through drawing.

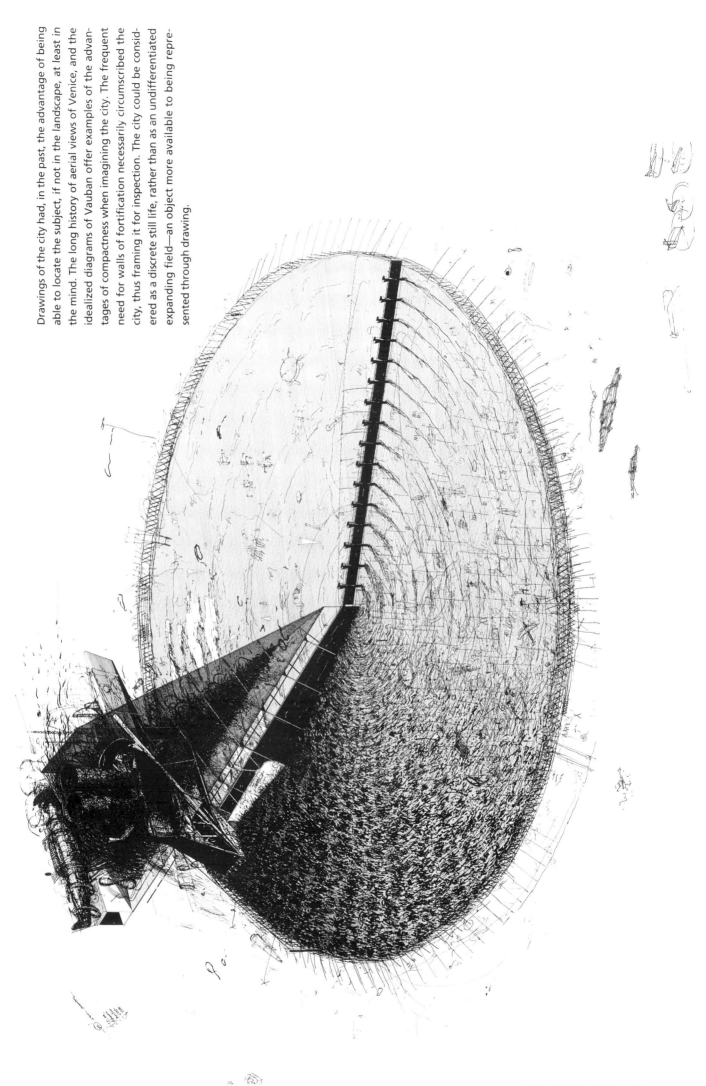

This study of the image of the city has eventually led to the most constricted of formats: the radial plan. Giving the appearance of being measured, these drawings are managed by the eye, thus requiring the reiteration of the center time and again. Disregarding issues of scale, the investigation has included porous, inwardly focused city-equivalents such as the Colosseum (virtually a model of the Roman Empire compressed into a single building type) and the reverse— opaque, supposedly impenetrable fortifications, both real and imagined. The former celebrates a known center, the latter monumentalizes a paranoia of the unseen. Due to the formality of the edge condition in each case, it is possible to identify the membrane as either an agent of containment for that within, or as a barrier to that without. Through the drawings, ratios of inclusion and repulsion are quantified for use in more precise conditions.

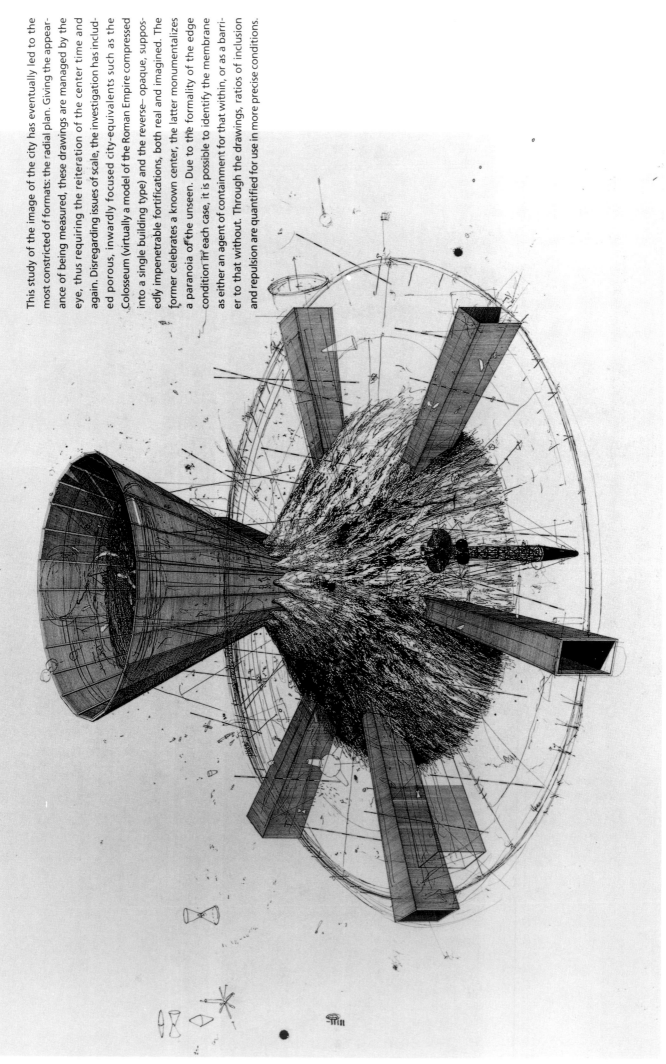

Donna Goodman

OFFSHORE STRUCTURES:

Islands for Industry and Food Production*

Victor Hugo once said that "the invention of the printing press destroyed the age of architecture." With this remark, he identified a very serious cultural change, the shift from the visual, intuitive, mysterious period of the Middle Ages, to the verbal, analytical period of the Renaissance, that eventually led to the current age of science, industry and invention.

The twentieth century has experienced more change than any other time in history. The invention of the automobile, television, computer, systems of mass production, mass transportation, and high rise construction have led to numerous cultural changes in rapid succession. Current urban environments could not have existed one hundred years ago.

We are now approaching a period in which many large scale, long term projects will be built. The Japanese are designing islands offshore, Europeans are completing the Channel Tunnel, and new towns are being planned in several developing countries. Many new inventions are also being created, such as ferry trains, solar power satellites, commuter airships, and offshore farms.

The architectural mainstream has, in recent years, focused on a series of movements—postmodernism, deconstructivism and other "isms"—that are not particularly inventive, but rather reflective of the materialism and surface conscious attitudes of the times. Architects, in general, have not been searching for new approaches to housing, transportation, industry and urban development that address current problems.

There have been several periods in history when architects played leading roles in social or technological transition. For Da Vinci and Brunelleschi, for example, the art and technology of architecture were inseparable and of equal importance. Our current lack of involvement with research and development could be extremely damaging to the profession. If it continues, we could easily slip behind the rest of our constantly changing culture and no longer be able to provide the appropriate structures for modern existence. We may end up like Charlie Chaplin in *Modern Times,* baffled by the world around us, ill equipped to address the problems of modern life.

It is anticipated that approximately forty percent of our resources will come from the ocean in the latter half of the next century. My own major ongoing project has been the design of a floating city based on the technologies of offshore industry and platform design, incorporating many new systems for underwater seafood farms, the production of kelp, drugs, pharmaceuticals, oil, minerals and masonry materials. Some of these resources, such as floating seafood farms, would offer quality products at a low cost.

The project utilizes the basic tension leg structure, an elegant, efficient approach to offshore design. Six different energy systems are employed, with a variety of concepts for recycling. The open seafood farms actually help to restore the natural ecology of the ocean. Urban and residential spaces are above water. Elevators and tethered vehicles connect the surface to underwater farms and factories.

Many of the concepts, such as housing piers, offshore ports, industrial or recreational islands, could also be applied to the expansion of existing cities, like New York, where the waterfront could again become an important area of the city.

Some of the structures are designed as flexible, modular elements that are seaworthy, and can be moved as the city grows or changes. The basic master plan could also be altered to include remote areas or subcenters, when the need for resources leads to additional offshore locations. The concept would then become a "dispersed city," to be linked through transportation systems to the urban center.

* Patent pending

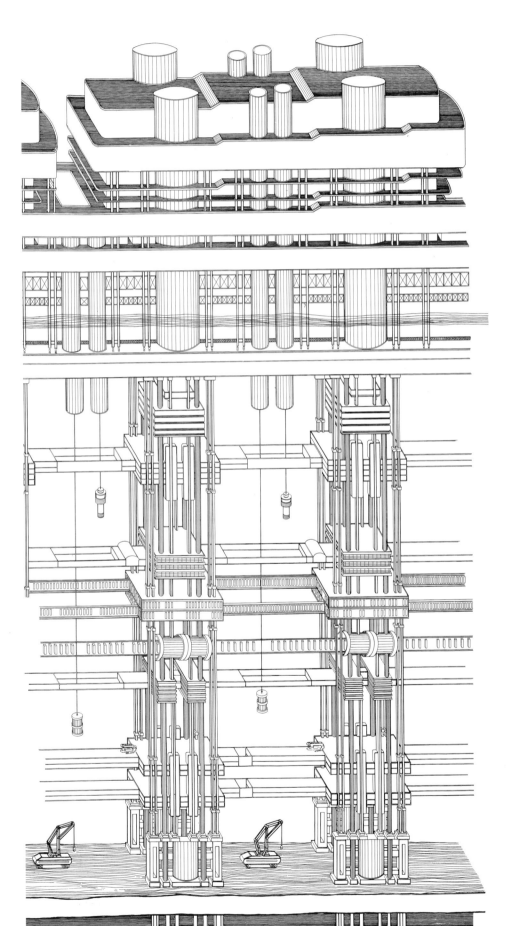

Upper Tiers and Roof Systems
Satellite Communications
Solar Collectors
Recreational and Residential Areas
Parks, Theatres, Arts Institutions
Public Service Cores
The Vertical University
The Vertical Corporation
Commercial Tiers
Urban Center
Public Transportation

Platform Structure
Service Transportation
Industrial Processes
Maintenance
Floating Drydocks
Wave Power

Water Level

Work Stations (Normal Atmospheric Pressure)
Packaging and Inspection
Warehouse and Distribution
Flotation Cylinders

Deck Substructure and Flotation Hull
Product Receiving
Final Processing
Chemicals and Pharmaceutical Production and
    Research
Tethered Research and Repair Vehicle
Ocean Thermal Power Processing Plants
Desalination, Hydrogen Power, Heating and
    Cooling, Water Treatment

Mooring System and Tension Legs
Fish Culture, Hatchery, Breeding
Oysters, Mussels
Lobsters, Crabs
Shrimps, Scallops, Clams
Cargo Lifts and Survey Equipment

**Lower Mechanical Systems,
Refining of Raw Materials**
Coral Farms with Simulated Sunlight
Manufacture of Building Materials,
Mining of Sand, Gravel, Minerals

Foundation at Ocean Floor
Ocean Floor Industries
Weighted Anchors, Steel Piles

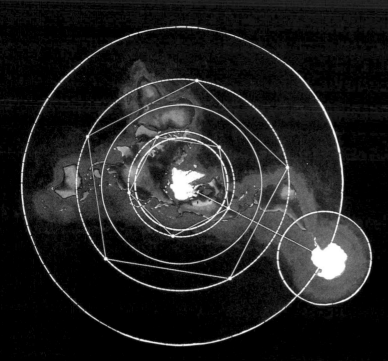

Studies of a universal city: the neighborhoods, the center, and the outer edge. In this drawing we took the natural land mass of the Earth and looked at it as one land, and each segment of that land we saw as a neighborhood. When you view the Earth from this position you see no boundaries, no cultures, and no class systems. There's a very large paradigm shift that has to occur in our collective thinking; we need a whole shift in our understanding of where we are.

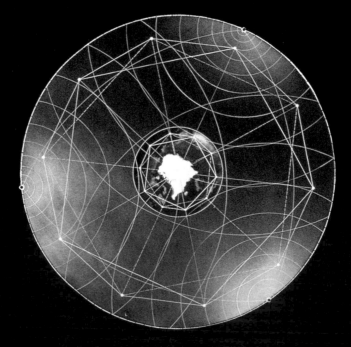

Floor plan of the universal city. We are looking at the Earth, at the center with its neighborhoods. This is also the floor plan of an electronic-age city, not an industrial-age city. The three points that are on the outer edge are three satellite stations, by which we communicate. When I call Los Angeles from New York, the person I am calling and I meet, so to speak, at one of these three points. We communicate at these centers. They have always been there; these satellites are the new village fountain, the market-place, or the cathedral of our time. The inner circle of twelve points, extended above the face of the Earth, are the Twelve New Moons of Earth–twelve new space stations. One could be the planned space station Freedom, and one could be a Disney recreation station, for example.

When we emerged from this planet we were global citizens. We then shifted local-ly into regional citizenship; tribal culture and simple architectures like Eskimo igloos are an aspect of that. We then grew into national citizenship. National citizenship colonized Manhattan and we changed the paradigm from a nationality to an inter-nationality. We have now left this planet, and we are in the paradigm shift from international to universal citizens. Manhattan was the primary architecture of the international citizen; our studio is examining what the architecture of universal citi-zenship will be. My co-workers and I are looking consciously at what humanity is building. What we all must not forget is that we were born from this planet and that we are now out in space giving birth to our next home. So home gives birth to humanity and humanity gives birth to its future home. These are the parts of the universal city/building. It is one piece of architecture.

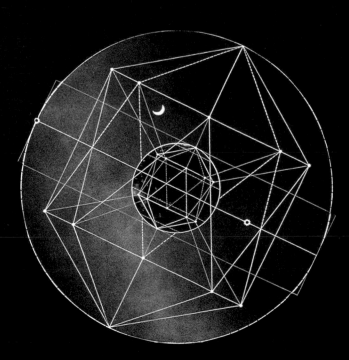

Elevation of the universal city. It is one building, not a series of buildings or a series of cities. What we're doing in this electronic age is structuring a major piece of architecture by interconnecting these different places. There are neighborhoods, which make up the land mass of the Earth, there is the meeting point–the village fountain–which is the center of the orbits of the satellites, and there are these twelve moons that will eventually be built; all of it is one ecological city.

Mark West

FABRIC-FORMED CONCRETE

My work with fabric-formed concrete started around 1984 with a project called the "Safe House." This was a model of a house that was completely "safe"; *absolutely* 100% *safe.* It was inspired indirectly by the start of Reagan's "Starwars" missile defense system research, and by the paranoia that was (and still is) on the rise in the United States.

The model of the Safe House was built by forcing several hundred pounds of plaster into a partially restrained fabric membrane to produce both the form of the house and its surrounding landscape. I thought of it as a "pressure building." This technique of using a soft material as formwork (for plaster, concrete, etc.) seemed like something that could be pursued at full scale with interesting results.

The columns shown here are the result of applying "pressure building" techniques to full scale concrete constructions. When traditional plywood or steel panels are replaced with a thin membrane, a vast, unexplored territory of architectural form and building practice opens up.

There are several interesting aspects to this discovery. One of the most illuminating is the way in which the materials themselves produce these forms. While a greater or lesser degree of tactical control can be exercised by the designer or builder, ultimately the final forms are arrived at by a private internal calculus performed by the liquid concrete and the tension membrane that surrounds it. The forms which result are not willfully produced (as they might be were they the work of a sculptor, for example), but are produced through the intelligence and desires of the materials themselves in the presence of gravity. As a result, the geometries they produce are perfectly precise, and somehow inevitable.

Unlike the planar surfaces produced by traditional formwork panels, the concrete in this work retains the memory of its liq-

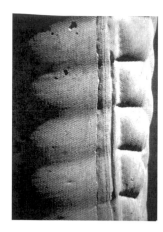

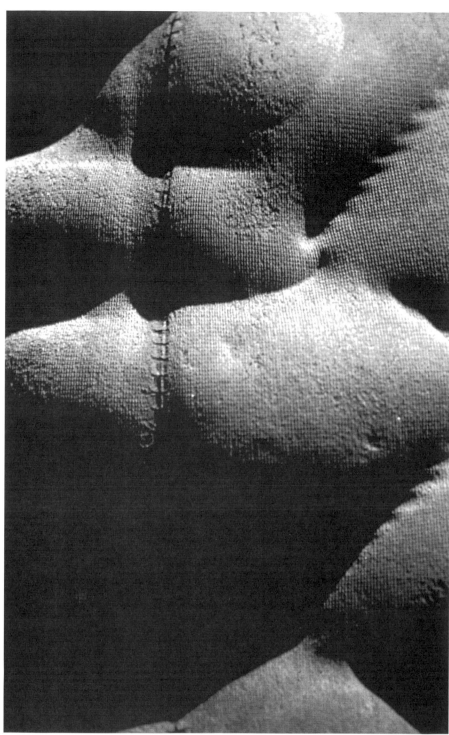

uid origins. The geometries produced are genetically different from those of traditional concrete architecture because they are given by the forces of a liquid under pressure bound in the continuous restraint of pure tension.

The geometries of traditional concrete forms are those of the milling machine, i.e. regular planar surfaces. It is worth noting that the great majority of structure supporting traditional formwork exists only to inhibit *deflection*. Inevitably, a high price (literally and figuratively) is paid to maintain *srtraightness* in the presence of pressure.

What I envision here is a way of building not only different in form, but in approach as well. While this method sets out certain precise limits and carefully exercises control over its results, these limits simultaneously provide a territory where the unpredictable precision of chance is allowed free reign. This territory is left open, so to speak, by staying out of the way and leaving the dynamics of the materials to "complete the work themselves."

Staying out of the way, however, is not a regular part of architectural training and practice. On the contrary, an understandable obsession with *control* is what dominates most architectural approaches to making. This desire for control, however, tends to overshadow or displace the great advantages and precision of chance events. My research over the past ten years has, in a sense, been about developing "technologies" of chance, forgetting and release, while maintaining the specific kinds of precision that building inevitably requires. The results seem to point to a new and unforseen freedom in the possibilities of what and how we might build.

James Carpenter

ARCH/TRUSS WALL

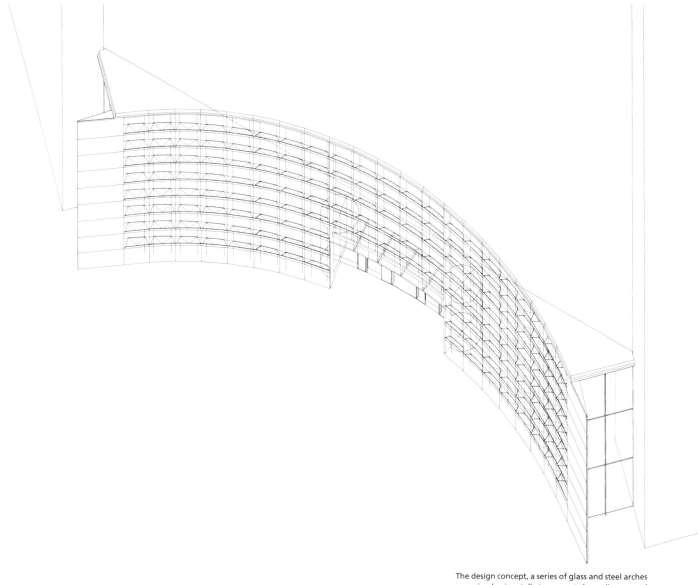

The design concept, a series of glass and steel arches spanning horizontally to support the wall, emerged from two conditions: the curve of the walls, and the requirement for sun screening (which was complicated by unequal sun exposure and shading along the length of the curved wall due to the building overhang). The glass walls create the weather and climate barrier for the main lobbies of the twin office towers and provide structure and sun screening for the entrance walls.

ARCH/TRUSS WALL Project Team:

James Carpenter Design Associates
James Carpenter
Janet Fink
Richard Kress
Neil Logan
Luke Lowings

Structural Engineers
Ove Arup and Partners
Tony Broomhead
Guy Nordenson
Greg Hodkinson

Component Engineer and Fabrication
Tripyramid Structures Inc.
Tim Eliassen
Michale Mulhern

Architect
Johnson, Fain and Pereira

Client
Hillman Properties West

Explorations of Structure

Our work is a synthesis of technical expertise, and aesthetic and tectonic values. Using glass, high-strength stainless steel alloys, aluminum, and wood, we attempt to work with material characteristics to create unique, primarily tensile structures, exploiting glass as an integral structural component. Systems for this work do not exist, so our work is a process of developing and integrating the structural concept, the means of production, and the aesthetic in order to build and achieve the things we want to do.

Each project explores interests in a slightly different way, expanding our vocabulary and abilities to explore the characteristics of materials, attempting to build form and space from an essential understanding of the behavior of materials. The fragments resulting from this process accumulate, leading ultimately to a more complete architectonic expression.

Many American municipalities now require new construction greater than a certain square footage to provide amenities that can be enjoyed by the public at large. Such a program has been adopted by the city of Los Angeles and was the primary impetus for Hillman Properties West to commission James Carpenter Design Associates to design the entrances to the Los Angeles Center Project.

Our solution comprises two matching, curved curtain walls facing south-east and south-west. The walls form the entrances to two office buildings; between them lies an outdoor public space. The glass walls provide the weather and climate barrier for the main lobbies and resolve issues of structure and sun screening, as dictated by their scale, sun exposure, and configuration.

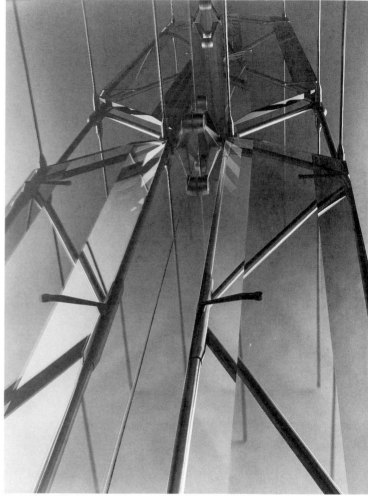

The glass wall activates the space between interior and exterior by the projection and transmission of light. What was formerly a thin and transparent boundary is transformed and expanded into an articulated presence.

Taking advantage of the curve, the wall structure functions alternately as an arch in negative (suction) pressure, and as a truss in positive (wind) pressure. The arch trusses provide stability to the arch elements. As Ove Arup's diagram indicates, the pattern of loading that gives rise to the most severe deformations of the arch truss is an unbalanced wind load. This type of loading suggests the need for connections that allow for the relative rotation of the glass vision panels in plan.

Because the glass wall experiences both suction and pressure, the truss chords and diagonals must be able to bear both tension and compression. The design of these members in collaboration with Ove Arup and Partners and TriPyramid Structures Inc. focused on the type and spacing of the connections to the glass, on which the diagonals rely for stability, as well as considerations of fabrication and installation.

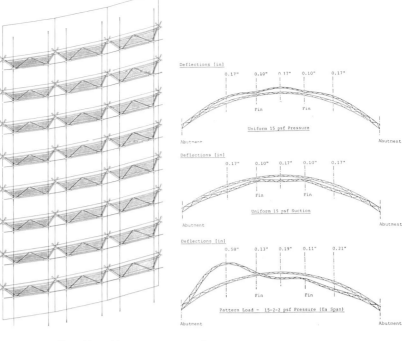

Each of the eight arches is made up of a series of machined stainless steel trusses and integrated dichroic glass blades, which vary in depth from twenty inches at the extreme end to nine inches at mid-span. The 1/4" diameter vertical hangers act in tension to support the weight of the glass panels and trusses.

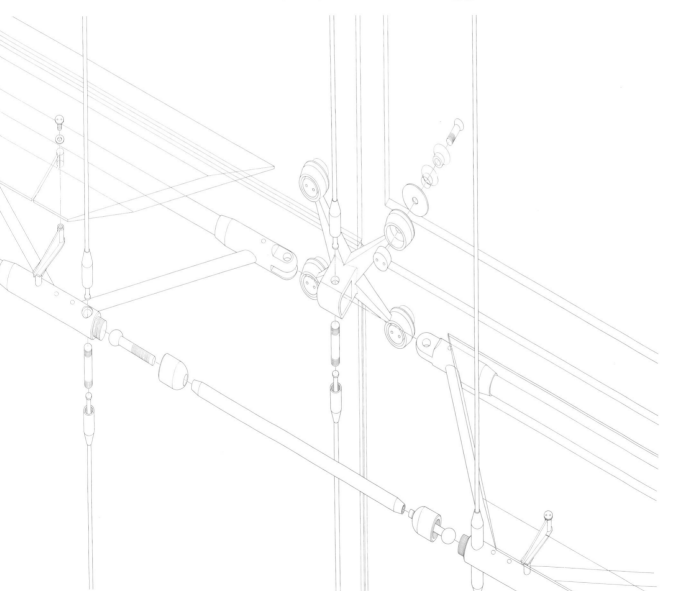

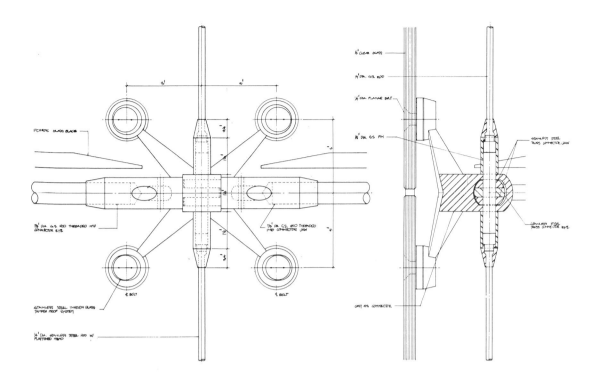

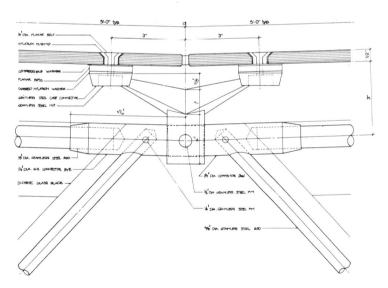

The load of the glass vision panels is transferred to the support structure through a stainless steel cast connector. This fitting accommodates thermal expansion of the vision panel both horizontally and vertically, as well as differential and seismic movements.

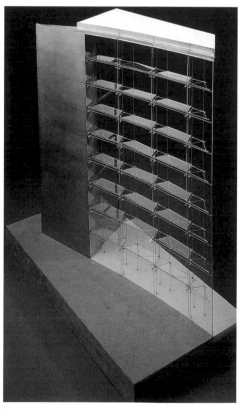

The mock-up not only provided a sense of the final appearance of the wall, but also indicated locations where further study was required on tolerances, joints, and allowance for movement.

Dan Hoffman

METROPLEX: THE EXPENDITURE OF DREAMS

The word *research* interests me in regard to architecture in part because it deals with a prejudice, a kind of lingering sense of guilt that architects carry over the relationship between architecture and science. Of course research has always been a part of science itself, and that's been a problem in architecture's relationship with science since the latter part of the seventeenth century. It's a problem that still is with us: architecture, the humanities, the works of people, have to be seen within a rational construct that sets itself toward an idealizing praxis, a means of making things in the world, a way that tends toward an ideal that is based on science. This remains a problem, for although we build with science, we inhabit architecture in a different way. We build with straight lines, but that doesn't mean that we perceive them as straight, or that we live in buildings in the context of straight lines. Our inhabitation is not scientific.

Much of my work deals with the difference between what is perceived as an idealized situation, and what is lived. These poems deal with the problem of inhabiting a city of science, made from technology and the speculations of science. The work seeks to produce a moist friction between the edifice, this city of science, and the dampness of the body.

METROPLEX HISTORY

Across the highway
stands a horizon
of ancient profiles
surmounted by soaring lattices
of wood and steel

The Historical Theme Park of Metroplex

Dry remnants of another age
when science was found
in cannon balls and fruit

It is twilight
and soon the switch will be thrown
bodies set into motion
accelerating along trajectories
with speeds robbed from the progress of time

An equation of physics
demonstrated
for the price of admission

But for now
all is still
the pendulum stopped
balanced upon its point
the place of silence and order
The mother referent of sublime momentums

Within the park
these mysteries of reason
bear the quaint maskes
of pirate galleons and swans
hovering upon the trajectories of a physicist's dream

A dream of absent frictions
a delerious marriage
of fact and fiction
revealed in the holy
vacuum of space

We now suffer the ecstacies
of the Universal Cause
lifted into the weightless moment
and screaming down the precise path
of the inevitable descent

From across the highway
the throbbing generators
remind us that this release
has become the burden of our days
that dreams are now measured
in dollars and sense

The inflationary cost
of forgetting
the history
of things

THE MOTOR INNS OF METROPLEX—THE EXPENDITURE OF DREAMS

My room is made from the foam of oils
that once rested here
the dark mud
of ancient shades

Electric
transformers
boil like bees
exciting the foam
in the warm currents
of deadly arrays.

The genius of this place
its contribution
is how so little
is spread
so far

The atomization of matter
the stuff of dark oceans
expanded into clouds of desire
a layer of time
burned in the spark of a circuit

A pile of ash
is removed at the beginning of each day

My room is haunted with smells
that strike between the eyes
the sour dust of memories
beyond the touch of fluids

I empty my pockets
and fold my clothes
for this place makes my skin damp
with the moisture of polycarbons

One can always feel the difference

The magnetic caress
stiffens my hair like a dog
and an arc of blue milk is expelled
dissolving into the light without heat
pulsing softly in the corner

The dark plastics stare without shame
for they have been neutered
electrons without temperatures
wearied by multiple deaths in dark fires
bearing the soulful masks of wood and
flowers

The bathroom waits
a white circuit of fluids
this is the place of greatest danger
for here the blood runs near the surface
seeking an open pore
to pool itself into a quiet circle of rest
from the endless business
the endless business

It is for this reason
that the bathroom is white
to suck
(like drops of blood in snow)
the amber halo of the body's warmth

The pool outside is carefully tended
each morning bits of leaf and grass are
removed
with deliberate care
it is curious
for no one swims here

At night
the waters burn
with a mineral silence
a radiant plasma
reflected upon the ceiling

I close my eyes
and damp machines
with efficient pumps
extract the moisture of my dreams
into the charged mists
of the electric night.

Allan Wexler

SEPTEMBER 18, 1990 — SEPTEMBER 28, 1990

SEPT. 18, 1990 7:24 AM

I feel the need to get something on paper defining the topic of architectural research. I'd rather continue building. Two people connected together through the hollows of the table and chairs. Is this research? I'm looking for something but don't know what. Sometimes I feel lost, only an urge keeps me going. Translate an adventure story of a search for foreign lands into a search for foreign ideas. Ideas at the edge. I hope I don't fall off. Keep working, keep moving. Once I stop I get too tired to get up again. Why am I working? Looking for what? Re-search, hints, clues. Four shirts sewn into a table-cloth. Am I designing a restaurant? Do I use a table saw like a surgeon uses a scalpel or an explorer uses a compass? Wouldn't it be nice if I could use a compass to tell me which direction I should move? What is my equivalent of a compass? A particular trend in the magazines? The words of a critic? Or does this compass tell you which direction not to take? I like the feeling of not knowing where I am going, of being pulled by the wood, the pencil, the clay, the fabric. These things tell me where to go. How can I make the surface of the table break apart and float away?

SEPT. 19, 1990 7:25 AM

Continue discussion on the topic of architectural research. I am trying to get into this gently without trying too hard, slipping between the meaning. Perhaps I should use the variables of this typewriter and this paper. But do I also need to use and explore the variables of the coffee that I am drinking now? Is it black, does it have milk, sugar? If I drink tea will this discussion be different? Should I fast for at least eight hours before I enter the studio each day? Wear the same clothing?

Do I eat the same meal each day using the same utensils? Marcel Duchamp, while living on 14th Street, would break each day at the same time and eat the same pasta with cream sauce. Artists and scientists need to hold everything constant that has nothing to do with the experimentation being pursued, the project being worked on. (Project, projection, running, jumping into an idea. A different approach to gently entering into an idea. I'll try this another time.)

I become interested in an area. Now it happens to be how four people come to a table and eat. A simple action. I eliminate many things from this exploration, but each day there seems to be more things I want to explore. Constants—things I try not to change—like the dimensions of the table, the height of the table, the dimensions of the chairs, their heights, the materials used, the surface treatments, the size of the nails, the actual people, the direction of the grain, the direction of the brush used when applying the surface finish. These constants are my vacuum, my petri dish. Within this petri dish I paint an idea, a culture. With each piece I make one change and one new element is added. I try to get lost in the work so that these new choices or germs that I insert into the building process are not preconceived, expected, or predetermined. Should my studio be empty with grey walls, no windows, constant temperature, no books? In fact it's cluttered with objects that I've picked up at yard sales, at the beach, in the woods, that have seemingly no relationship to my work, but nevertheless they are all objects that I love, that are silly, that are serious, that are sensuous. Looking back at my work, I can now see how each project has been influenced by some object that I've found and displayed in my studio. I know that Man Ray was also a flea market fanatic. Perhaps it's the flea market where things from all cultures, times, states of mind, ages, economic brackets come together in nonpreconceived ways. I like this word *recreation*, which we should pronounce **RE**(*long* e)-CREATION. This is as important an activity as creation. Next week is Yom Kippur, which is a fast. It's an entire day of no food. We should also have a day of no sound, a day of no touch, a day of no seeing, a day of no pencils, a day of no reading, of no subway. It's only on those days that we begin to understand.

I've always been interested in the idea of a scar, the break, the repair. In Recycled Conference Room, which I did in response to Merle Ukales's *Garbage* Up Front exhibition, I found twelve broken chairs, and a broken glass conference table, and repaired them. For instance, an antique arm chair had one arm missing, so I replaced it with corrugated cardboard to try to make it look like the other arm. Another metal leg chair had one leg bent, so I straightened it with a wooden leg, which I tried to hide by painting it black. The broken glass table top had some pieces of glass missing, which I replaced with wood. I like repairs that are still visible. I love white-out. A layering takes place, a memory; the past can never be completely whited-out.

Sept. 25, 1990 7:29 AM

The hollow table piece has something to do with attempting to suck the energy out of the individuals through the attached hat and shoes through ductwork into the legs of the table and into the tabletop where one person's energy—not necessarily energy: spirit, medium, whatever—mixes with the other person's. I found some old vacuum bags that are beautiful in a sculptural way, and I'd like to use them in another set of table and chairs. Perhaps I'll paint these paper vacuum cleaner bags with polyester resin in order to stiffen them. If they are stiff does that destroy the possibility of them ever filling with air, or meta-air? Inflated or deflated—which would look better? That would give the answer as to which is conceptually stronger. Four flannel shirts, different sizes and patterns of fabric, are going to be sewn into the edge of a white tablecloth. I think I'll try the same thing, but in the second version of this piece, I'll resin-impregnate the shirts in their "occupied-unoccupied" 3-D state. I will then try once again to make these shirts flexible by making all the joints hinged so that a person can fit into them and eat a meal, bending his or her arms, moving his or her hand.

Sept. 26, 1990 about 7:30 AM

The shoes have been built and they are now attached to the chair. The head unit is almost complete. I'd like to attach all the ductwork today and see if I can get the piece completed with the exception of the paint. The paint will attempt (but not very well) to imitate mahogany, like the table worn by the four people that I did last spring, so that the piece looks as if I'm not trying to make a piece of sculpture, but a table with two chairs. Is this really a discussion of architectural research? I hate this type of imprecision. I should require myself to write exactly 250 words every day, beginning at 7:30 AM and stopping at 8:00. John Cage did a project like this called *Indeterminacy* where he wrote several stories, almost like Zen koans, and read each one before an audience in exactly one minute. If a story had a few lines, he slowed his speech when telling the story to fill a minute. If the story was very long he had to speak very fast. Sol Lewitt did a similar project: two opposite walls of the same gallery that were the same size had the same amount of lines painted on each wall, except that one wall's lines were twice the length of those on the opposite side. Don Judd's plywood boxes, which seemingly look the same are, in fact, very different from each other because of the different shadows cast by the boxes themselves and variations in the grain of the plywood. I was probably more influenced by these people as a student in architecture than by architects. I want to pursue this issue of outsider influence, and if it happens to others as it happens to me. Should we have doctors, writers, scientists teaching our future architects?

Sept. 29, 1990 7:25 AM

I realized that the last line went up to the margin and I had to push the margin release. This allows the information, the writing to flow through. I wish I had a margin and a margin release. Margins are important to focus, to build up the energy on one side of the margin until you can't stand it any longer, and then release it.
No dead air,
      no dead space on this paper,
           keep going until the end,
                don't look back and reread,
                  keep moving,
                        don't be afraid to repeat things,
                          make mistakes,
                              spell things wrong,
                                  sound stupid.
                                      Spin around,
                                          get disoriented,
                                              look back some other time.

Now I lost my train of thought.
What happens when the train derails and falls off, and runs out of fuel, and the train cars get musty-smelling, and the windows get dirty, and the cars are too cold? You are out of control, you are being driven. When I'm in the middle of a project, I feel that way too. The project is driving me, I'm out of control. I'm there for the enjoyable ride. Sometimes the train breaks down and has to be fixed up, but eventually it gets started again and drives me until I get to my destination. But as soon as I think I've arrived, I realize there is someplace else I'd rather be. Is there never any end to this? I'm getting tired, my fingers are beginning to burn, my back hurts. I'm dying for a cup of coffee. The paper is running out. Only a little bit left. But I still have so much I want to say. Matisse at the end of his life was so arthritic that a brush had to be taped to his hands so that he could continue to work.

                            I want to be Matisse when I grow up.

Discussion

AUDIENCE Does anyone have anything to say on the difference between inspiration and research? Do they lead to different places? Do you consider that there could be such a thing as inspiration? Is there a way of finding a method for research?

WELLINGTON REITER Inspiration might be that initial motivating force that causes you to act. In the course of research you may possibly kill off that which first inspired the investigation. I think creation is really a cycle, working between research and inspiration.

ALLAN WEXLER I think of inspiration as being objects stored in your attic that you find interesting at some point in your life. At some other point you go up to the attic and look at the collection again. You say, this has something to do with what I'm working on now, and you bring it down to your studio. At that point the inspiration becomes research. Inspiration is sometimes not part of your conscious present.

JAMES CARPENTER There are two levels. One is inspiration, one is producing reality from conception. Research is really just secondary, aiming towards the inspiring goal. In my endeavors, it is the interpretation of light that is the inspiring fact. Research is simply steps that I take to create something that actually achieves or manifests that inspiration.

Research is not necessarily specific to a project, to be measured in levels of productivity and accomplishment. I think we are attempting to create a new basis—attempting to devise, to structure, to resculpture and elaborate our interpretation of information. These structures of glass and steel necessarily become complex. We have particular expertise in certain materials, and we rely on the expertise of others in collaboration.

DAN HOFFMAN Jamie talked about inspiration being one thing, and research being this kind of necessary act that brings to bear the proper codes, sign-offs, etc., as if research is a filter that legitimizes inspiration in terms of liability exposure, code constraints, infrastructural engineering, etc. In this sense, research has to translate inspiration into a legal entity. In some way or other people have to attempt to circumnavigate that filter, make an end run around it, but it is still there because any time we want to build today, one builds into a system of instrumental complexes. Knowledge is constrained, it exists in certain ways, forming an instrumental whole. This has been the case since the eighteenth century, since the idea of the modern sciences was born, wherein knowledge is rendered in the form of mathesis, universal form that can be translated and repeated at another place and another time, providing the necessary certainty for production. The difficulty is that at many times this translation is served up as "truth." The panelists' presentations revealed a deep suspicion of that "truth," hinting that there may possibly be other truths. In Jamie's case, where he deals with glass connections, those connections, their truth and legitimization exist in a formula which is codified in some national standards test. This test is sustained by a recognized scientific theory. There is this infinitude of formulaic relations and in the end no one really knows how Jamie's actually going to form the joint, and everybody has this proprietary interest in different parts of the formula. So no one really knows what is going to go on until it goes up and everybody wants to make sure the liability is spread around. This, for me, is what research really boils down to in architecture, and I think it's unfortunate.

Husserl, in his writing at the turn of the century, pointed

out a problem in scientific reason: there is a mathematic certainty to scientific argument, but it is not necessarily accompanied by a human certainty, as it were, a certainty of human consciousness, of all that is not mathematical. Husserl attempted to find some—he wouldn't use this word—essence, an origin from which one could understand the mathematically described phenomena at hand. So, for example, one speaks of acceleration due to gravity, a mathematical construct. He would attempt to reduce that construct to some essence that would enable us to understand outside of the realm of mathematics. If there is research to be performed by architects it is research that attempts to deal with this landscape of science, translating it back to phenomena that are describable in human terms. The division between universal mathematics and the soul's universality is an essential split. Husserl attempted to establish two parallel sciences so that every advance in science comes with a research as to where in our consciousness that advance may be understood. We must ask what is it in ourselves that allows our world to exist.

I put emphasis on the first syllable: RE-search. I look at research as re-searching, going over again a territory, attempting to locate ourselves and find a place within that territory, instead of research being a positive condition which presumably expands the field of knowledge. This re-searching is a necessary activity. Always in our culture there is this notion of horizon, of advancing toward a horizon; research presumes this mechanism of advance. It is a first condition of science that we are reaching forward to a more true, more accurate description of the real. We use tools to come closer to the ideal; the more accurate our tools are the closer we are to the truth. The very notion of the truth is based on this infinite regression of inaccuracy. How can we ever reach the truth? It's an infinite regression.

What I see as remarkable about Jamie's work is not its ritual observances on the altar of technology, but rather that despite all the technique the work inspires vision. In the end these constructions are miraculous visual things that show me again that I can see, I have sight, sight is there. I am aware that I see despite the rational fact of these incredible constructions. The quality of the work for me always surpasses its engineering.

STEVEN FRANKEL (New York Department of City Planning) I believe that the fundamental question that all architects must deal with is how should we live? In our present moment there is all this research being done on form and materials. It would be lovely and interesting to talk about texture and form and how it reflects light, all of which are necessary for us as human beings in living our lives in our houses and cities. But the more fundamental question that I think needs to be asked along with—maybe before—those, is how is this research, this architecture going to affect how we live?

HOFFMAN What Steve is saying appears very naive and simple. When someone gets up and asks an architect, "Well, how shall we live?" everybody shudders, as if living had been pure at one point. But in part the question belies that assumption; it shows how complex things are today. One cannot simply live. The difficulty of the situation and its tragedy is that we cannot extricate ourselves from the net of instrumental complexes that precondition our lives and, ultimately, our work.

We went through a time when architects were very successful propagandists for ways of living. But we began to see,

for example, Corbusier running on top of his Unité, adoring the sun as part of a justificatory mythology for Western expansion in the Third World. The power relationships that underwrite architecture in building are evident to anyone today. We are in a time when most people are suspect of advocating a way of living that is based upon architecture.

AUDIENCE In architecture there is an objective side (developing materials that, for instance, have greater strength) that can be tested, but there is also a subjective side of architectural research. How would this fit in, research as constructing myths? Or are we dealing with a different problem?

JOAN OCKMAN I think you are making a traditional distinction between "hard" science and social sciences, human sciences. There is the myth of objective science, on the one hand, and on the other a more cultural kind of description which is scientific in a sense, but that doesn't have the same pretense to objectivity. What is interesting of course is that even pure scientific research will necessarily include all kinds of subjective elements. The very "givens," the personal biography that any researcher brings to the enterprise necessarily creates those kinds of subjective presences in the work.

KEN SAYLOR One of the things that I noticed about the variety of work presented today is the challenge of how research is disseminated. Perhaps the work itself is such that it really can't find any mode of reaching out, of getting out publicly.

OCKMAN In regard to this question of dissemination: at what point in research does the collecting and gathering of data and information turn into a project? It was interesting to me how in the presentations everybody slid very nicely from a research problem they had set for themselves into the project that emerges from that research, and how that project also was presented as research. The article I presented earlier is called "Reinventing Jefim Golyscheff"[1] because I realized that I wasn't presenting an objective history and that any history involves as much fiction as it does science. The point is that research flips and becomes a project, becomes a problem of design.

SAYLOR I think the distinction isn't so clear-cut. It is a methodological question. If one's methodology allows for a variety of discursive or research strategies to take place simultaneously, some become objectified while others only exist discursively; others become graphic material, a kind of collage and montage of information, but always mediated.

MICHAEL KALIL I think research needs necessity first in order to exist. It is the necessity of the projects which initiates research and somehow I think that its essence, some percentage, belongs to human memory. Maybe that is what subjectivity is, that percentage.

BYRON BRONSTON (Harvard Architecture Review) But in your work for NASA you were given a particular program, you did not develop your own program, deciding whether or not we should move into space, which remains an open question. The ideological, economic, and ecological factors of such a move are many. By doing this work, aren't you buying into this system, these goals?

KALIL No, we are taking responsibility for our existence. Our move into space—I'm not naive—could be a total human disaster, but it could also be the next Manhattan in its day. The responsibility is within this room as to which direction we are going to take. It's the same thing that happened here in America. We came over here bringing all of European architecture with us. But then we developed an international architecture which has colonized the rest of the planet. We again see this process, but only now it's in space.

SHEILA KENNEDY You can choose the kinds of research you do in architecture and outside of architecture. You may choose to pursue "necessary" research, or to pursue a superfluous architecture. Only a certain section of the population actually builds, or is able to enjoy research. There is only a section of the population, not just in this country, that has the ability to do it, has the education to do it, and is in a position where they can understand research. So there is a question of access and control. Research is intimately and complicitously connected with systems of power. Research has lost its purity, if it ever had any, and it enjoys a very awkward and delicate balance that we all need to attend to. It throws an enormous amount of responsibility on the individual who is conducting research.

I wonder if in fact the notion of the product of our research is in question. I am not sure that we can produce new things in our research; it is rather a personal inquiry to question and expose systems that are already in place. The idea of creating a new Manhattan, of creating progress, is itself an historical idea. If we are to effect change, we must question the systems that are at work, the way in which cultural productions take place, are validated and disseminated.

DONNA GOODMAN Changes happen for economic reasons. For instance, we needed oil, so built drilling platforms in the ocean. We may want to go into space to collect solar energy or manufacture perfect crystals. Europe came to America to develop resources and create a different style of life. Economics play a large part in these decisions. Architects ought to be ready with new concepts for when there is an economic reason to develop a new environment. We will continue to build on the ocean because we will need food and pharmaceutical products. We will go into space for other resources. Our role as architects is to try to create environments and systems that will make the ocean and space habitable. We might even engender a dialogue about traditional cities, raising general questions about urban change.

OCKMAN Back in the sixties architectural research was very much in the air because research, and the architect as analyst, were being proposed as a critique of the author theory, of the architect as creator, inventor, genius figure. The ideal architect was the patient worker analyzing typologies and so forth who is very much the hero of books like Aldo Rossi's *The Architecture of the City*, where the city is material for analysis; from there the problem was to get to the project. This project vision of research sees architecture as less of an intuitive invention than as the result of some scientifically rooted, methodologically rigorous approach to a problem. Some resonances of that discussion are creeping back today, but I think the difference twenty-five years has made is found in the questions of information, dissemination, and reception, and in this idea of research as a kind of resistance to strategies of power. That kind of concern gives research its relevance to present conditions.

1. Joan Ockman, "Reinventing Jefim Golyscheff: Lives of a Minor Modernist," *Assemblage* 11 (April 1990): 71-106.

Contributors

Stan Allen is a practicing architect in New York City, and assistant professor of architecture at Columbia University Graduate School of Architecture, Planning and Preservation. Mr. Allen has published numerous theoretical and critical papers in journals in the U.S. and abroad. His work has received support from the National Endowment for the Arts and the New York Foundation for the Arts.

Preston Scott Cohen is assistant professor of architecture at the Graduate School of Design, Harvard University. He also maintains a private practice in Boston. His work has been featured in numerous exhibitions in the U.S. and Europe, and has been published most recently in *Assemblage* 13, and in the catalogue of the Third International Exhibition of Architecture: Venice Project, Biennale di Venezia. Mr. Cohen is also the recipient of a 1992 Young Architects Award from the Architectural League of New York.

Bill Hillier is professor of Architecture and Urban Morphology in the University of London, and Director of the Unit for Architectural Studies in the Bartlett School of Architecture and Planning, University College London. Professor Hillier has written extensively on research in architecture, urban design and space syntax, including *The Social Logic of Space* (Cambridge: Cambridge University Press, 1984). In addition to serving as a consultant for the design of major urban development projects in London, Professor Hillier has most recently directed several investigations sponsored by the Science and Research Council of the U.K. and the Department of Education and Science.

Sheila Kennedy co-founded Kennedy and Violich Architecture in 1988, and is an assistant professor of architecture at the Harvard University Graduate School of Design. Ms. Kennedy's research has been supported by several grants, including a Design Arts grant from the National Endowment for the Arts, and a Project Support Grant from the Massachusetts Council for the Arts for the construction of the Interim Bridges Prototype. Kennedy Violich Architects has participated in gallery and site specific installations throughout the U.S.

Lars Lerup is an architect and professor of architecture at the University of California, Berkeley. Professor Lerup, a native of Sweden, has written on and conducted research on a wide range of subjects from fire safety studies done in the 1970s for the National Bureau of Standards and the National Science Foundation, to more recent articles on architectural education and design. A volume of his speculative investigations on the single family house was published as a book, *Planned Assaults: No Family house, Love/House, Texas Zero* (Cambridge: MIT Press, 1987). He is presently serving as the director of the Southern California Institute of Architecture program in Vico Marcote, Switzerland.

Christopher Macdonald has been in private practice with Peter Salter since 1982, and has taught architecture at the Architectural Association in London and at the University of Texas at Austin.

Peter Salter is co-founder of Macdonald and Salter in London, and a teacher at the Architectural Association in London. Macdonald and Salter's work has been published widely and exhibited in galleries in New York, Europe and Japan.

Fernando Pérez-Oyarzún is dean of the Facultad de Arquitectura y Belles Aretes at the Escuela de Arquitectura de la Universidad Catolica de Chile. He has taught at universities throughout South America. and his writings have appeared regularly in South American and Spanish publications. His most recent book, *Le Corbusier y Sud-america: Viases y Protectos* was published in 1991.

Hashim Sarkis is a lecturer in the Department of Architecture at the Massachusetts Institute of Technology and a practicing architect in partnership with Hani Asfour. He is currently pursuing a Ph.D. in architecture at Harvard University. Mr. Sarkis is a founding member of the Center for Research and Comparative Studies in Lebanon and the Levant, and was a research fellow at the Chicago Insitute for Architecture and Urbanism from 1989 to 1990.

Billie Tsien is co-principal, with Tod Williams, of Tod Williams, Billie Tsien & Associates in New York. Ms. Tsien, who has a background in painting and graphic design, has taught and lectured at schools throughout the U.S. She has pursued her particular interest in work that bridges art and architecture through numerous gallery exhibits, and several projects done in collaboration with partner Tod Williams and artists Jackie Ferrera, Mary Miss, and Dan Graham funded by grants from the National Endowment for the Arts, and the New York State Council for the Arts.

Juan Frano Violich is co-founder of Kennedy and Violich Architecture in Boston, a practice dedicated to the exploration of affordable design in the public realm and the public use of small scale urban structures and spaces. As a member of the faculty of the Department of Architecture at the Rhode Island School of Design, Mr. Violich obtained initial funding for the Interim Bridges Project through a grant provided by the R.I.S.D. Faculty Development Fund.

John Whiteman, architect and educator, was director of the Glasgow School of Art from 1990 to 1991. Prior to returning to his native Scotland, Mr. Whiteman served as director of the Chicago Insitute for Architecture and Urbanism. Mr. Whiteman's projects and writings on architectural theory have been published throughout the United States and Europe.

Tod Williams established his architectural practice in 1974. His built commissions, exhibitions, installations, and teachings have been motivated by an examination of the physical and philosophical nature of construction. His work has attracted widespread attention and commendation both in the U.S. and abroad, and in 1983 he was the recipient of the Prix de Rome. Mr. Williams has taught at schools throughout the U.S., and since 1984 has been adjunct professor of Architecture at the Irwin Chanin School of Architecture at the Cooper Union.

Lebbeus Woods lives in New York City where, since 1976, he has concentrated on architectural theory, experimental projects and teaching. Mr. Woods' speculative projects have been widely exhibited in galleries in Europe and the U.S., and published in a series of monographs including *Einstein Tomb* (*Pamphlet Architecture* 6, 1980), *Origins* (1986) and *Centricity: The Unified Urban Field* (1987). Mr. Woods is an adjunct professor at the Irwin Chanin School of Architecture at the Cooper Union and the founding director of the Research Institute for Experimental Architecture (RIEA), a not-for-profit organization dedicated to the advancement of architecture through experimentation and research. Among his recent collaborations is the development of the conceptual architecture for the film *Alien³* (1990).

This book was designed with the Sabon and Frutiger type families.
It was composed on a Macintosh IIci computer using Quark XPress page layout software.